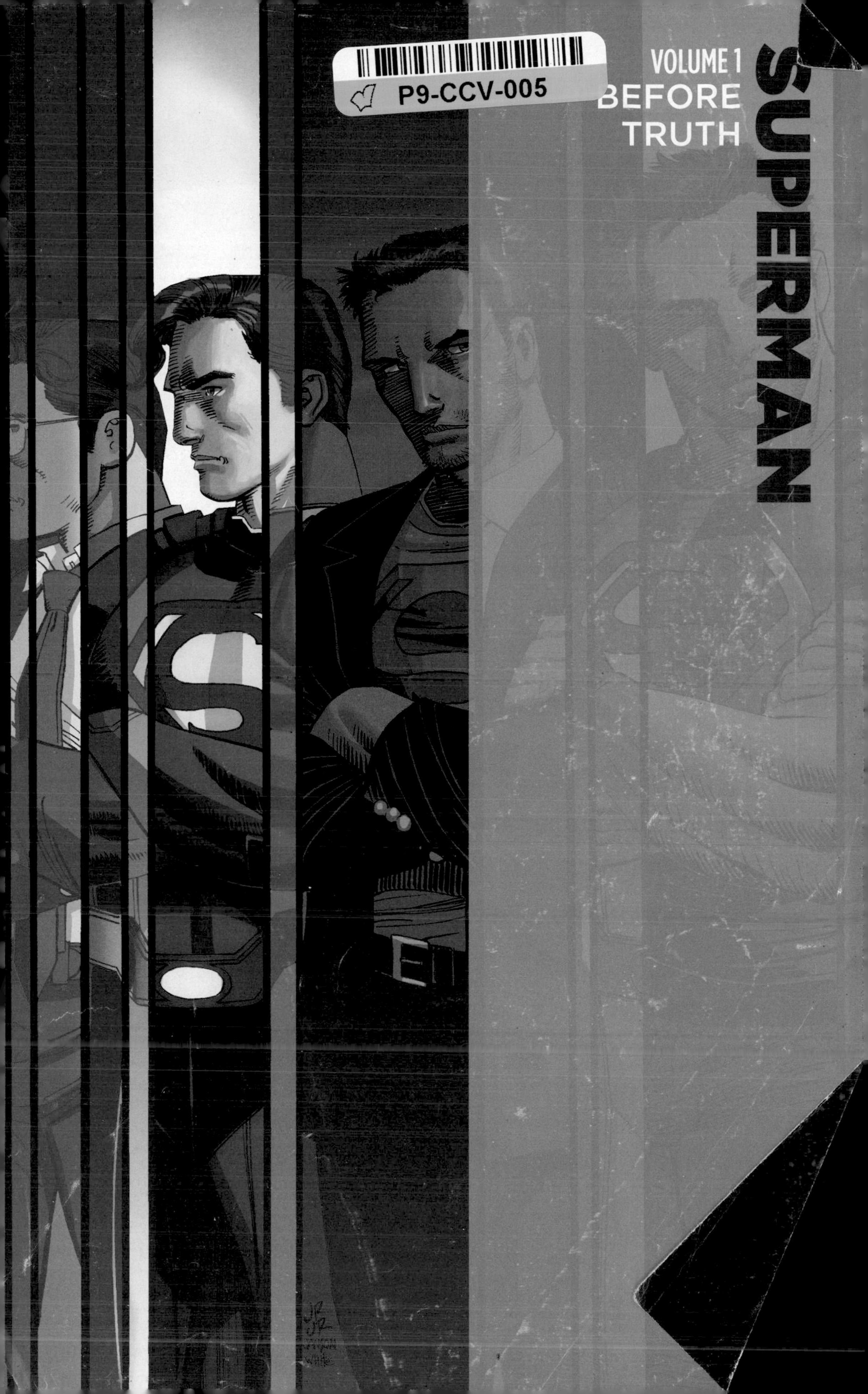
SUPERMAN
VOLUME 1
BEFORE TRUTH

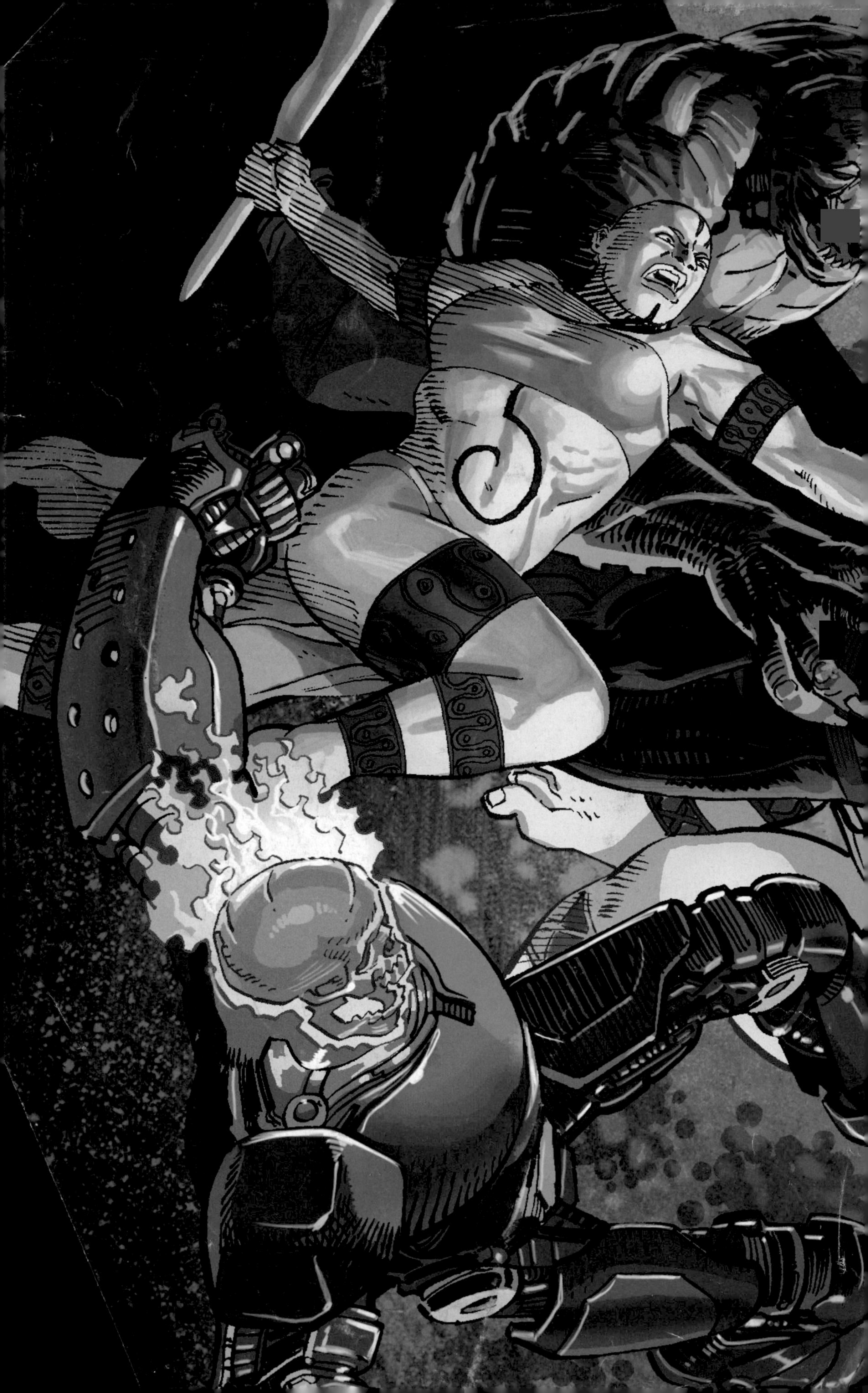

SUPERMAN

VOLUME 1 BEFORE TRUTH

WRITTEN BY
GENE LUEN YANG

ART BY
JOHN ROMITA JR.
KLAUS JANSON
SCOTT HANNA

COLOR BY
DEAN WHITE
WIL QUINTANA
TOMEU MOREY
LEONARDO OLEA
BLOND
HI-FI

LETTERS BY
ROB LEIGH
TRAVIS LANHAM

COLLECTION COVER ART BY
JOHN ROMITA JR.
KLAUS JANSON
DEAN WHITE

ORIGINAL SERIES COVERS
KLAUS JANSON
AARON KUDER
DEAN WHITE

SUPERMAN CREATED BY
JERRY SIEGEL
AND **JOE SHUSTER**
SUPERGIRL BASED ON
CHARACTERS CREATED BY
JERRY SIEGEL
AND **JOE SHUSTER**
BY SPECIAL ARRANGEMENT WITH
THE JERRY SIEGEL FAMILY.

ANDREW MARINO JEREMY BENT Assistant Editors - Original Series
RICKEY PURDIN Associate Editor - Original Series
EDDIE BERGANZA Editor - Original Series
JEB WOODARD Group Editor - Collected Editions
SCOTT NYBAKKEN Editor - Collected Edition
STEVE COOK Design Director - Books
DAMIAN RYLAND Publication Design

BOB HARRAS Senior VP - Editor-in-Chief, DC Comics

DIANE NELSON President
DAN DIDIO and JIM LEE Co-Publishers
GEOFF JOHNS Chief Creative Officer
AMIT DESAI Senior VP - Marketing & Global Franchise Management
NAIRI GARDINER Senior VP - Finance
SAM ADES VP - Digital Marketing
BOBBIE CHASE VP - Talent Development
MARK CHIARELLO Senior VP - Art, Design & Collected Editions
JOHN CUNNINGHAM VP - Content Strategy
ANNE DEPIES VP - Strategy Planning & Reporting
DON FALLETTI VP - Manufacturing Operations
LAWRENCE GANEM VP - Editorial Administration & Talent Relations
ALISON GILL Senior VP - Manufacturing & Operations
HANK KANALZ Senior VP - Editorial Strategy & Administration
JAY KOGAN VP - Legal Affairs
DEREK MADDALENA Senior VP - Sales & Business Development
JACK MAHAN VP - Business Affairs
DAN MIRON VP - Sales Planning & Trade Development
NICK NAPOLITANO VP - Manufacturing Administration
CAROL ROEDER VP - Marketing
EDDIE SCANNELL VP - Mass Account & Digital Sales
COURTNEY SIMMONS Senior VP - Publicity & Communications
JIM (SKI) SOKOLOWSKI VP - Comic Book Specialty & Newsstand Sales
SANDY YI Senior VP - Global Franchise Management

SUPERMAN VOL. 1: BEFORE TRUTH

DC Comics, 2900 West Alameda Ave., Burbank, CA 91505
Printed by RR Donnelley, Salem, VA, USA. 8/26/16. First Printing.
ISBN: 978-1-4012-6510-6

Library of Congress Cataloging-in-Publication Data

Names: Romita, John, author, illustrator. | Yang, Gene Luen, author. | Janson, Klaus, illustrator. | Hanna, Scott, illustrator. | White, Dean (Dean V.) illustrator. | Quintana, Wil, illustrator. | Morey, Tomeu, illustrator. | Olea, Leonardo, illustrator. | Blond, illustrator. | Leigh, Rob, illustrator. | Lanham, Travis, illustrator.
Title: Superman. Volume 1, Before Truth / John Romita Jr., Gene Luen Yang, writers ; John Romita Jr., Klaus Janson, Scott Hanna, artists ; Dean White, Wil Quintana, Tomeu Morey, Leonardo Olea, Blond, colorists ; Rob Leigh, Travis Lanham, letterers ; John Romita Jr., Klaus Janson, Dean White, collection Cover Art.
Other titles: Before Truth
Description: Burbank, CA : DC Comics, [2016]
Identifiers: LCCN 2015049454 | ISBN 9781401265106
Subjects: LCSH: Graphic novels. | Superhero comic books, strips, etc.
Classification: LCC PN6728.S9 R66 2016 | DDC 741.5/973—dc23
LC record available at http://lccn.loc.gov/2015049454

PEFC Certified
Printed on paper from sustainably managed forests and controlled sources
PEFC
PEFC/29-31-75
www.pefc.org

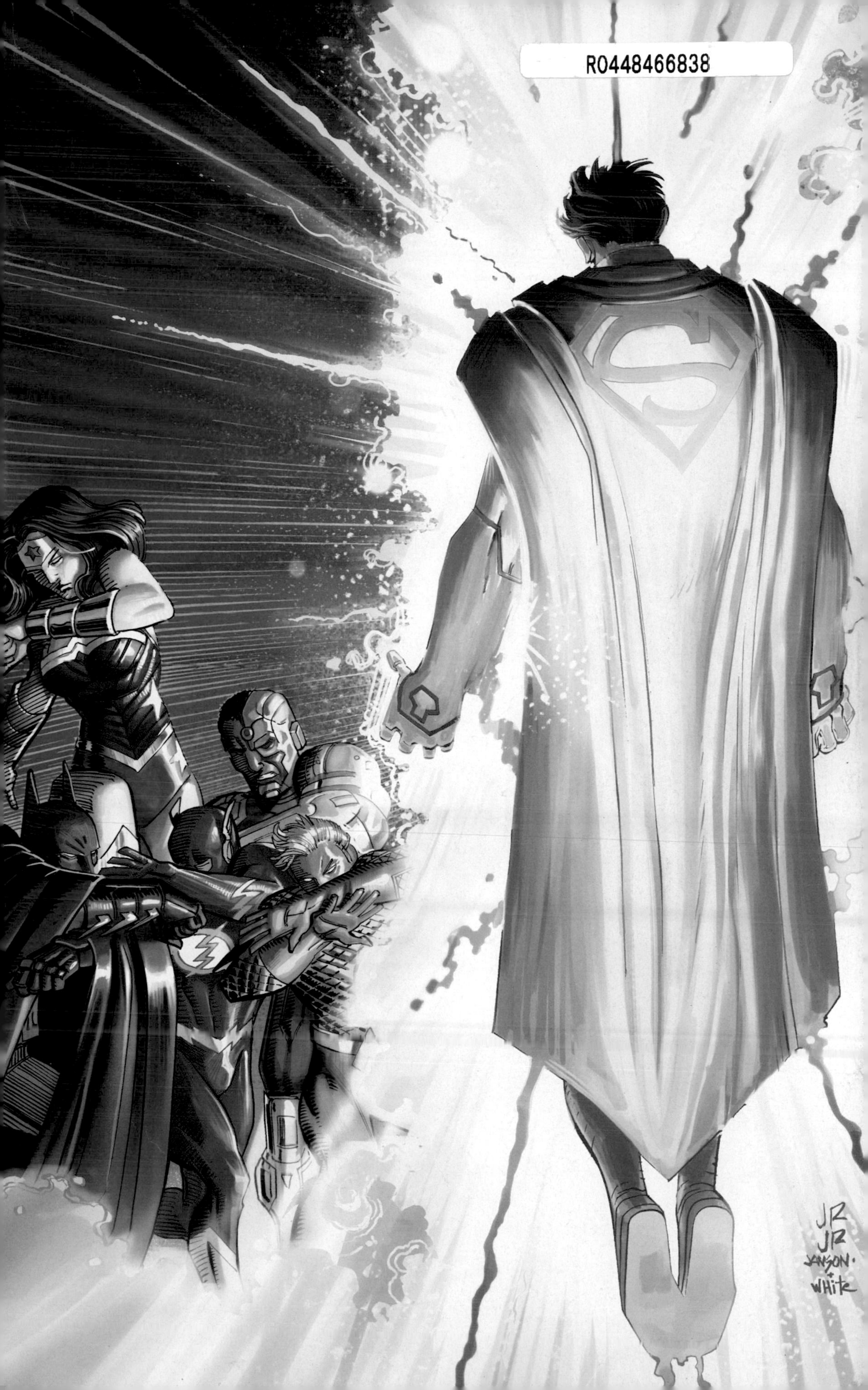
JR
JR
JANSON
+
WHITE

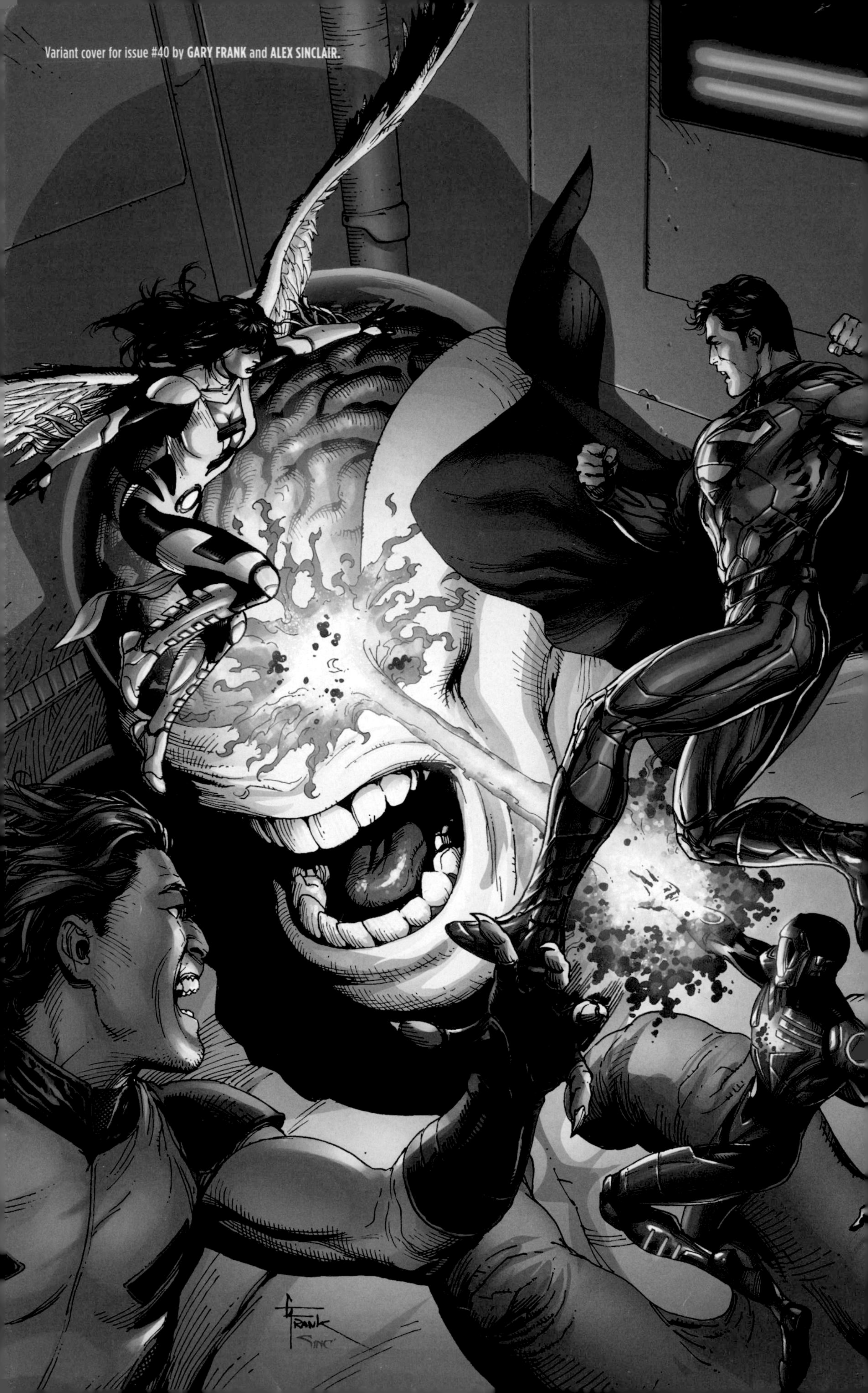

Variant cover for issue #40 by **GARY FRANK** and **ALEX SINCLAIR.**

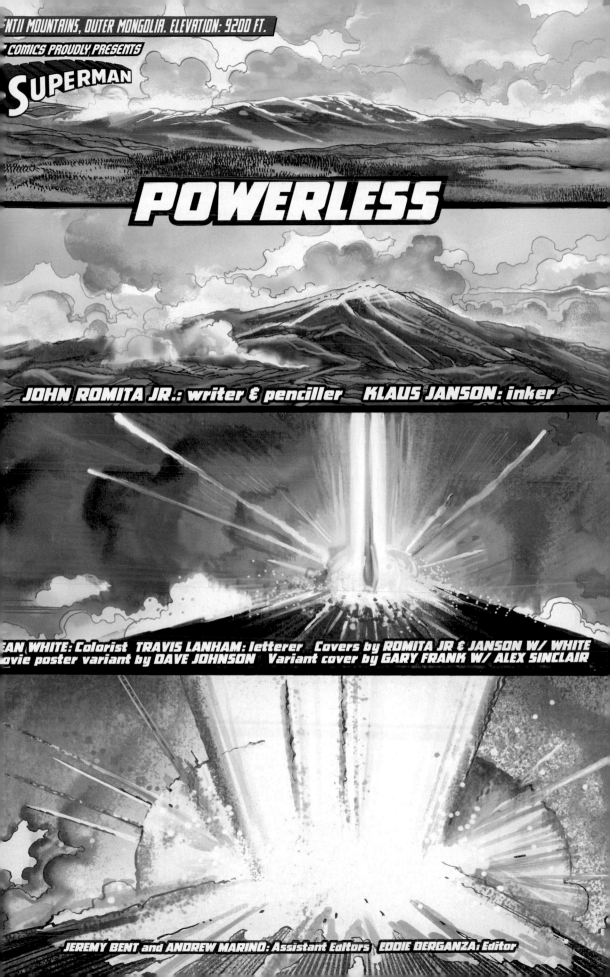

ALTII MOUNTAINS, OUTER MONGOLIA. ELEVATION: 9200 FT.

COMICS PROUDLY PRESENTS

SUPERMAN

POWERLESS

JOHN ROMITA JR.: writer & penciller   **KLAUS JANSON:** inker

EAN WHITE: Colorist   TRAVIS LANHAM: letterer   Covers by ROMITA JR & JANSON W/ WHITE
ovie poster variant by DAVE JOHNSON   Variant cover by GARY FRANK W/ ALEX SINCLAIR

JEREMY BENT and ANDREW MARINO: Assistant Editors   EDDIE BERGANZA: Editor

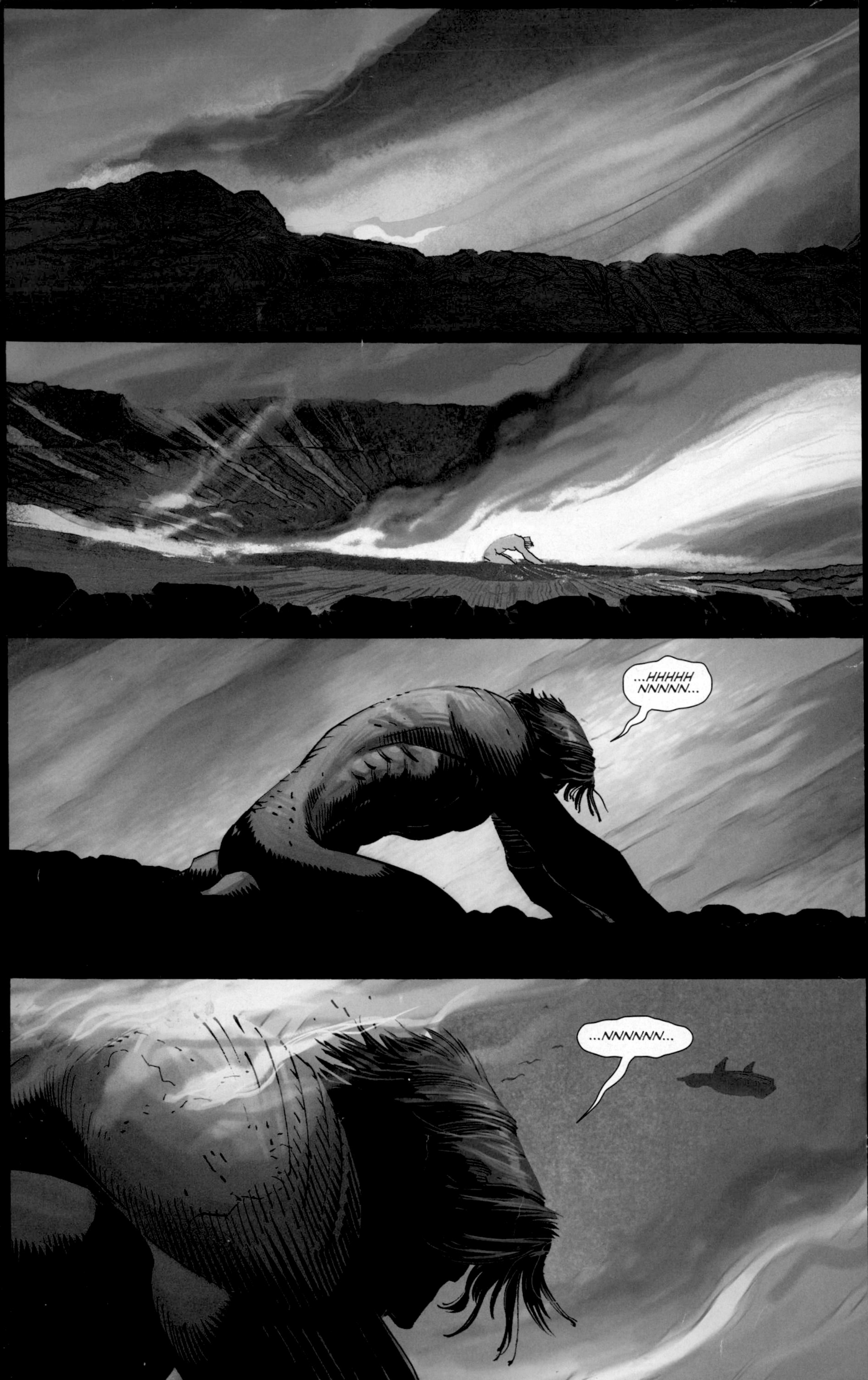
...HHHHH NNNNN...
...NNNNNN...

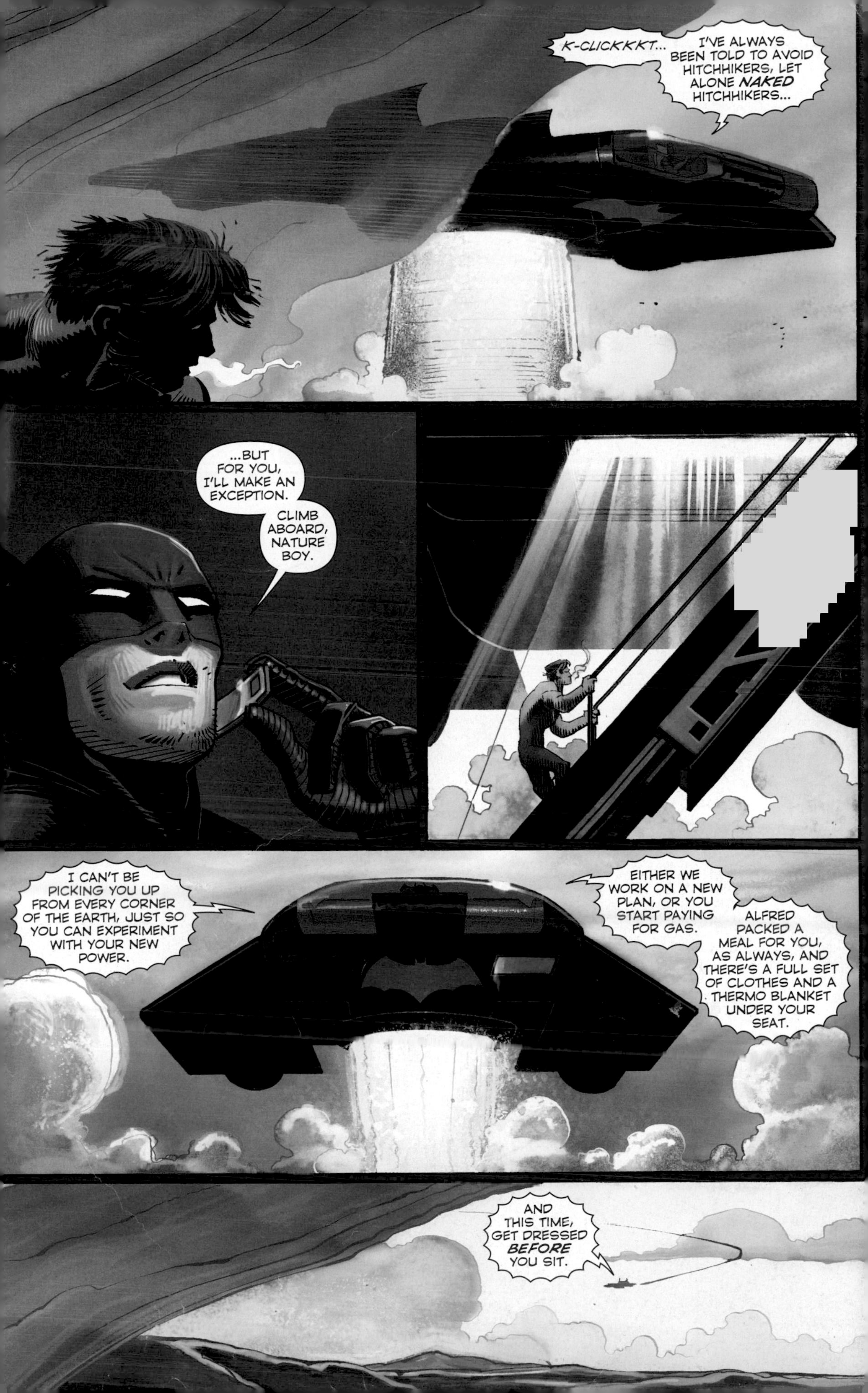
K-CLICKKKT...
I'VE ALWAYS BEEN TOLD TO AVOID HITCHHIKERS, LET ALONE NAKED HITCHHIKERS...
...BUT FOR YOU, I'LL MAKE AN EXCEPTION.
CLIMB ABOARD, NATURE BOY.
I CAN'T BE PICKING YOU UP FROM EVERY CORNER OF THE EARTH, JUST SO YOU CAN EXPERIMENT WITH YOUR NEW POWER.
EITHER WE WORK ON A NEW PLAN, OR YOU START PAYING FOR GAS.
ALFRED PACKED A MEAL FOR YOU, AS ALWAYS, AND THERE'S A FULL SET OF CLOTHES AND A THERMO BLANKET UNDER YOUR SEAT.
AND THIS TIME, GET DRESSED BEFORE YOU SIT.

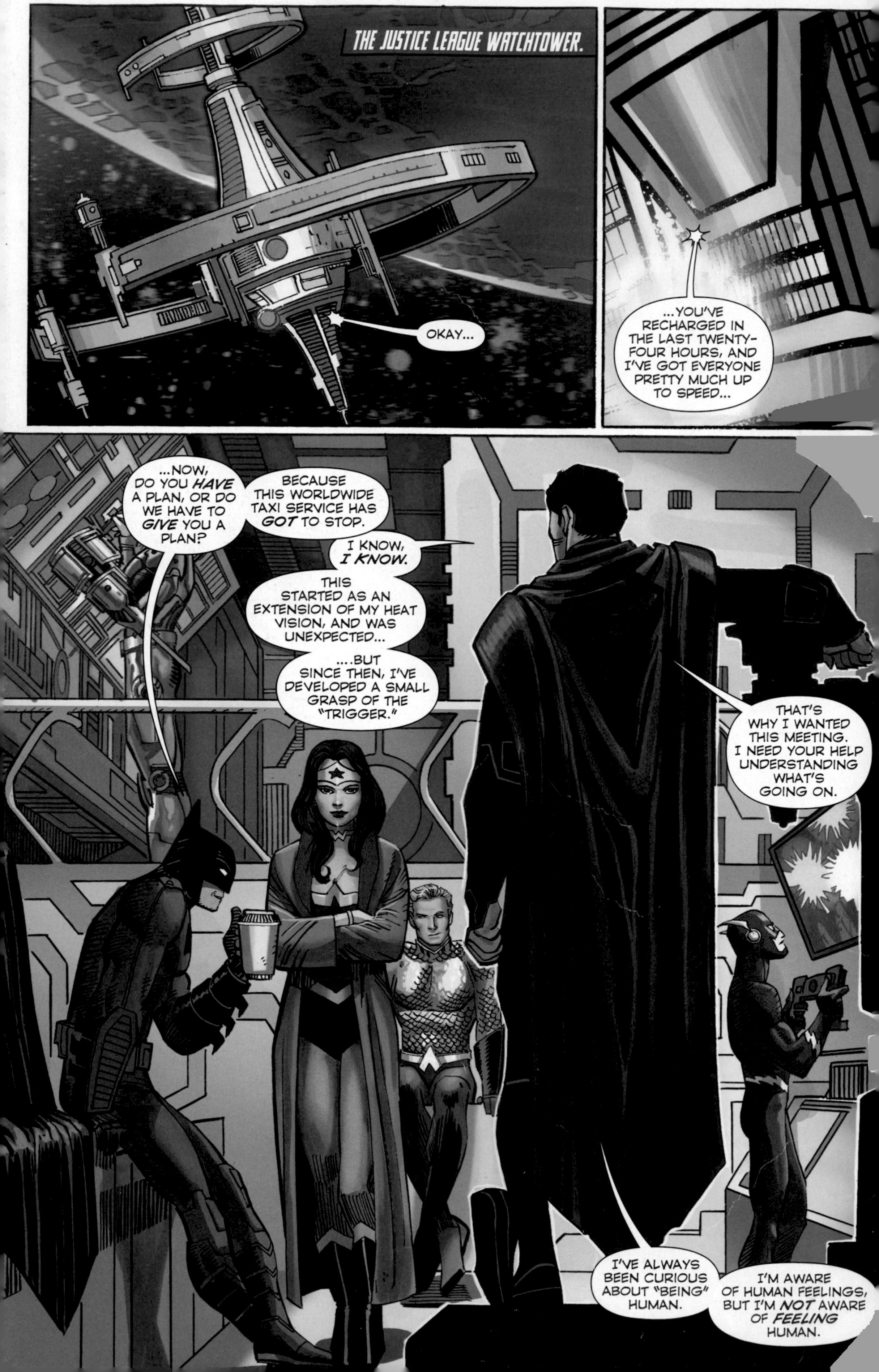
THE JUSTICE LEAGUE WATCHTOWER.
OKAY...
...YOU'VE RECHARGED IN THE LAST TWENTY-FOUR HOURS, AND I'VE GOT EVERYONE PRETTY MUCH UP TO SPEED...
...NOW, DO YOU HAVE A PLAN, OR DO WE HAVE TO GIVE YOU A PLAN?
BECAUSE THIS WORLDWIDE TAXI SERVICE HAS GOT TO STOP.
I KNOW, I KNOW.
THIS STARTED AS AN EXTENSION OF MY HEAT VISION, AND WAS UNEXPECTED...
....BUT SINCE THEN, I'VE DEVELOPED A SMALL GRASP OF THE "TRIGGER."
THAT'S WHY I WANTED THIS MEETING. I NEED YOUR HELP UNDERSTANDING WHAT'S GOING ON.
I'VE ALWAYS BEEN CURIOUS ABOUT "BEING" HUMAN.
I'M AWARE OF HUMAN FEELINGS, BUT I'M NOT AWARE OF FEELING HUMAN.

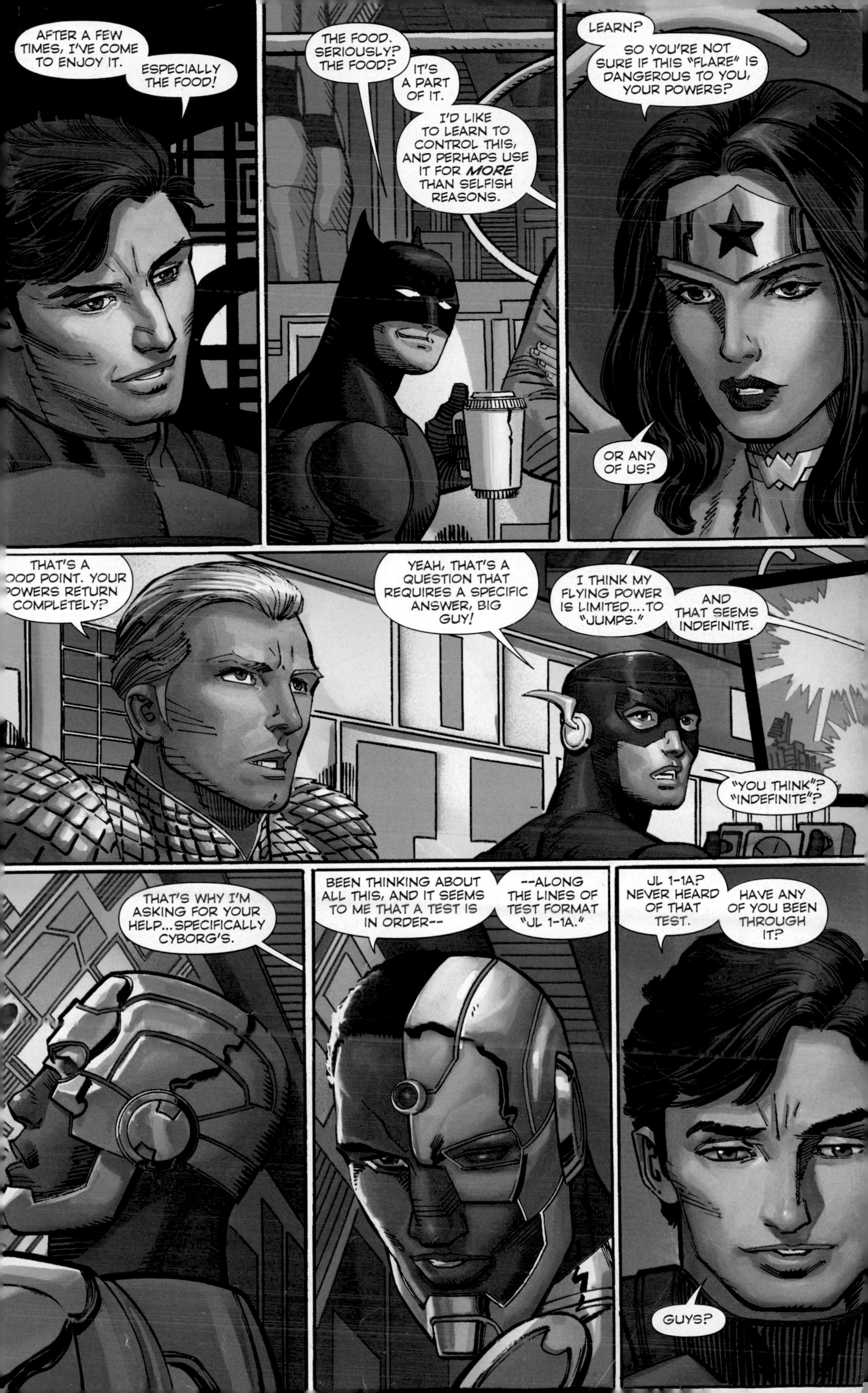
AFTER A FEW TIMES, I'VE COME TO ENJOY IT.
ESPECIALLY THE FOOD!
THE FOOD. SERIOUSLY? THE FOOD?
IT'S A PART OF IT.
I'D LIKE TO LEARN TO CONTROL THIS, AND PERHAPS USE IT FOR MORE THAN SELFISH REASONS.
LEARN?
SO YOU'RE NOT SURE IF THIS "FLARE" IS DANGEROUS TO YOU, YOUR POWERS?
OR ANY OF US?
THAT'S A OOD POINT. YOUR OWERS RETURN COMPLETELY?
YEAH, THAT'S A QUESTION THAT REQUIRES A SPECIFIC ANSWER, BIG GUY!
I THINK MY FLYING POWER IS LIMITED....TO "JUMPS."
AND THAT SEEMS INDEFINITE.
"YOU THINK"? "INDEFINITE"?
THAT'S WHY I'M ASKING FOR YOUR HELP...SPECIFICALLY CYBORG'S.
BEEN THINKING ABOUT ALL THIS, AND IT SEEMS TO ME THAT A TEST IS IN ORDER--
--ALONG THE LINES OF TEST FORMAT "JL 1-1A."
JL 1-1A? NEVER HEARD OF THAT TEST.
HAVE ANY OF YOU BEEN THROUGH IT?
GUYS?

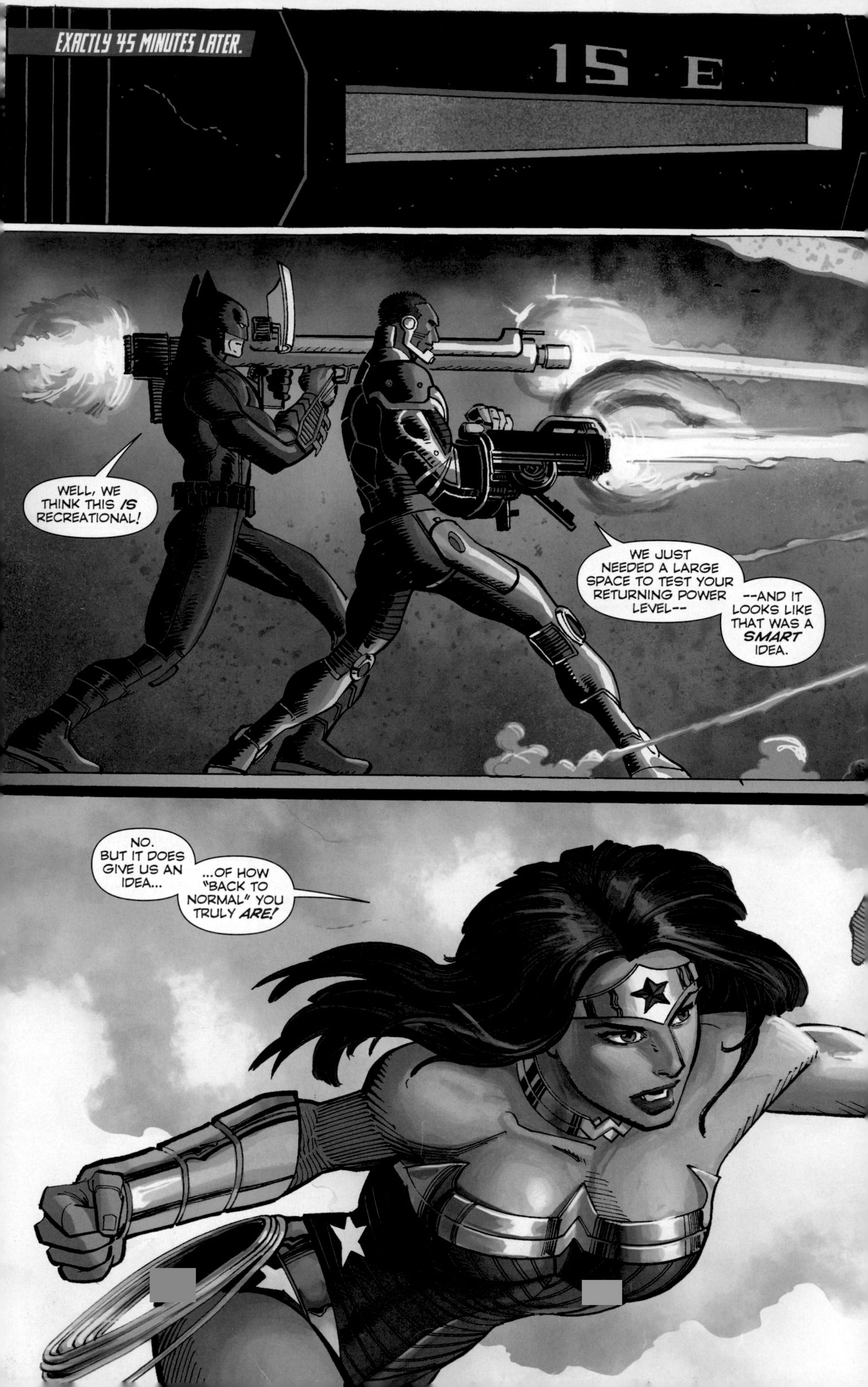
EXACTLY 45 MINUTES LATER.
WELL, WE THINK THIS *IS* RECREATIONAL!
WE JUST NEEDED A LARGE SPACE TO TEST YOUR RETURNING POWER LEVEL--
--AND IT LOOKS LIKE THAT WAS A ***SMART*** IDEA.
NO. BUT IT DOES GIVE US AN IDEA...
...OF HOW "BACK TO NORMAL" YOU TRULY ***ARE!***

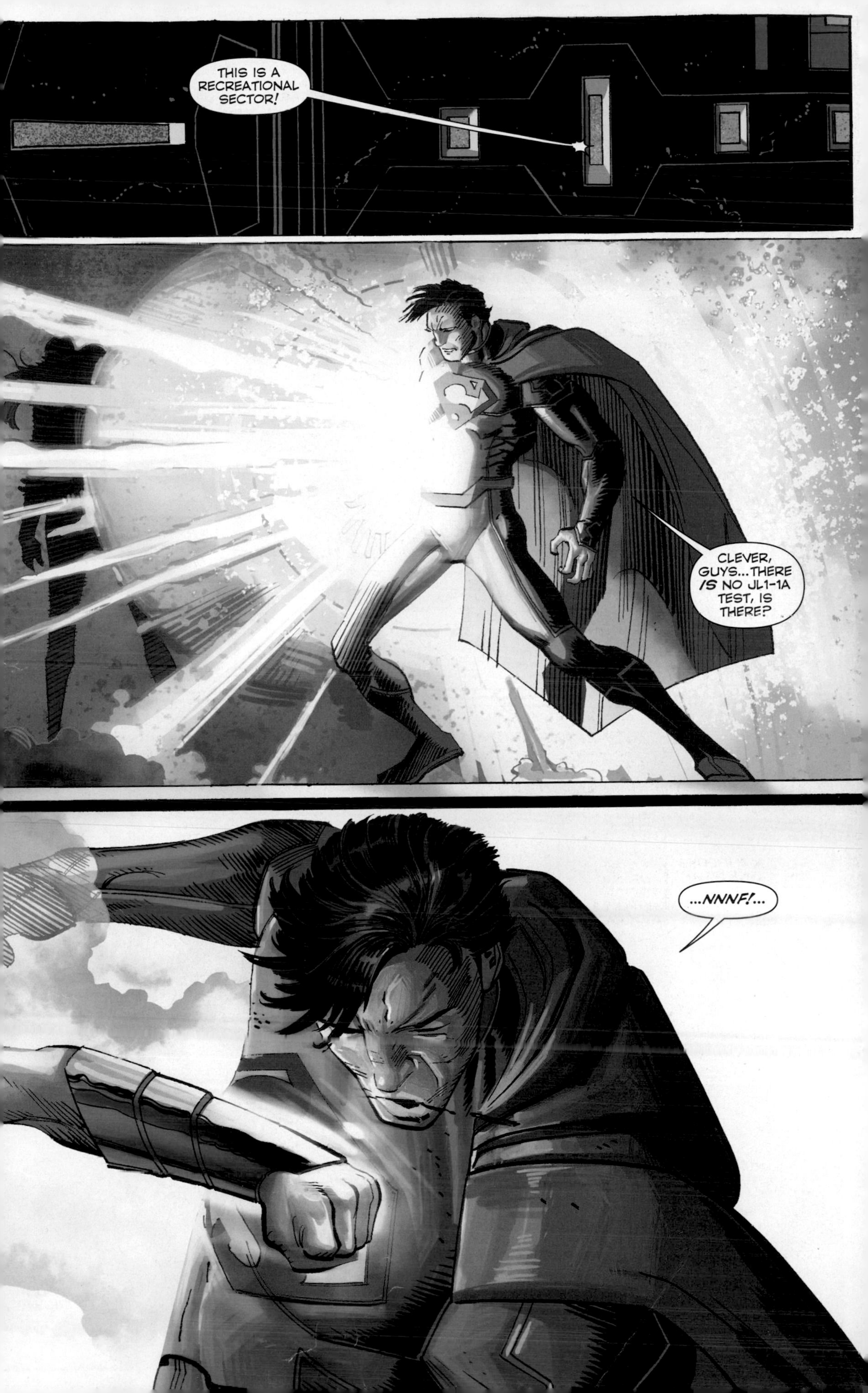
THIS IS A RECREATIONAL SECTOR!
CLEVER, GUYS...THERE IS NO JL1-1A TEST, IS THERE?
...NNNF!...

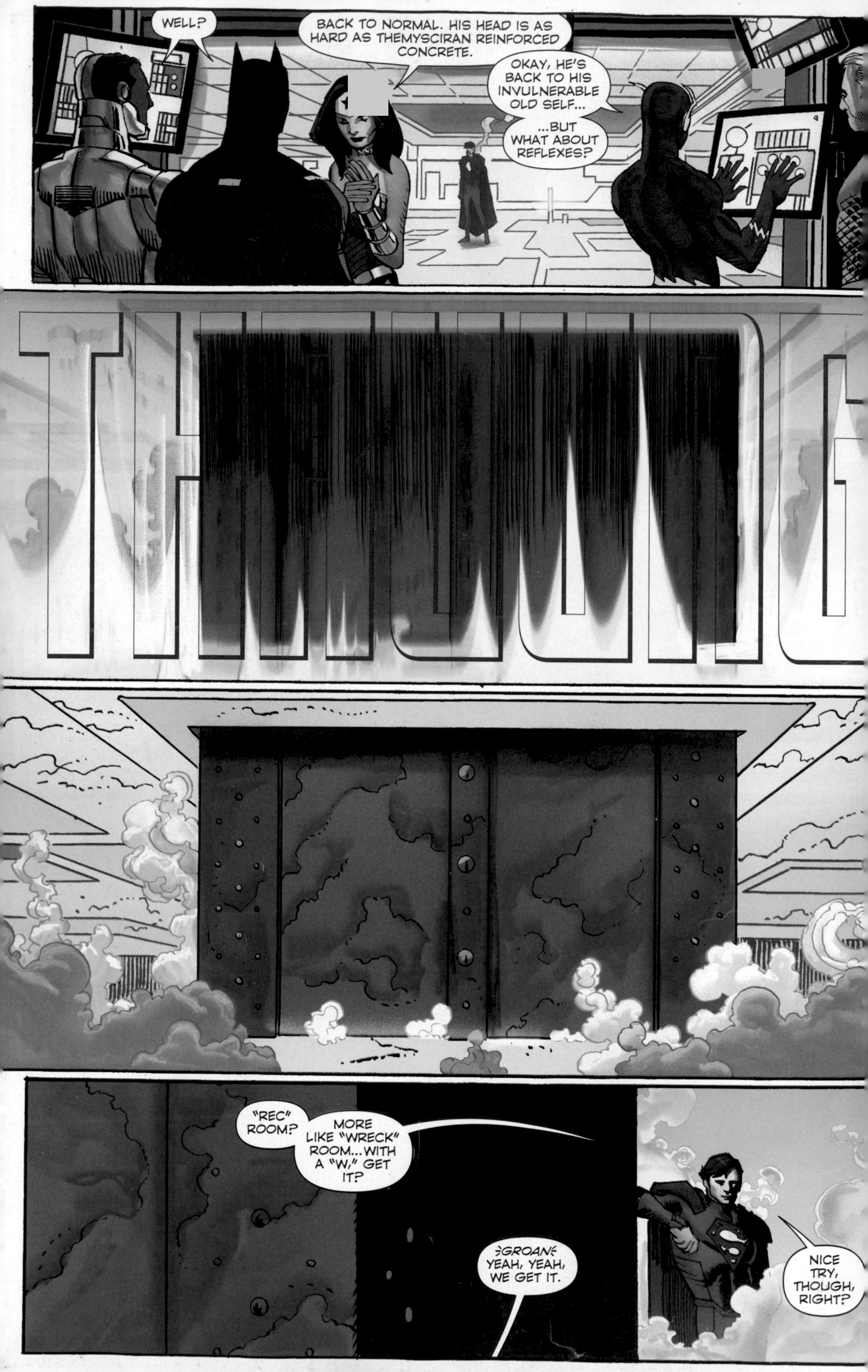
WELL?
BACK TO NORMAL. HIS HEAD IS AS HARD AS THEMYSCIRAN REINFORCED CONCRETE.
OKAY, HE'S BACK TO HIS INVULNERABLE OLD SELF...
...BUT WHAT ABOUT REFLEXES?
"REC" ROOM?
MORE LIKE "WRECK" ROOM...WITH A "W," GET IT?
GROAN YEAH, YEAH, WE GET IT.
NICE TRY, THOUGH, RIGHT?

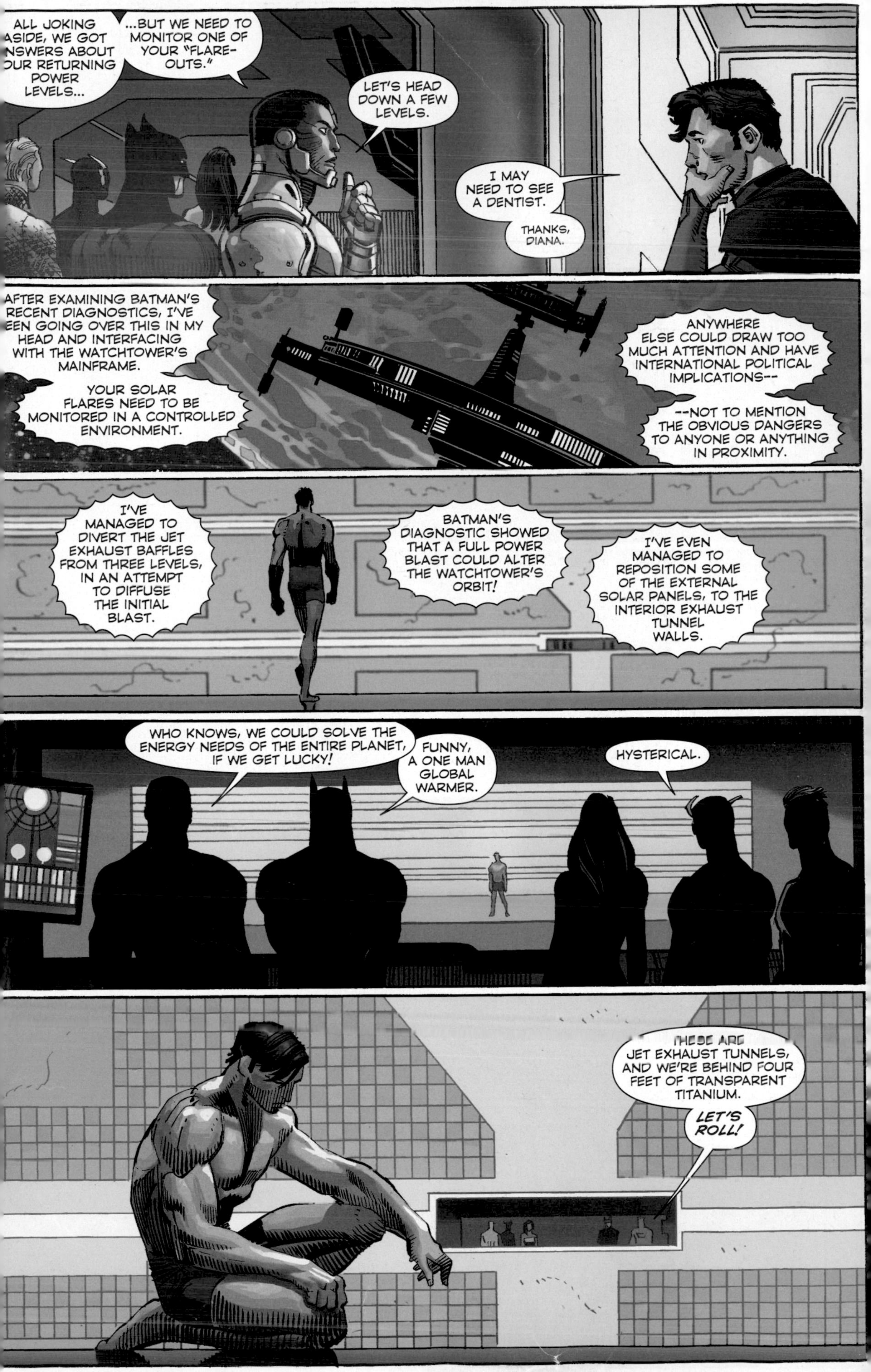
ALL JOKING ASIDE, WE GOT NSWERS ABOUT OUR RETURNING POWER LEVELS...
...BUT WE NEED TO MONITOR ONE OF YOUR "FLARE-OUTS."
LET'S HEAD DOWN A FEW LEVELS.
I MAY NEED TO SEE A DENTIST.
THANKS, DIANA.
AFTER EXAMINING BATMAN'S RECENT DIAGNOSTICS, I'VE EEN GOING OVER THIS IN MY HEAD AND INTERFACING WITH THE WATCHTOWER'S MAINFRAME.
YOUR SOLAR FLARES NEED TO BE MONITORED IN A CONTROLLED ENVIRONMENT.
ANYWHERE ELSE COULD DRAW TOO MUCH ATTENTION AND HAVE INTERNATIONAL POLITICAL IMPLICATIONS--
--NOT TO MENTION THE OBVIOUS DANGERS TO ANYONE OR ANYTHING IN PROXIMITY.
I'VE MANAGED TO DIVERT THE JET EXHAUST BAFFLES FROM THREE LEVELS, IN AN ATTEMPT TO DIFFUSE THE INITIAL BLAST.
BATMAN'S DIAGNOSTIC SHOWED THAT A FULL POWER BLAST COULD ALTER THE WATCHTOWER'S ORBIT!
I'VE EVEN MANAGED TO REPOSITION SOME OF THE EXTERNAL SOLAR PANELS, TO THE INTERIOR EXHAUST TUNNEL WALLS.
WHO KNOWS, WE COULD SOLVE THE ENERGY NEEDS OF THE ENTIRE PLANET, IF WE GET LUCKY!
FUNNY, A ONE MAN GLOBAL WARMER.
HYSTERICAL.
THESE ARE JET EXHAUST TUNNELS, AND WE'RE BEHIND FOUR FEET OF TRANSPARENT TITANIUM.
LET'S ROLL!

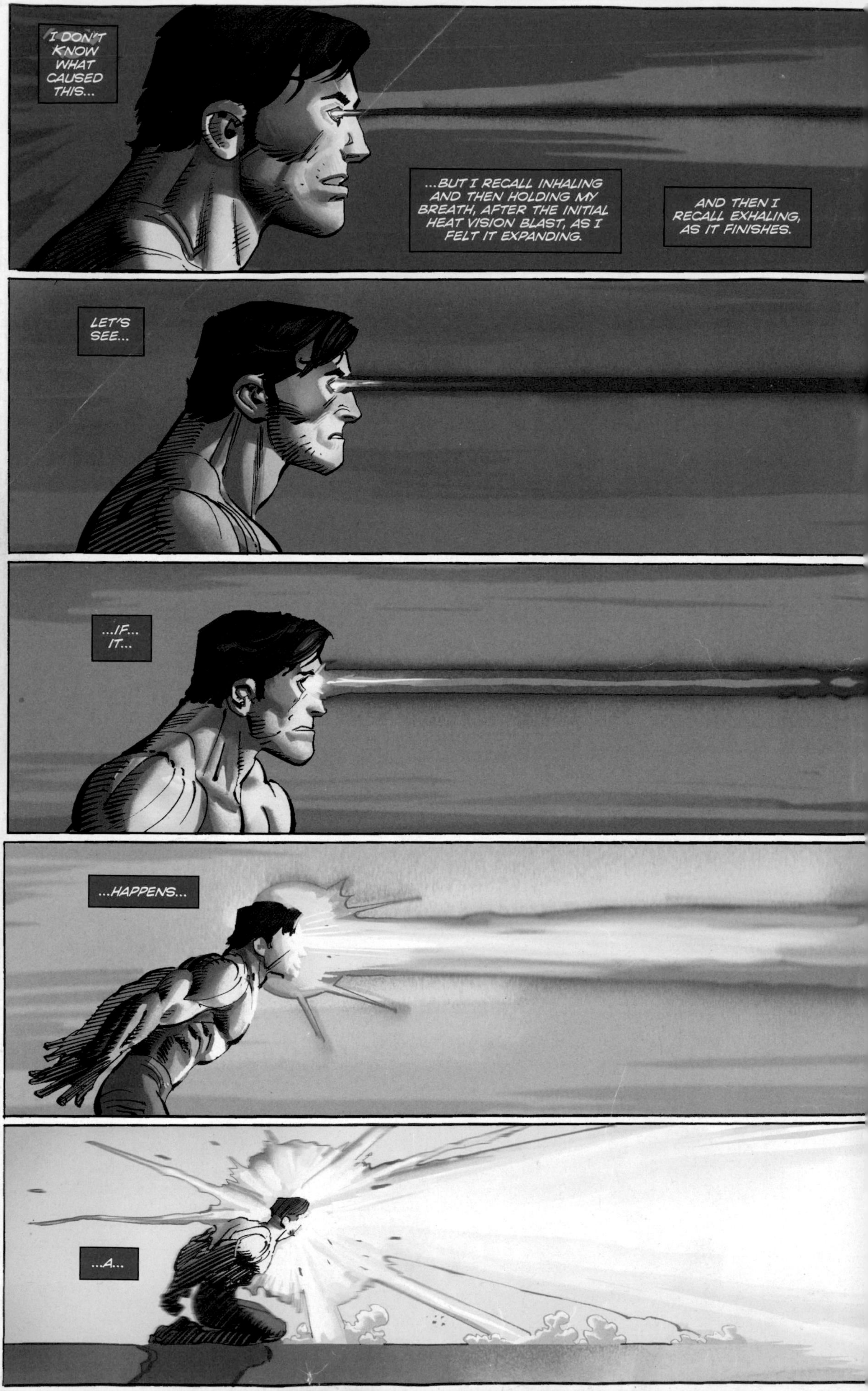
I DON'T KNOW WHAT CAUSED THIS...
...BUT I RECALL INHALING AND THEN HOLDING MY BREATH, AFTER THE INITIAL HEAT VISION BLAST, AS I FELT IT EXPANDING.
AND THEN I RECALL EXHALING, AS IT FINISHES.
LET'S SEE...
...IF... IT...
...HAPPENS...
...A...

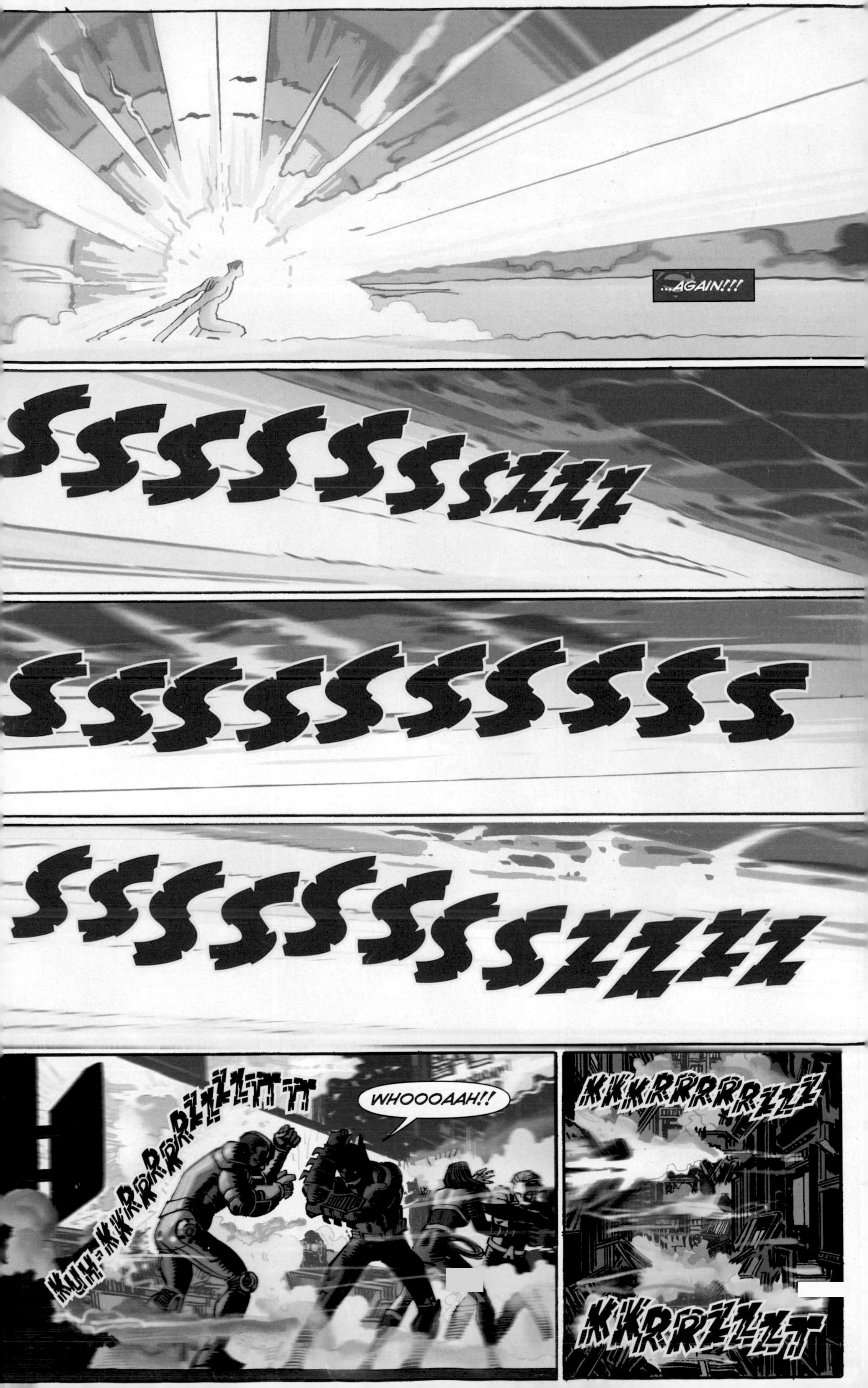
...AGAIN!!!
SSSSSSSZZZZ
SSSSSSSSSS
SSSSSSSSZZZZZ
KUH-KKRRRRRZZZZTTTT
WHOOOAAH!!
KKKRRRRRRZZZ
KKRRZZZT

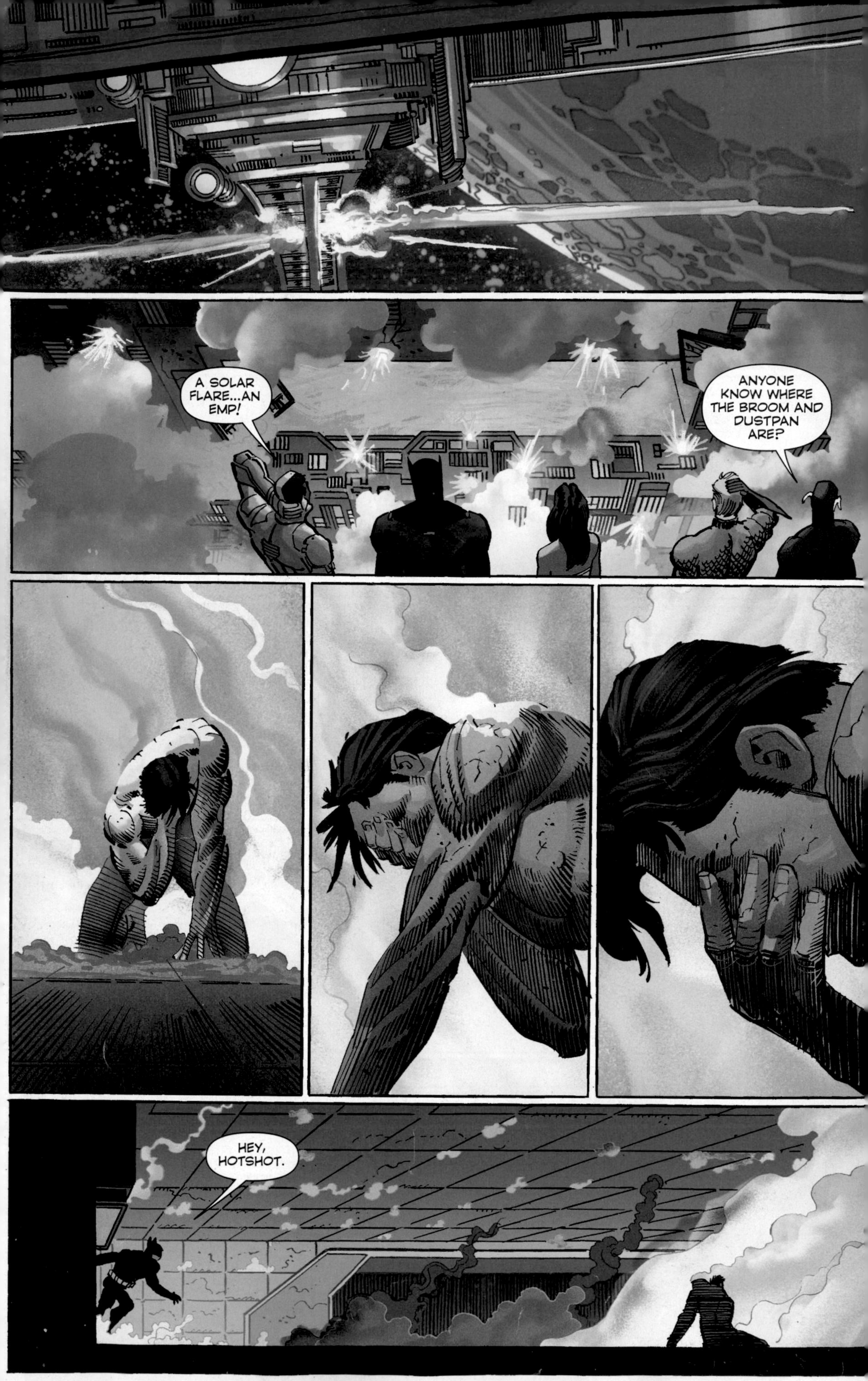
A SOLAR FLARE...AN EMP!
ANYONE KNOW WHERE THE BROOM AND DUSTPAN ARE?
HEY, HOTSHOT.

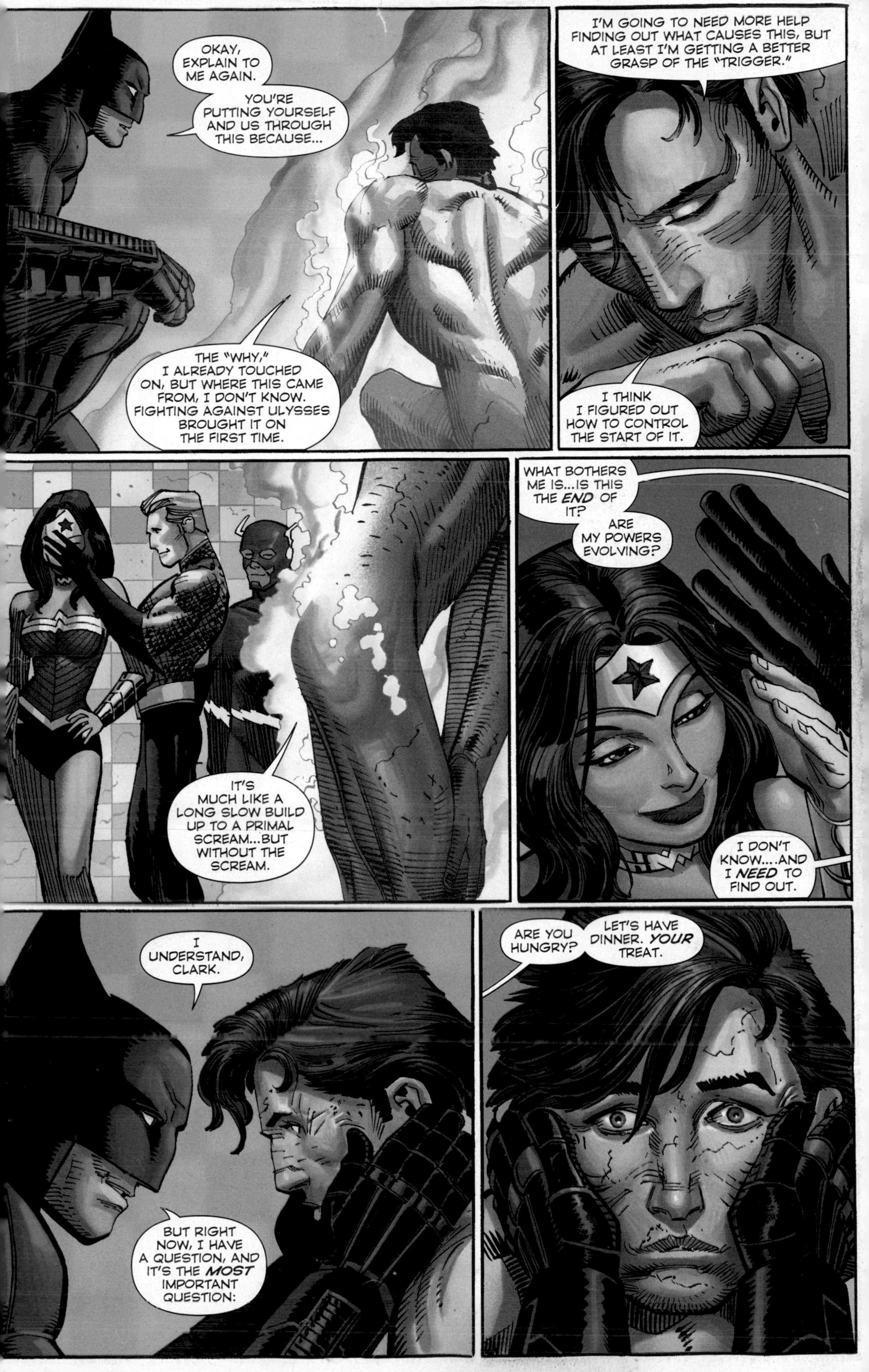
OKAY, EXPLAIN TO ME AGAIN.
YOU'RE PUTTING YOURSELF AND US THROUGH THIS BECAUSE...
THE "WHY," I ALREADY TOUCHED ON, BUT WHERE THIS CAME FROM, I DON'T KNOW. FIGHTING AGAINST ULYSSES BROUGHT IT ON THE FIRST TIME.
I'M GOING TO NEED MORE HELP FINDING OUT WHAT CAUSES THIS, BUT AT LEAST I'M GETTING A BETTER GRASP OF THE "TRIGGER."
I THINK I FIGURED OUT HOW TO CONTROL THE START OF IT.
IT'S MUCH LIKE A LONG SLOW BUILD UP TO A PRIMAL SCREAM...BUT WITHOUT THE SCREAM.
WHAT BOTHERS ME IS...IS THIS THE *END* OF IT?
ARE MY POWERS EVOLVING?
I DON'T KNOW....AND I *NEED* TO FIND OUT.
I UNDERSTAND, CLARK.
BUT RIGHT NOW, I HAVE A QUESTION, AND IT'S THE *MOST* IMPORTANT QUESTION:
ARE YOU HUNGRY?
LET'S HAVE DINNER. *YOUR* TREAT.

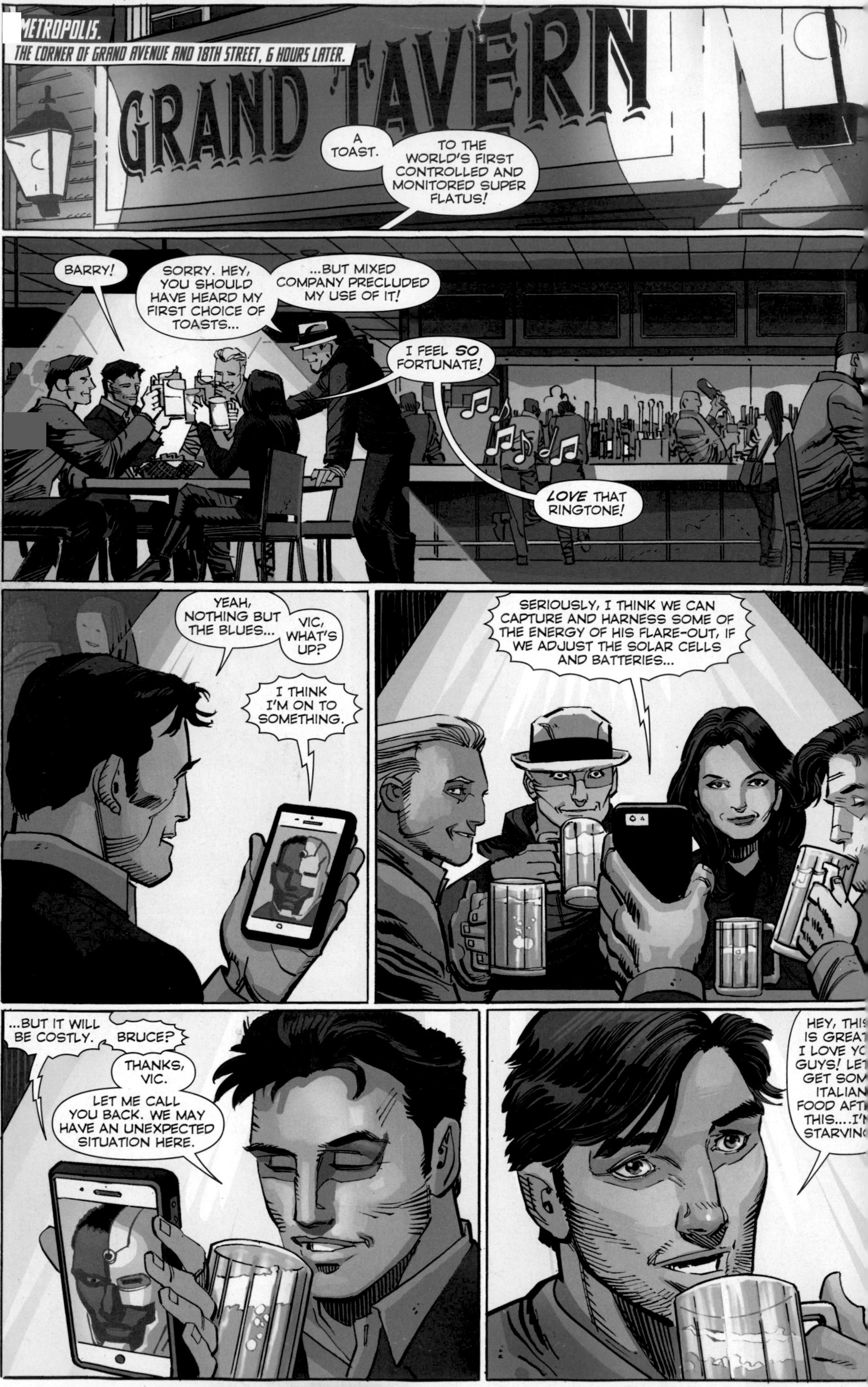
METROPOLIS.
THE CORNER OF GRAND AVENUE AND 18TH STREET, 6 HOURS LATER.
GRAND TAVERN
A TOAST.
TO THE WORLD'S FIRST CONTROLLED AND MONITORED SUPER FLATUS!
BARRY!
SORRY. HEY, YOU SHOULD HAVE HEARD MY FIRST CHOICE OF TOASTS...
...BUT MIXED COMPANY PRECLUDED MY USE OF IT!
I FEEL SO FORTUNATE!
LOVE THAT RINGTONE!
YEAH, NOTHING BUT THE BLUES...
VIC, WHAT'S UP?
I THINK I'M ON TO SOMETHING.
SERIOUSLY, I THINK WE CAN CAPTURE AND HARNESS SOME OF THE ENERGY OF HIS FLARE-OUT, IF WE ADJUST THE SOLAR CELLS AND BATTERIES...
...BUT IT WILL BE COSTLY.
BRUCE?
THANKS, VIC.
LET ME CALL YOU BACK. WE MAY HAVE AN UNEXPECTED SITUATION HERE.
HEY, THIS IS GREAT I LOVE YO GUYS! LET GET SOM ITALIAN FOOD AFT THIS....I'M STARVIN

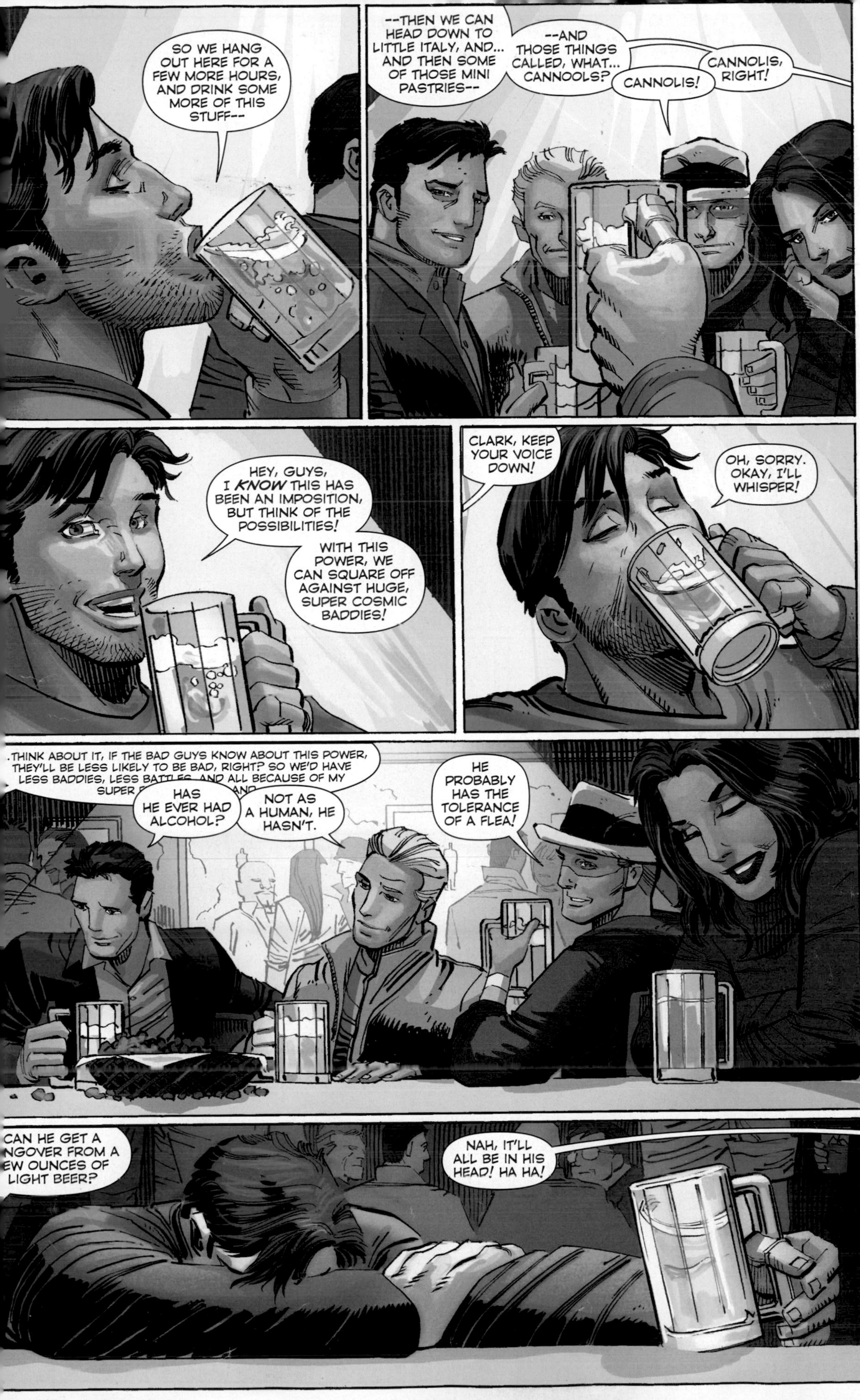
SO WE HANG OUT HERE FOR A FEW MORE HOURS, AND DRINK SOME MORE OF THIS STUFF--
--THEN WE CAN HEAD DOWN TO LITTLE ITALY, AND... AND THEN SOME OF THOSE MINI PASTRIES--
--AND THOSE THINGS CALLED, WHAT... CANNOOLS?
CANNOLIS!
CANNOLIS, RIGHT!
HEY, GUYS, I *KNOW* THIS HAS BEEN AN IMPOSITION, BUT THINK OF THE POSSIBILITIES!
WITH THIS POWER, WE CAN SQUARE OFF AGAINST HUGE, SUPER COSMIC BADDIES!
CLARK, KEEP YOUR VOICE DOWN!
OH, SORRY. OKAY, I'LL WHISPER!
.THINK ABOUT IT, IF THE BAD GUYS KNOW ABOUT THIS POWER, THEY'LL BE LESS LIKELY TO BE BAD, RIGHT? SO WE'D HAVE LESS BADDIES, LESS BATTLES, AND ALL BECAUSE OF MY SUPER
HAS HE EVER HAD ALCOHOL?
NOT AS A HUMAN, HE HASN'T.
HE PROBABLY HAS THE TOLERANCE OF A FLEA!
CAN HE GET A NGOVER FROM A EW OUNCES OF LIGHT BEER?
NAH, IT'LL ALL BE IN HIS HEAD! HA HA!

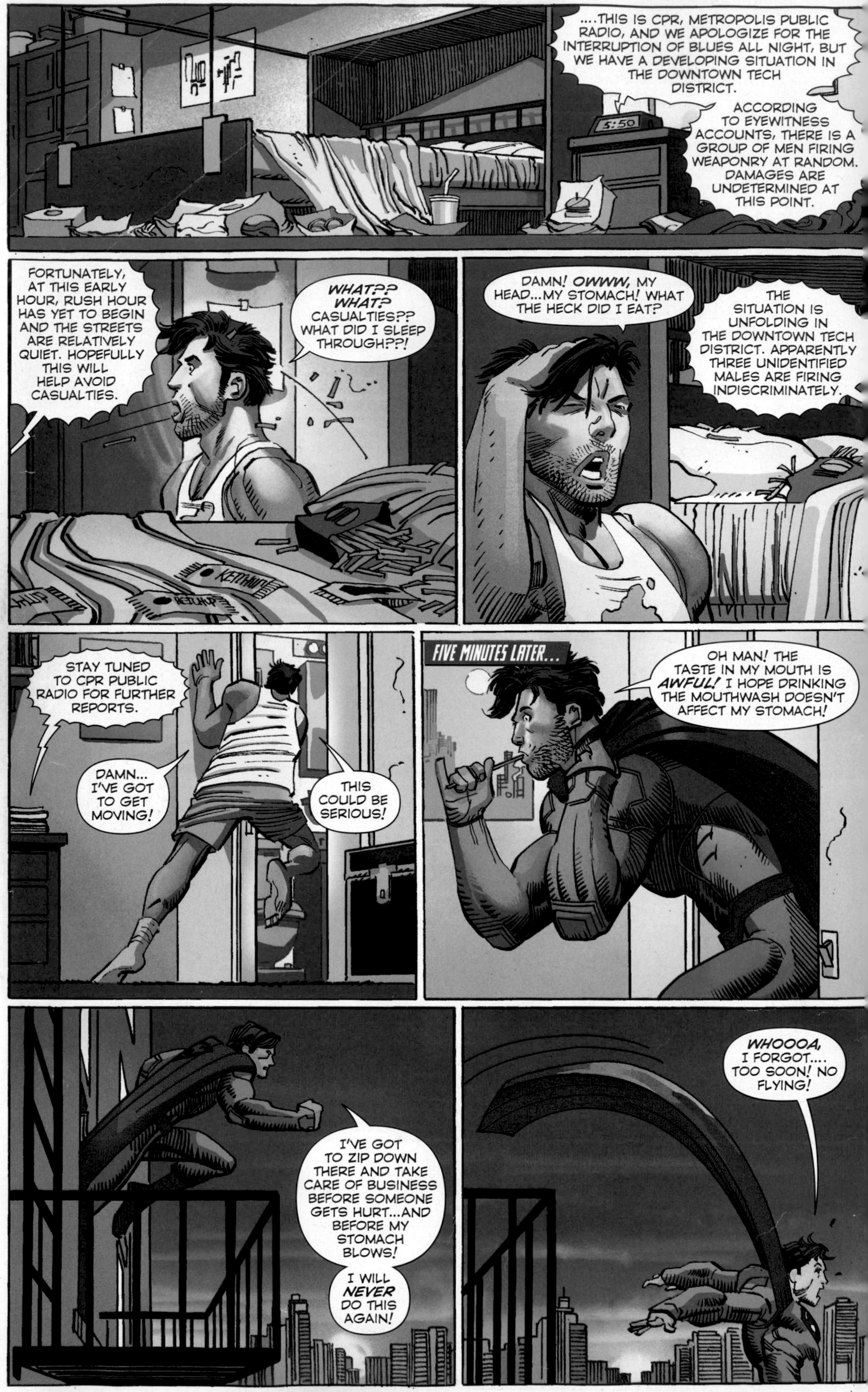
....THIS IS CPR, METROPOLIS PUBLIC RADIO, AND WE APOLOGIZE FOR THE INTERRUPTION OF BLUES ALL NIGHT, BUT WE HAVE A DEVELOPING SITUATION IN THE DOWNTOWN TECH DISTRICT.
ACCORDING TO EYEWITNESS ACCOUNTS, THERE IS A GROUP OF MEN FIRING WEAPONRY AT RANDOM. DAMAGES ARE UNDETERMINED AT THIS POINT.
5:50
FORTUNATELY, AT THIS EARLY HOUR, RUSH HOUR HAS YET TO BEGIN AND THE STREETS ARE RELATIVELY QUIET. HOPEFULLY THIS WILL HELP AVOID CASUALTIES.
WHAT?? WHAT? CASUALTIES?? WHAT DID I SLEEP THROUGH??!
KETCHUP
DAMN! OWWW, MY HEAD...MY STOMACH! WHAT THE HECK DID I EAT?
THE SITUATION IS UNFOLDING IN THE DOWNTOWN TECH DISTRICT. APPARENTLY THREE UNIDENTIFIED MALES ARE FIRING INDISCRIMINATELY.
STAY TUNED TO CPR PUBLIC RADIO FOR FURTHER REPORTS.
DAMN... I'VE GOT TO GET MOVING!
THIS COULD BE SERIOUS!
FIVE MINUTES LATER...
OH MAN! THE TASTE IN MY MOUTH IS AWFUL! I HOPE DRINKING THE MOUTHWASH DOESN'T AFFECT MY STOMACH!
I'VE GOT TO ZIP DOWN THERE AND TAKE CARE OF BUSINESS BEFORE SOMEONE GETS HURT...AND BEFORE MY STOMACH BLOWS!
I WILL NEVER DO THIS AGAIN!
WHOOOA, I FORGOT.... TOO SOON! NO FLYING!

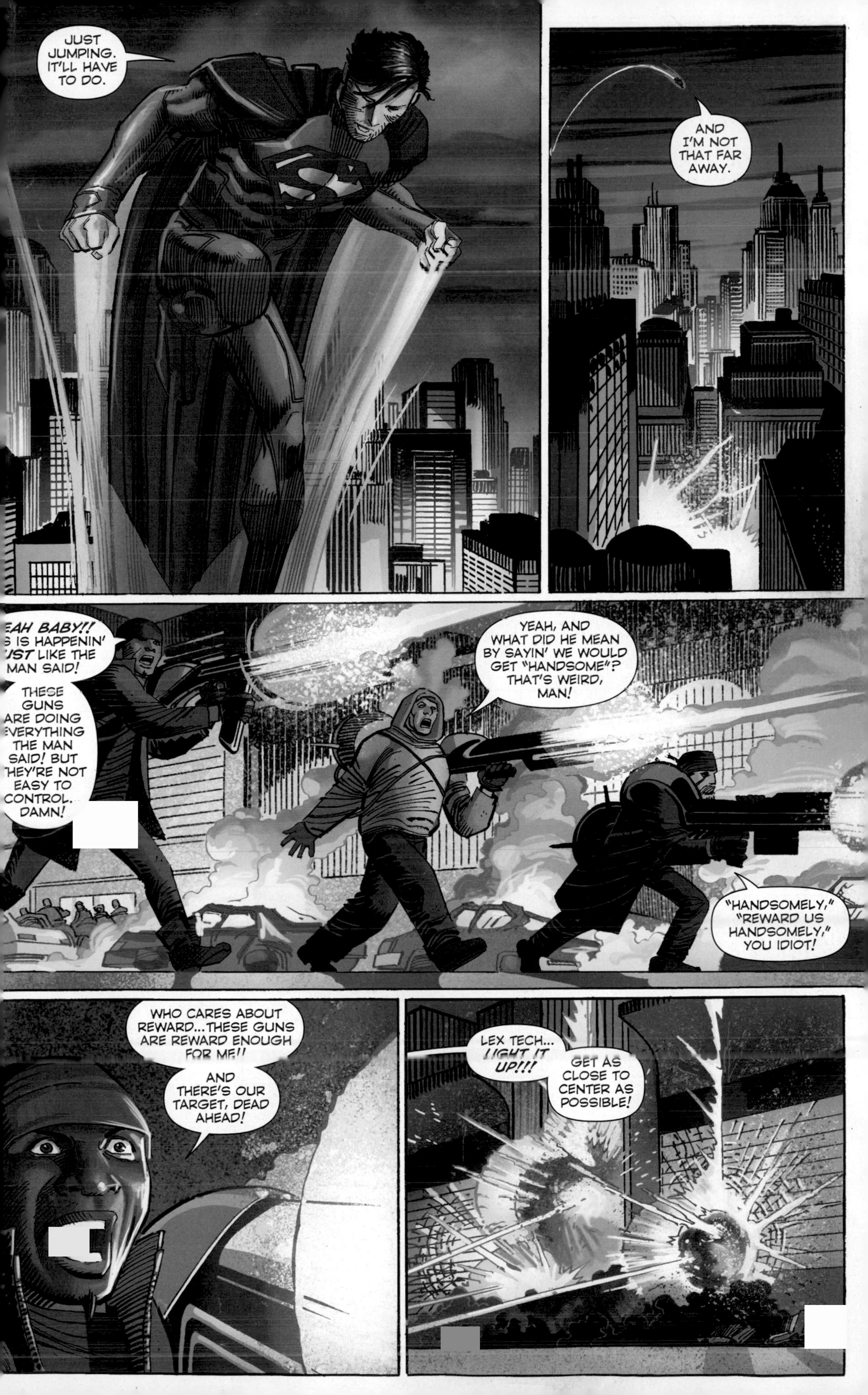
JUST JUMPING. IT'LL HAVE TO DO.
AND I'M NOT THAT FAR AWAY.
EAH BABY!! S IS HAPPENIN' UST LIKE THE MAN SAID!
THESE GUNS ARE DOING EVERYTHING THE MAN SAID! BUT THEY'RE NOT EASY TO CONTROL... DAMN!
YEAH, AND WHAT DID HE MEAN BY SAYIN' WE WOULD GET "HANDSOME"? THAT'S WEIRD, MAN!
"HANDSOMELY," "REWARD US HANDSOMELY," YOU IDIOT!
WHO CARES ABOUT REWARD...THESE GUNS ARE REWARD ENOUGH FOR ME!!
AND THERE'S OUR TARGET, DEAD AHEAD!
LEX TECH... LIGHT IT UP!!!
GET AS CLOSE TO CENTER AS POSSIBLE!

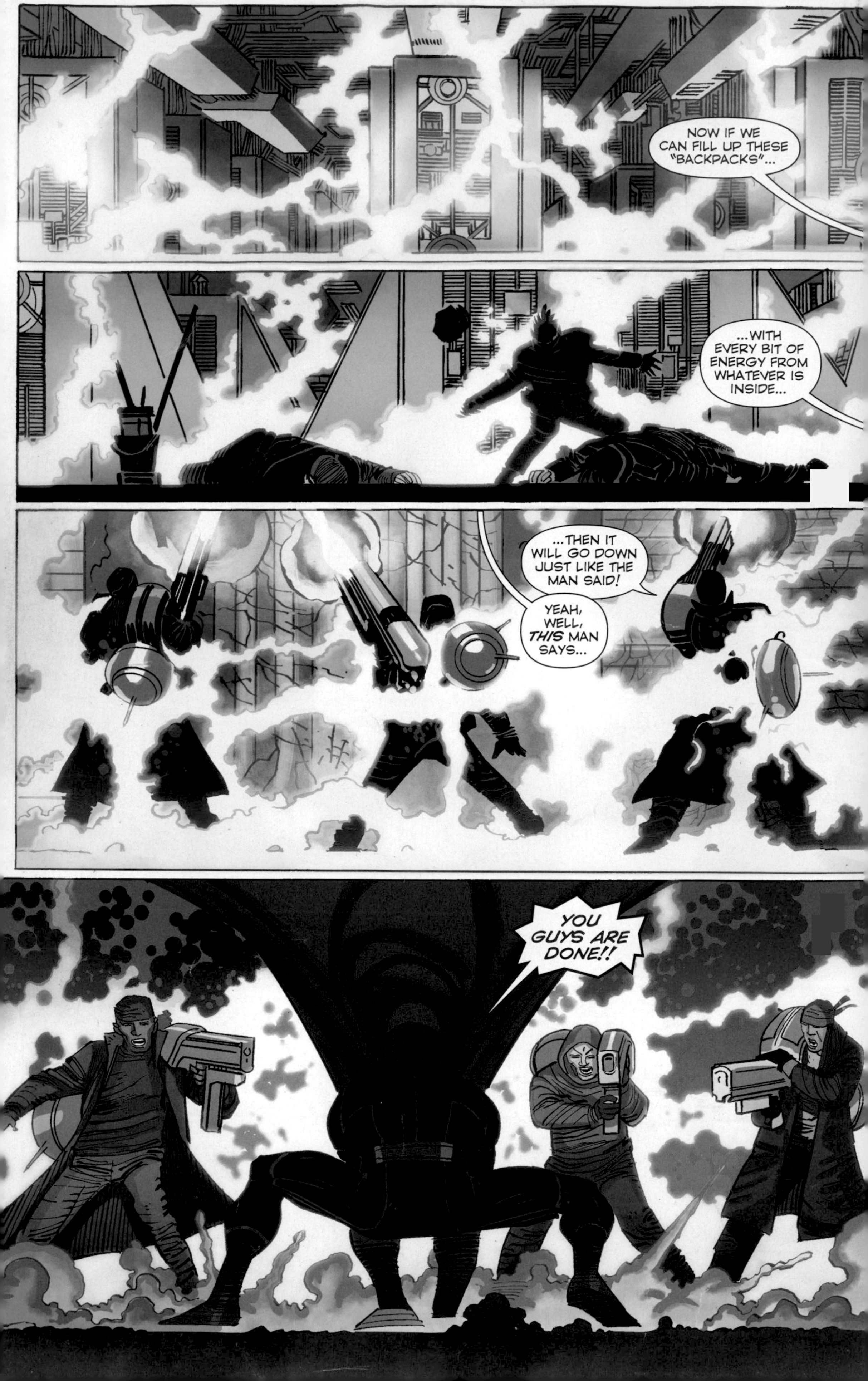
NOW IF WE CAN FILL UP THESE "BACKPACKS"...
...WITH EVERY BIT OF ENERGY FROM WHATEVER IS INSIDE...
...THEN IT WILL GO DOWN JUST LIKE THE MAN SAID!
YEAH, WELL, THIS MAN SAYS...
YOU GUYS ARE DONE!!

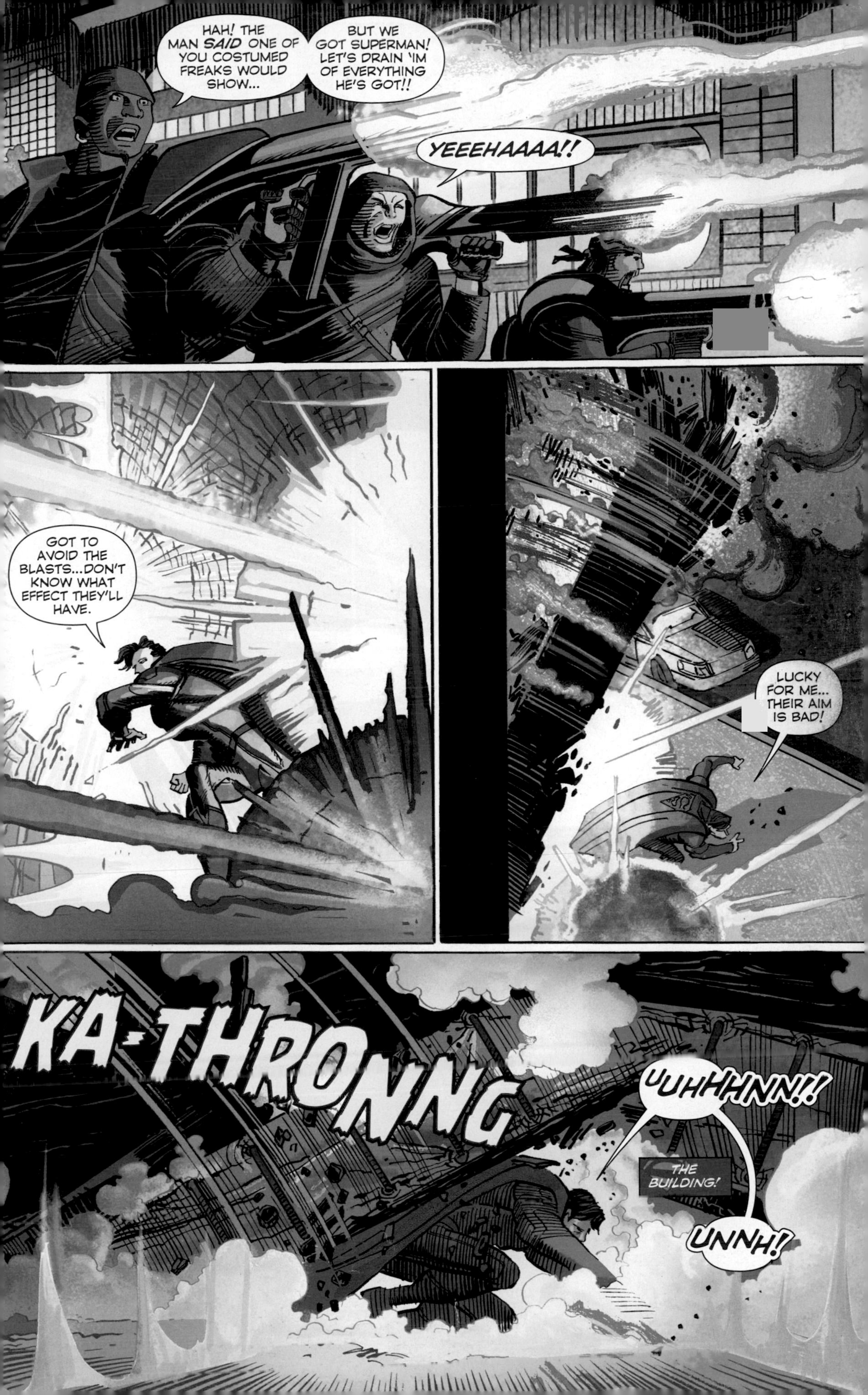
HAH! THE MAN SAID ONE OF YOU COSTUMED FREAKS WOULD SHOW...
BUT WE GOT SUPERMAN! LET'S DRAIN 'IM OF EVERYTHING HE'S GOT!!
YEEEHAAAA!!
GOT TO AVOID THE BLASTS...DON'T KNOW WHAT EFFECT THEY'LL HAVE.
LUCKY FOR ME... THEIR AIM IS BAD!
KA-THRONNG
UUHHHNN!!
THE BUILDING!
UNNH!

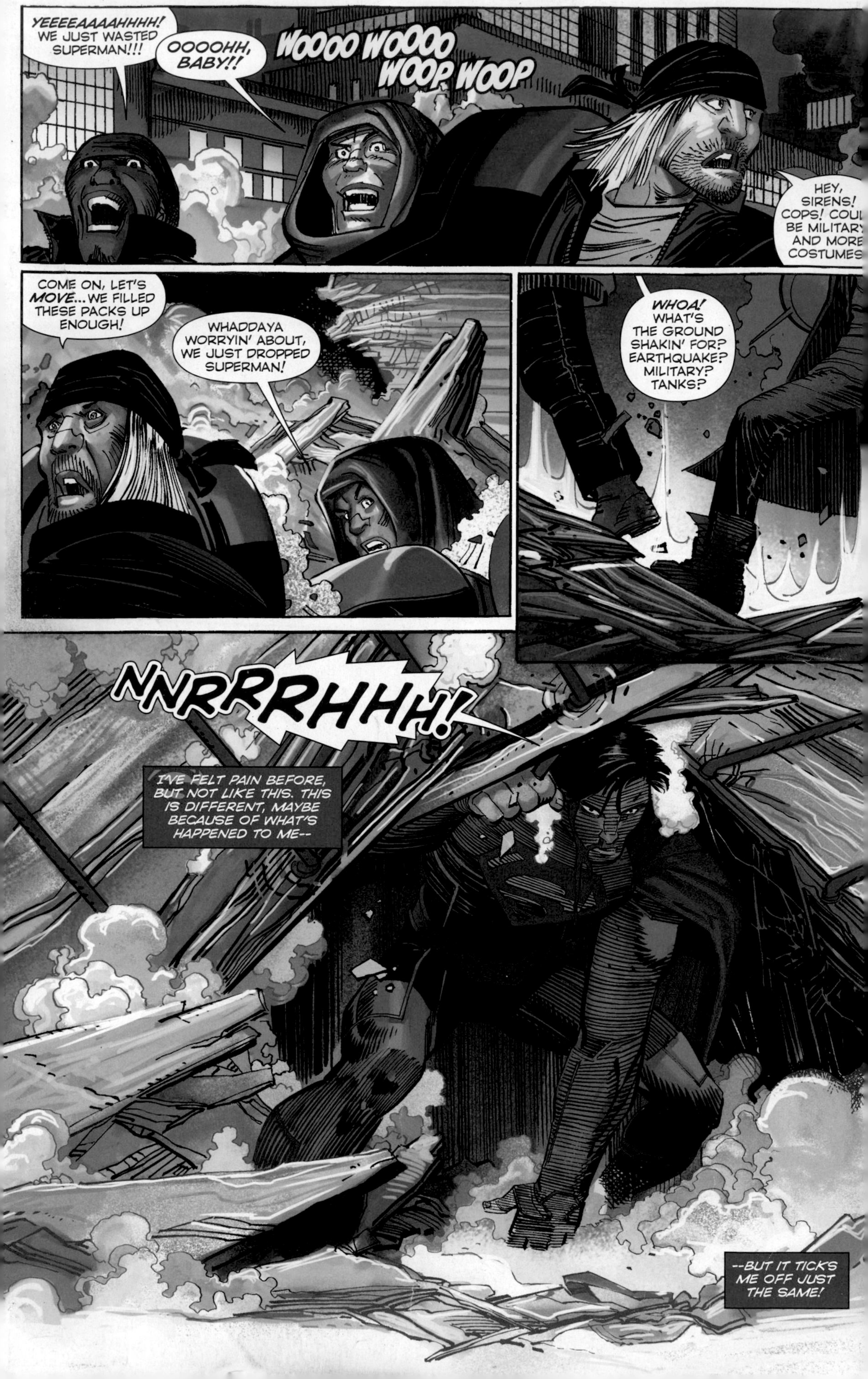
YEEEEAAAAHHHH! WE JUST WASTED SUPERMAN!!!
OOOOHH, BABY!!
WOOOO WOOOO WOOP WOOP
HEY, SIRENS! COPS! COUL BE MILITARY AND MORE COSTUMES
COME ON, LET'S MOVE... WE FILLED THESE PACKS UP ENOUGH!
WHADDAYA WORRYIN' ABOUT, WE JUST DROPPED SUPERMAN!
WHOA! WHAT'S THE GROUND SHAKIN' FOR? EARTHQUAKE? MILITARY? TANKS?
NNRRRHHH!
I'VE FELT PAIN BEFORE, BUT NOT LIKE THIS. THIS IS DIFFERENT, MAYBE BECAUSE OF WHAT'S HAPPENED TO ME--
--BUT IT TICKS ME OFF JUST THE SAME!

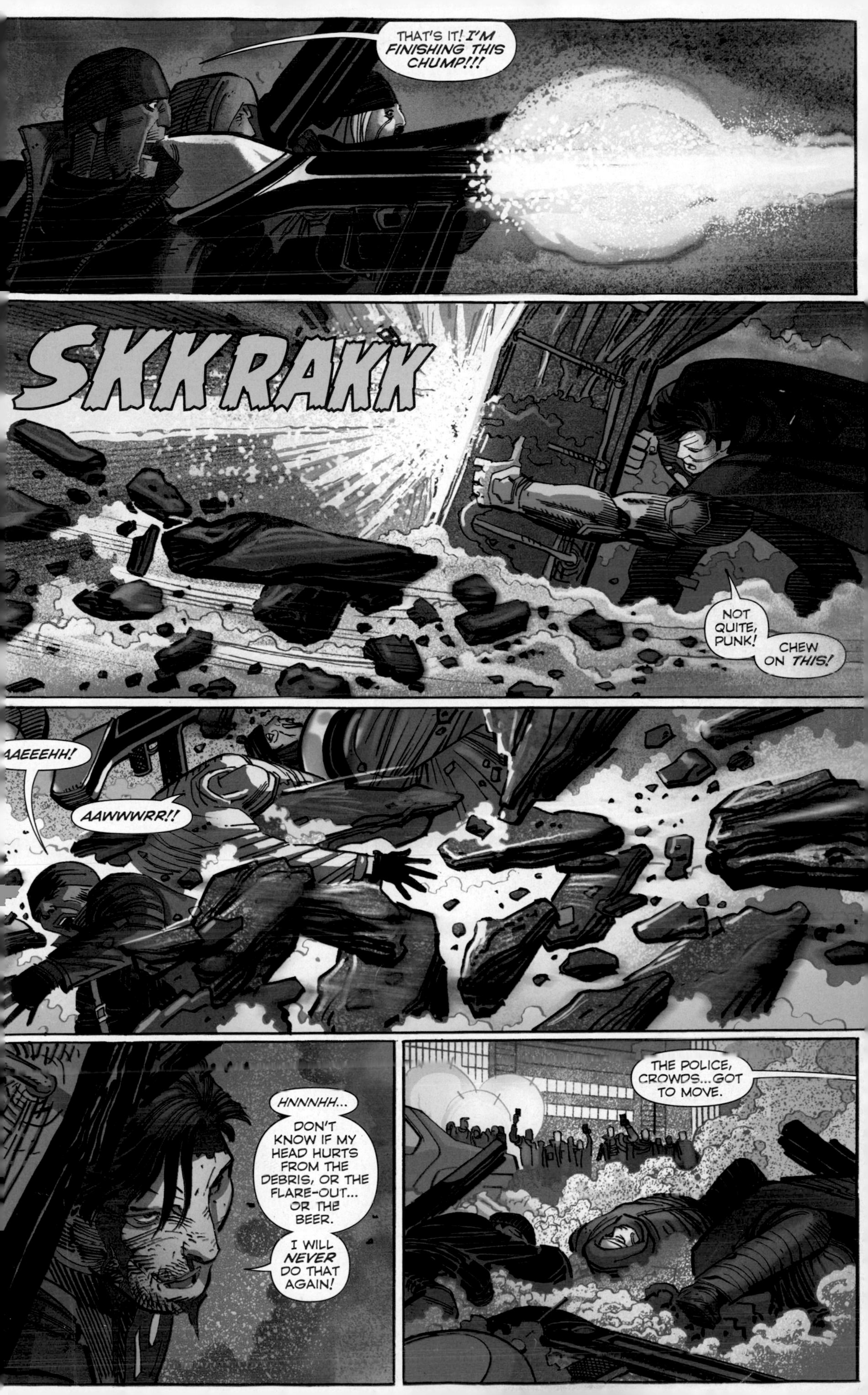
THAT'S IT! I'M FINISHING THIS CHUMP!!!
SKKRAKK
NOT QUITE, PUNK!
CHEW ON THIS!
AAEEEHH!
AAWWWRR!!
HNNNHH...
DON'T KNOW IF MY HEAD HURTS FROM THE DEBRIS, OR THE FLARE-OUT... OR THE BEER.
I WILL NEVER DO THAT AGAIN!
THE POLICE, CROWDS...GOT TO MOVE.

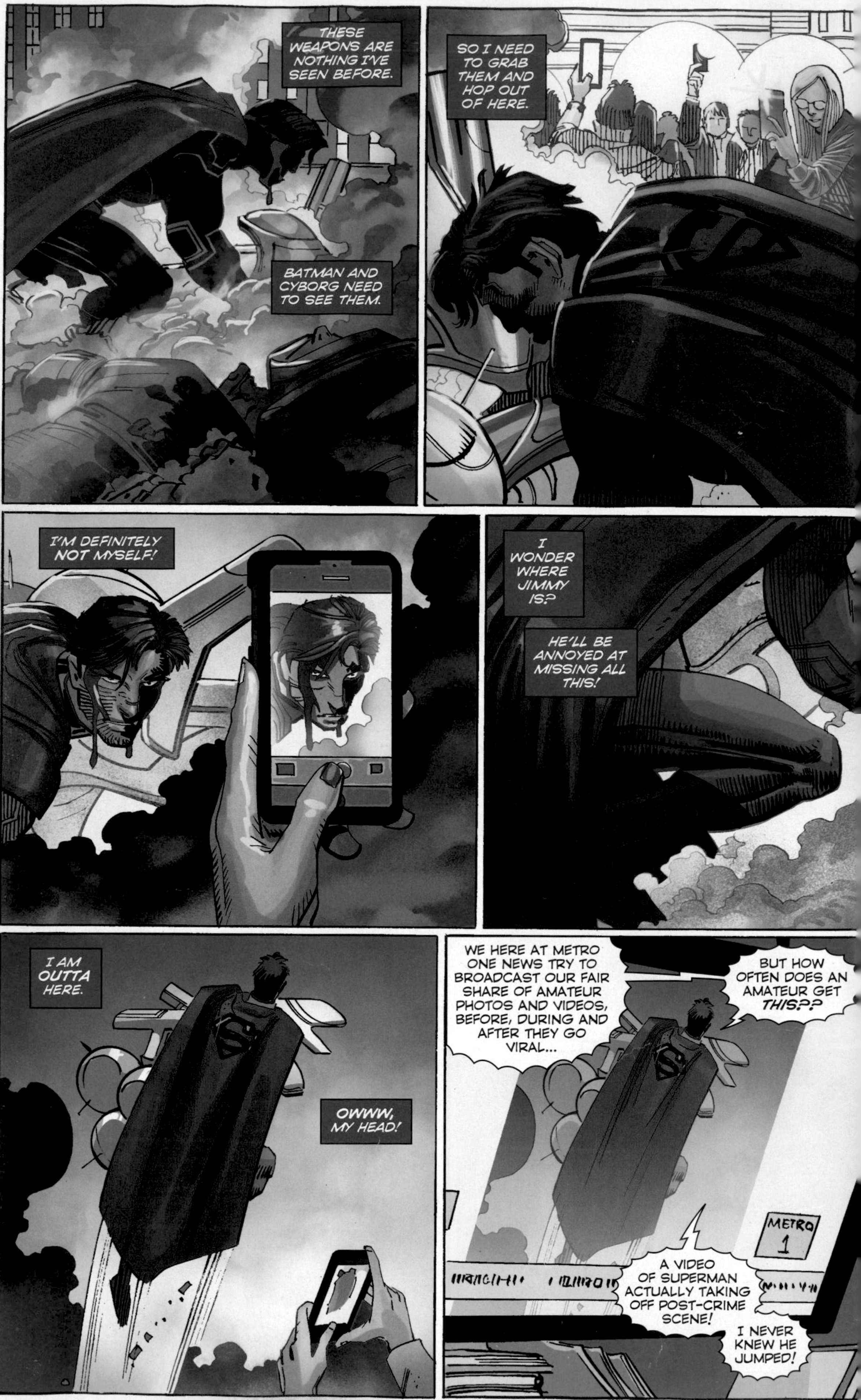
THESE WEAPONS ARE NOTHING I'VE SEEN BEFORE.
BATMAN AND CYBORG NEED TO SEE THEM.
SO I NEED TO GRAB THEM AND HOP OUT OF HERE.
I'M DEFINITELY NOT MYSELF!
I WONDER WHERE JIMMY IS?
HE'LL BE ANNOYED AT MISSING ALL THIS!
I AM OUTTA HERE.
OWWW, MY HEAD!
WE HERE AT METRO ONE NEWS TRY TO BROADCAST OUR FAIR SHARE OF AMATEUR PHOTOS AND VIDEOS, BEFORE, DURING AND AFTER THEY GO VIRAL...
BUT HOW OFTEN DOES AN AMATEUR GET THIS??
METRO 1
A VIDEO OF SUPERMAN ACTUALLY TAKING OFF POST-CRIME SCENE!
I NEVER KNEW HE JUMPED!

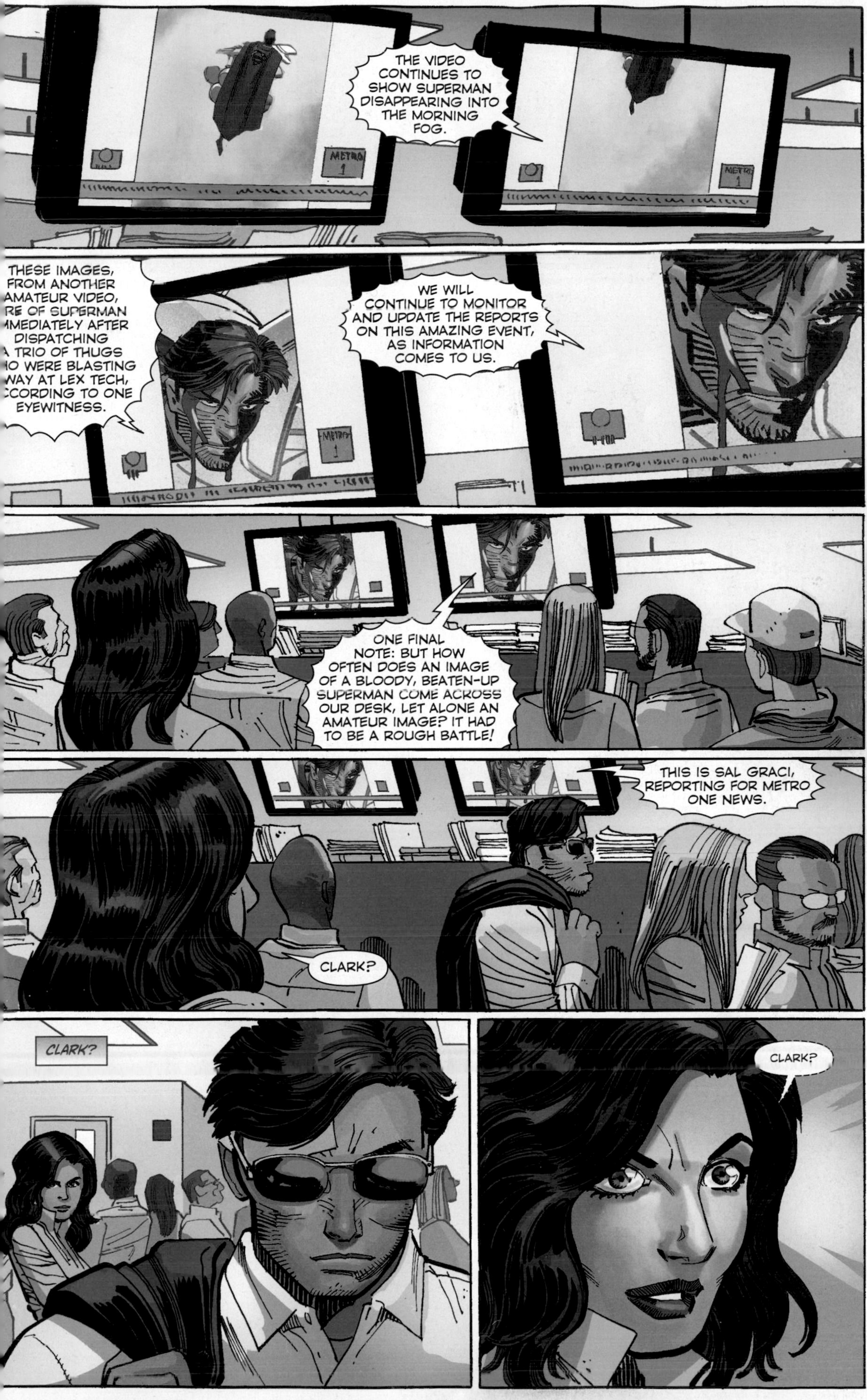

THE VIDEO CONTINUES TO SHOW SUPERMAN DISAPPEARING INTO THE MORNING FOG.
METRO 1
THESE IMAGES, FROM ANOTHER AMATEUR VIDEO, RE OF SUPERMAN MMEDIATELY AFTER DISPATCHING A TRIO OF THUGS IO WERE BLASTING WAY AT LEX TECH, CCORDING TO ONE EYEWITNESS.
WE WILL CONTINUE TO MONITOR AND UPDATE THE REPORTS ON THIS AMAZING EVENT, AS INFORMATION COMES TO US.
ONE FINAL NOTE: BUT HOW OFTEN DOES AN IMAGE OF A BLOODY, BEATEN-UP SUPERMAN COME ACROSS OUR DESK, LET ALONE AN AMATEUR IMAGE? IT HAD TO BE A ROUGH BATTLE!
THIS IS SAL GRACI, REPORTING FOR METRO ONE NEWS.
CLARK?
CLARK?
CLARK?

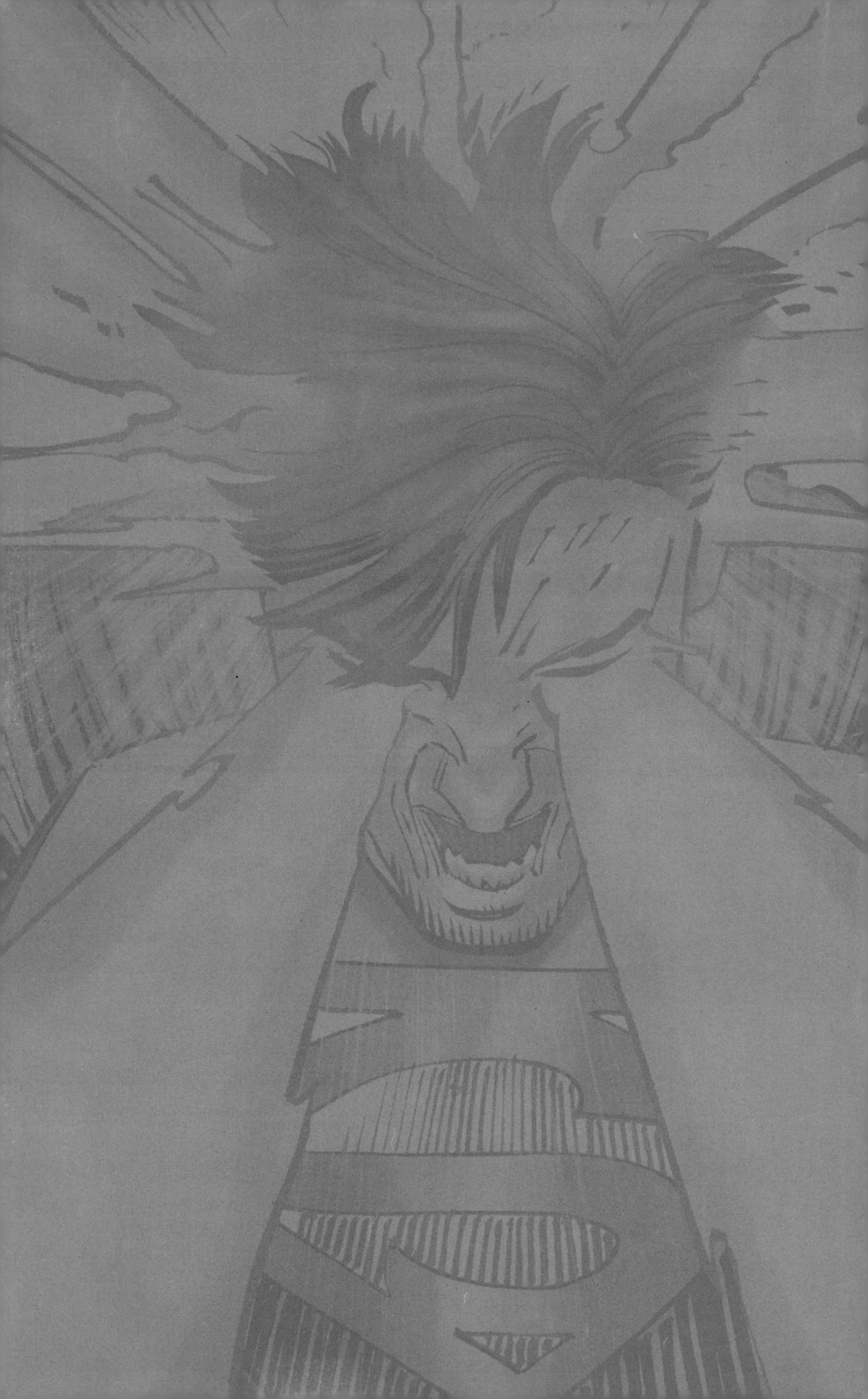

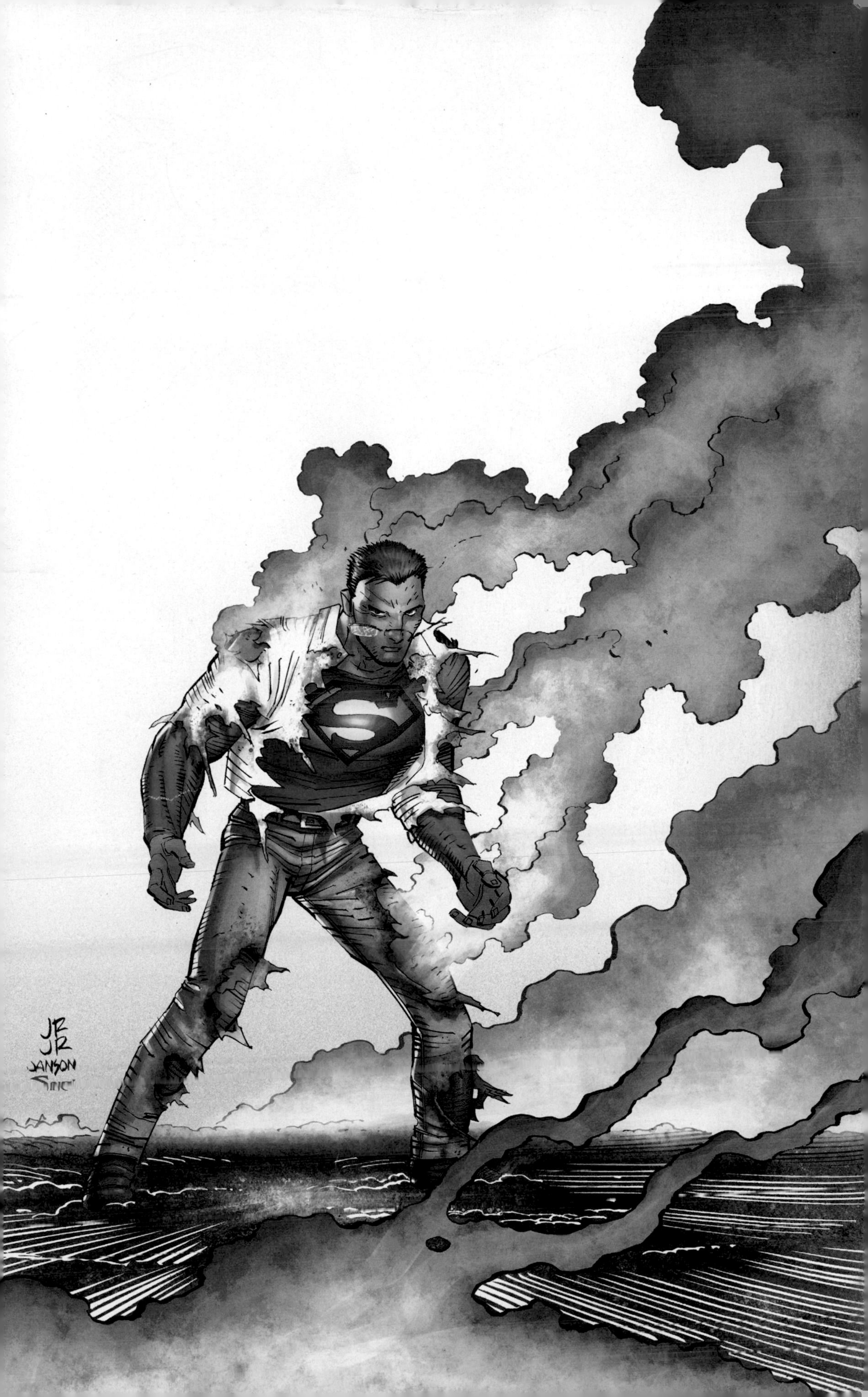
JR
JR
JANSON

The Joker 75th Anniversary variant cover for issue #41 by **KARL KERSCHL.**

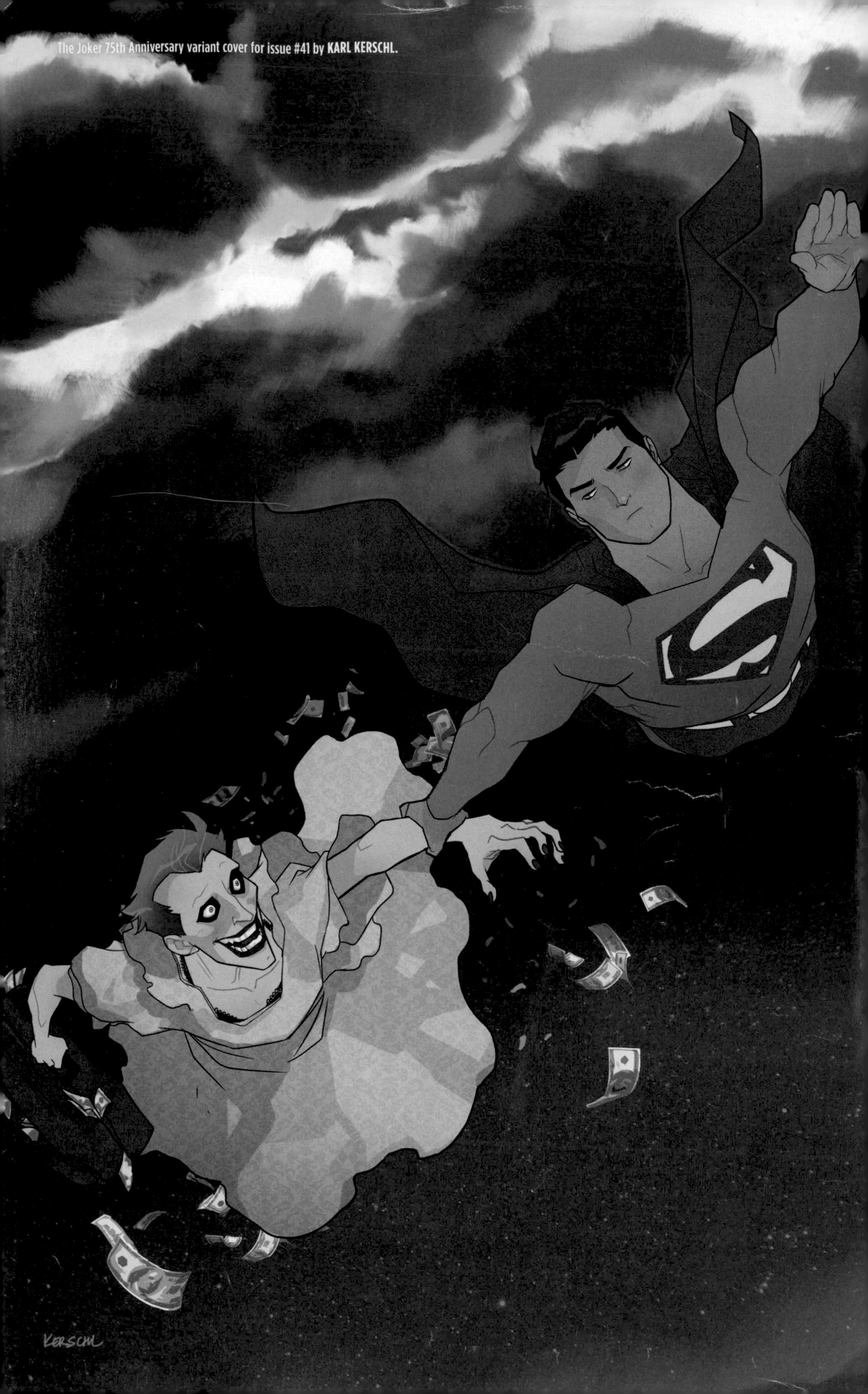
KERSCHL

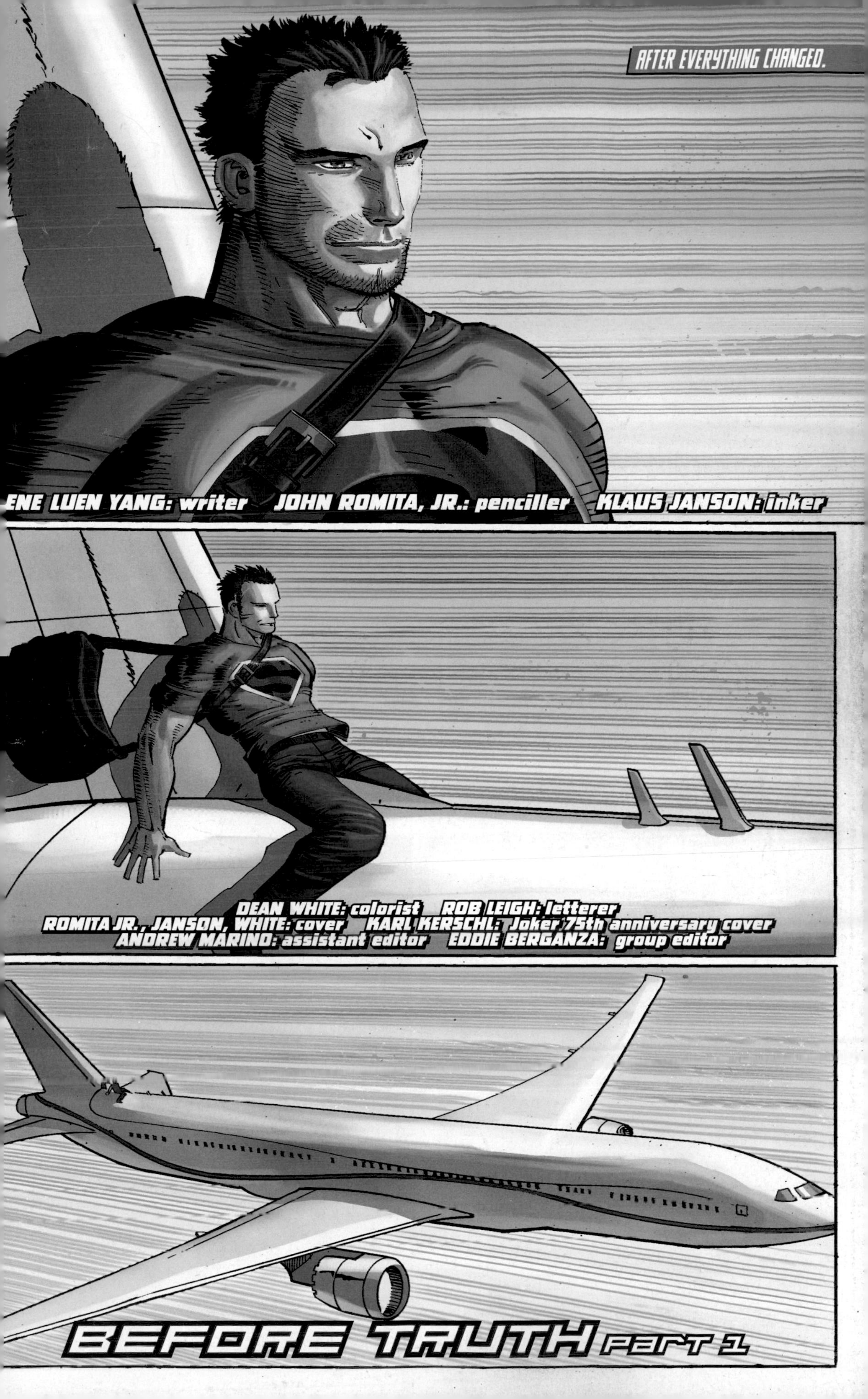
AFTER EVERYTHING CHANGED.
ENE LUEN YANG: writer JOHN ROMITA, JR.: penciller KLAUS JANSON: inker
DEAN WHITE: colorist ROB LEIGH: letterer
ROMITA JR., JANSON, WHITE: cover KARL KERSCHL: Joker 75th anniversary cover
ANDREW MARINO: assistant editor EDDIE BERGANZA: group editor
BEFORE TRUTH PART 1

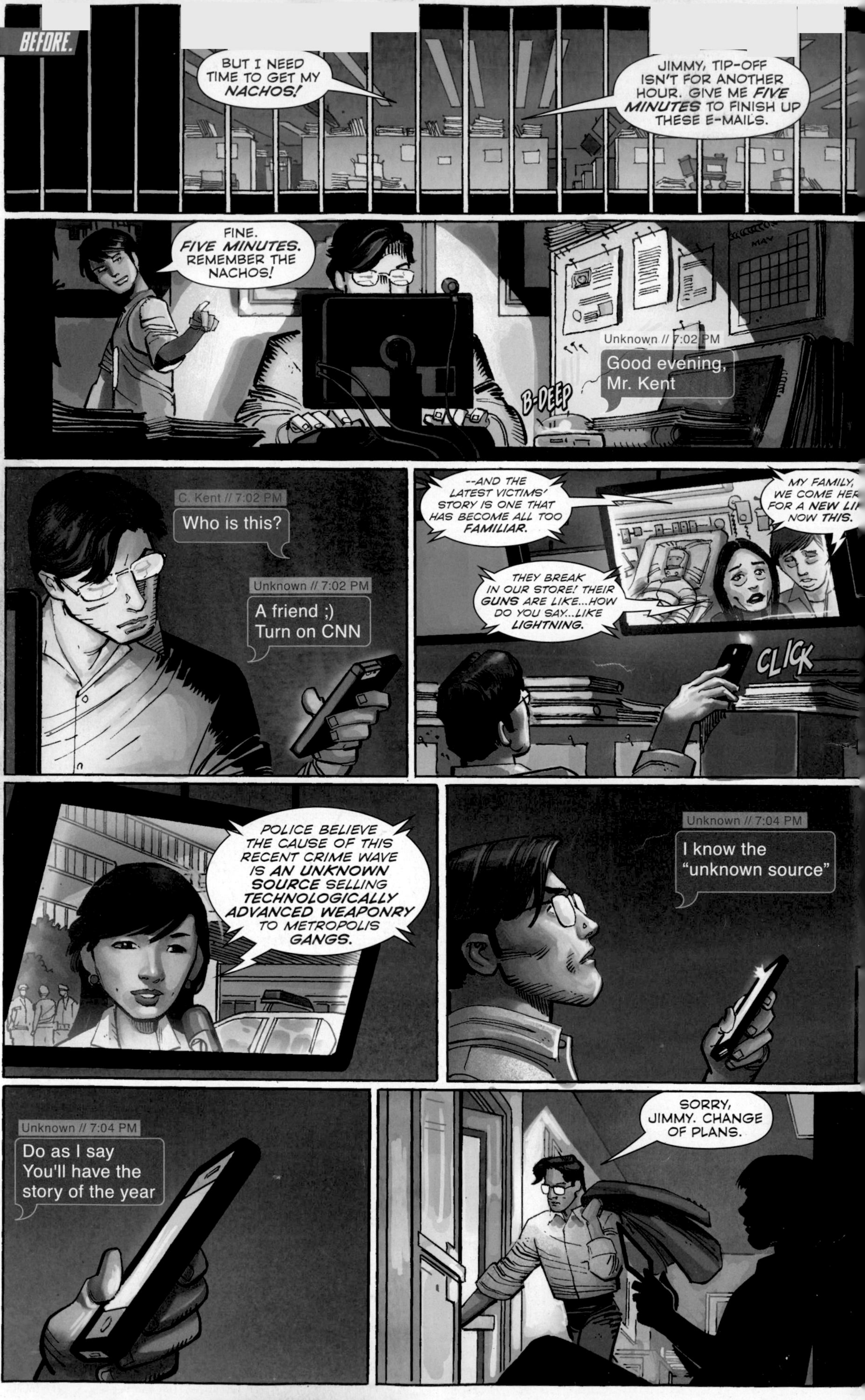
BEFORE.
BUT I NEED TIME TO GET MY *NACHOS!*
JIMMY, TIP-OFF ISN'T FOR ANOTHER HOUR. GIVE ME *FIVE MINUTES* TO FINISH UP THESE E-MAILS.
FINE. *FIVE MINUTES.* REMEMBER THE NACHOS!
B-DEEP
Unknown // 7:02 PM
Good evening, Mr. Kent
C. Kent // 7:02 PM
Who is this?
Unknown // 7:02 PM
A friend ;) Turn on CNN
--AND THE LATEST VICTIMS' STORY IS ONE THAT HAS BECOME ALL TOO *FAMILIAR.*
MY FAMILY, WE COME HER FOR A *NEW LI* NOW *THIS.*
THEY BREAK IN OUR STORE! THEIR *GUNS* ARE LIKE...HOW DO YOU SAY...LIKE *LIGHTNING.*
CLICK
POLICE BELIEVE THE CAUSE OF THIS RECENT CRIME WAVE IS *AN UNKNOWN SOURCE* SELLING *TECHNOLOGICALLY ADVANCED WEAPONRY* TO METROPOLIS *GANGS.*
Unknown // 7:04 PM
I know the "unknown source"
Unknown // 7:04 PM
Do as I say You'll have the story of the year
SORRY, JIMMY. CHANGE OF PLANS.

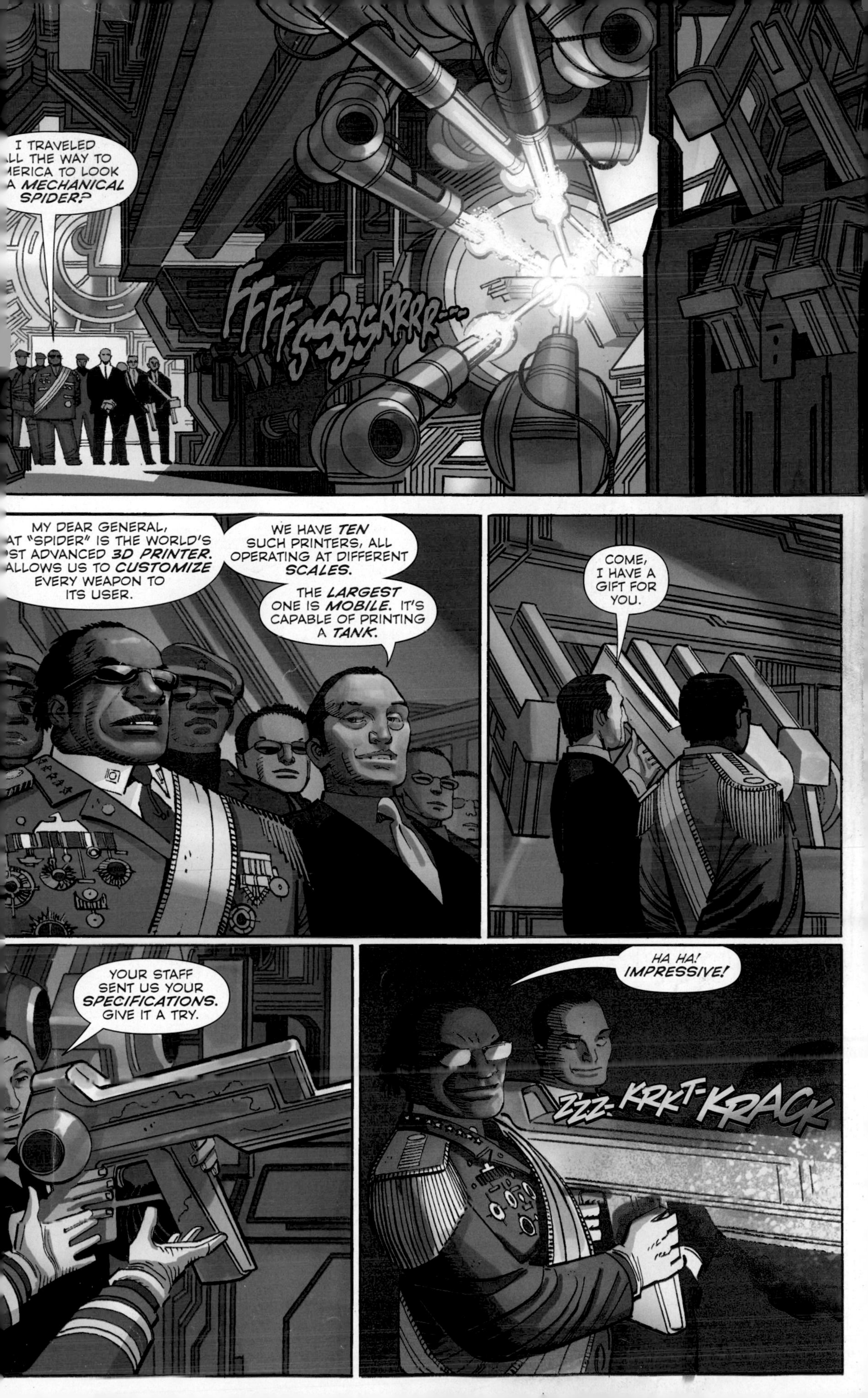
I TRAVELED LL THE WAY TO MERICA TO LOOK A MECHANICAL SPIDER?
FFFFSSSSRRRR--
MY DEAR GENERAL, AT "SPIDER" IS THE WORLD'S ST ADVANCED 3D PRINTER. ALLOWS US TO CUSTOMIZE EVERY WEAPON TO ITS USER.
WE HAVE TEN SUCH PRINTERS, ALL OPERATING AT DIFFERENT SCALES.
THE LARGEST ONE IS MOBILE. IT'S CAPABLE OF PRINTING A TANK.
COME, I HAVE A GIFT FOR YOU.
YOUR STAFF SENT US YOUR SPECIFICATIONS. GIVE IT A TRY.
HA HA! IMPRESSIVE!
ZZZ-KRKT-KRACK

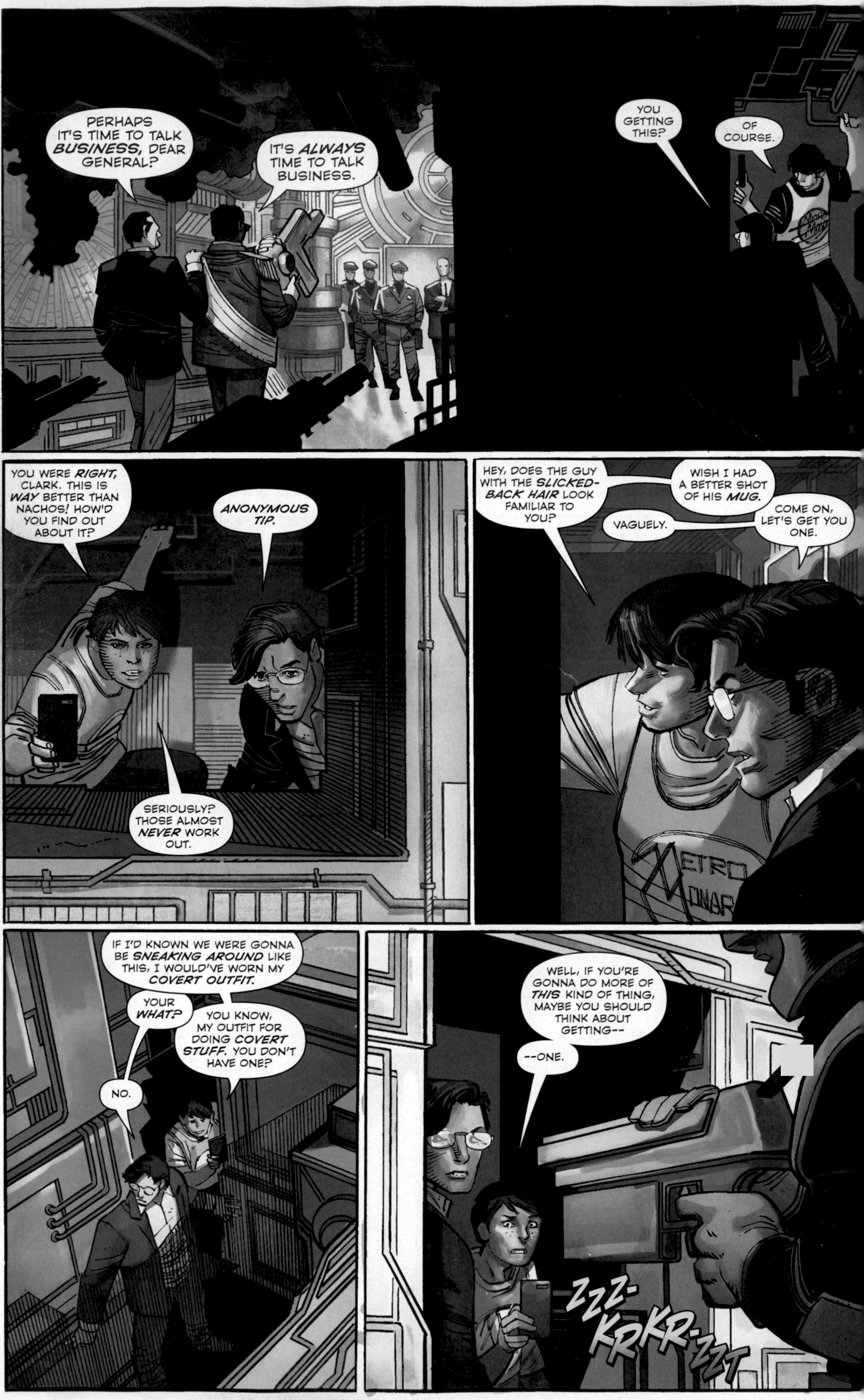
PERHAPS IT'S TIME TO TALK BUSINESS, DEAR GENERAL?
IT'S ALWAYS TIME TO TALK BUSINESS.
YOU GETTING THIS?
OF COURSE.
YOU WERE RIGHT, CLARK. THIS IS WAY BETTER THAN NACHOS! HOW'D YOU FIND OUT ABOUT IT?
ANONYMOUS TIP.
SERIOUSLY? THOSE ALMOST NEVER WORK OUT.
HEY, DOES THE GUY WITH THE SLICKED-BACK HAIR LOOK FAMILIAR TO YOU?
VAGUELY.
WISH I HAD A BETTER SHOT OF HIS MUG.
COME ON, LET'S GET YOU ONE.
IF I'D KNOWN WE WERE GONNA BE SNEAKING AROUND LIKE THIS, I WOULD'VE WORN MY COVERT OUTFIT.
YOUR WHAT?
YOU KNOW, MY OUTFIT FOR DOING COVERT STUFF. YOU DON'T HAVE ONE?
NO.
WELL, IF YOU'RE GONNA DO MORE OF THIS KIND OF THING, MAYBE YOU SHOULD THINK ABOUT GETTING--
--ONE.
ZZZ-KRKR-ZZT

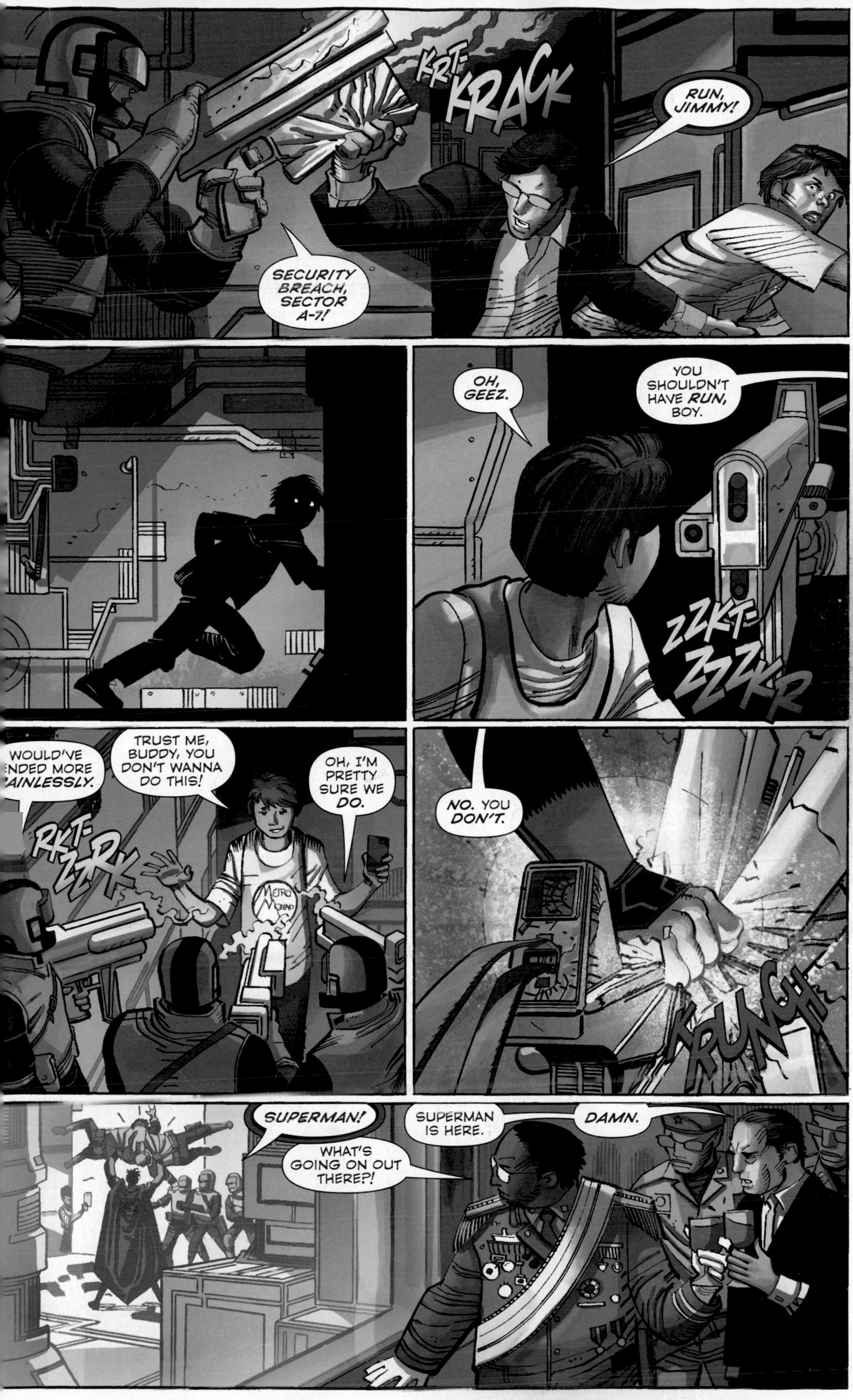
KRT-KRACK
RUN, JIMMY!
SECURITY BREACH, SECTOR A-7!
OH, GEEZ.
YOU SHOULDN'T HAVE RUN, BOY.
ZZKT-ZZZKR
WOULD'VE ENDED MORE PAINLESSLY.
TRUST ME, BUDDY, YOU DON'T WANNA DO THIS!
RKT-ZZRK
OH, I'M PRETTY SURE WE DO.
NO. YOU DON'T.
KRUNCH
SUPERMAN!
WHAT'S GOING ON OUT THERE?!
SUPERMAN IS HERE.
DAMN.

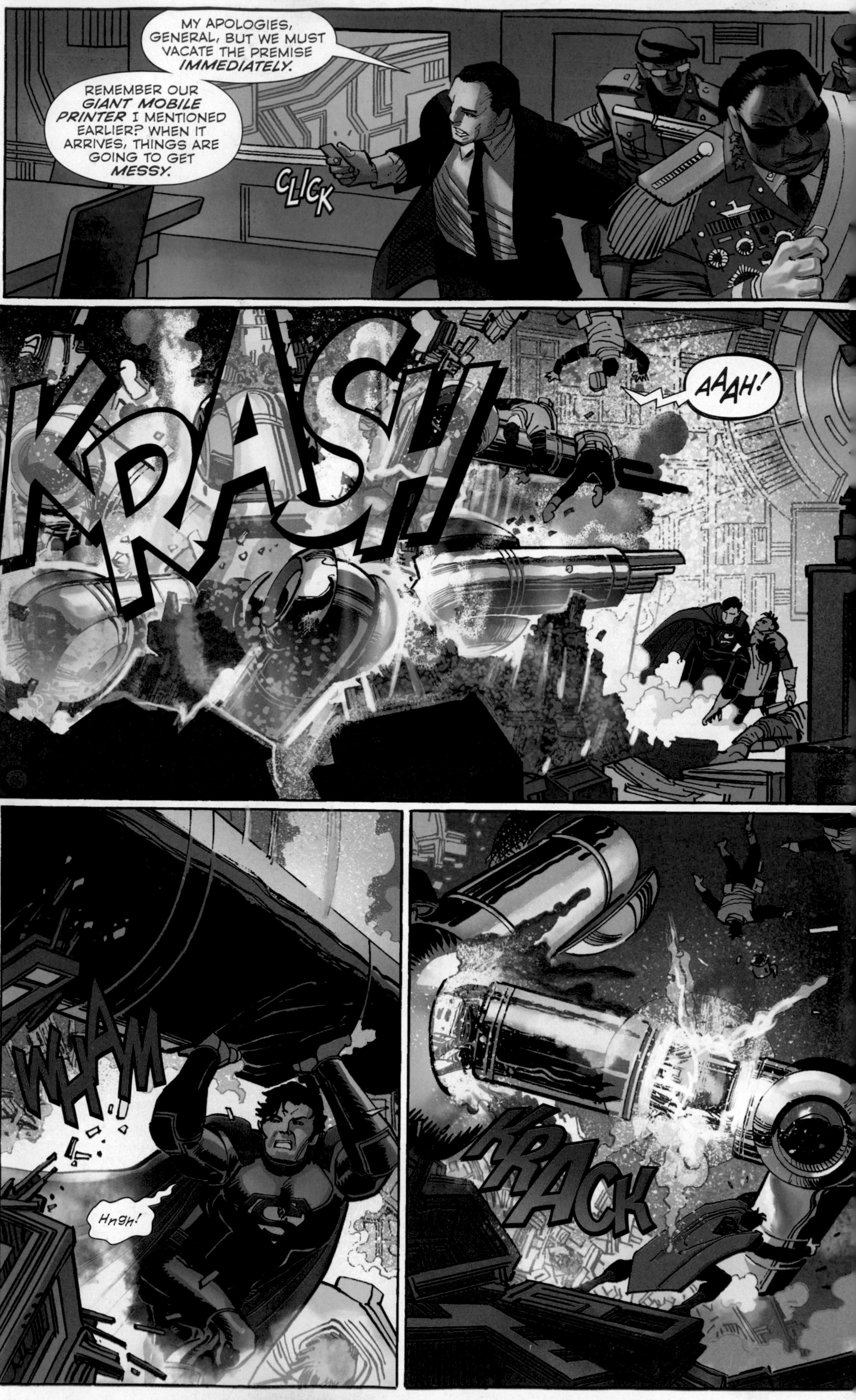
MY APOLOGIES, GENERAL, BUT WE MUST VACATE THE PREMISE *IMMEDIATELY.*
REMEMBER OUR *GIANT MOBILE PRINTER* I MENTIONED EARLIER? WHEN IT ARRIVES, THINGS ARE GOING TO GET *MESSY.*
CLICK
KRASH!
AAAH!
WHAM
Hngh!
KRACK

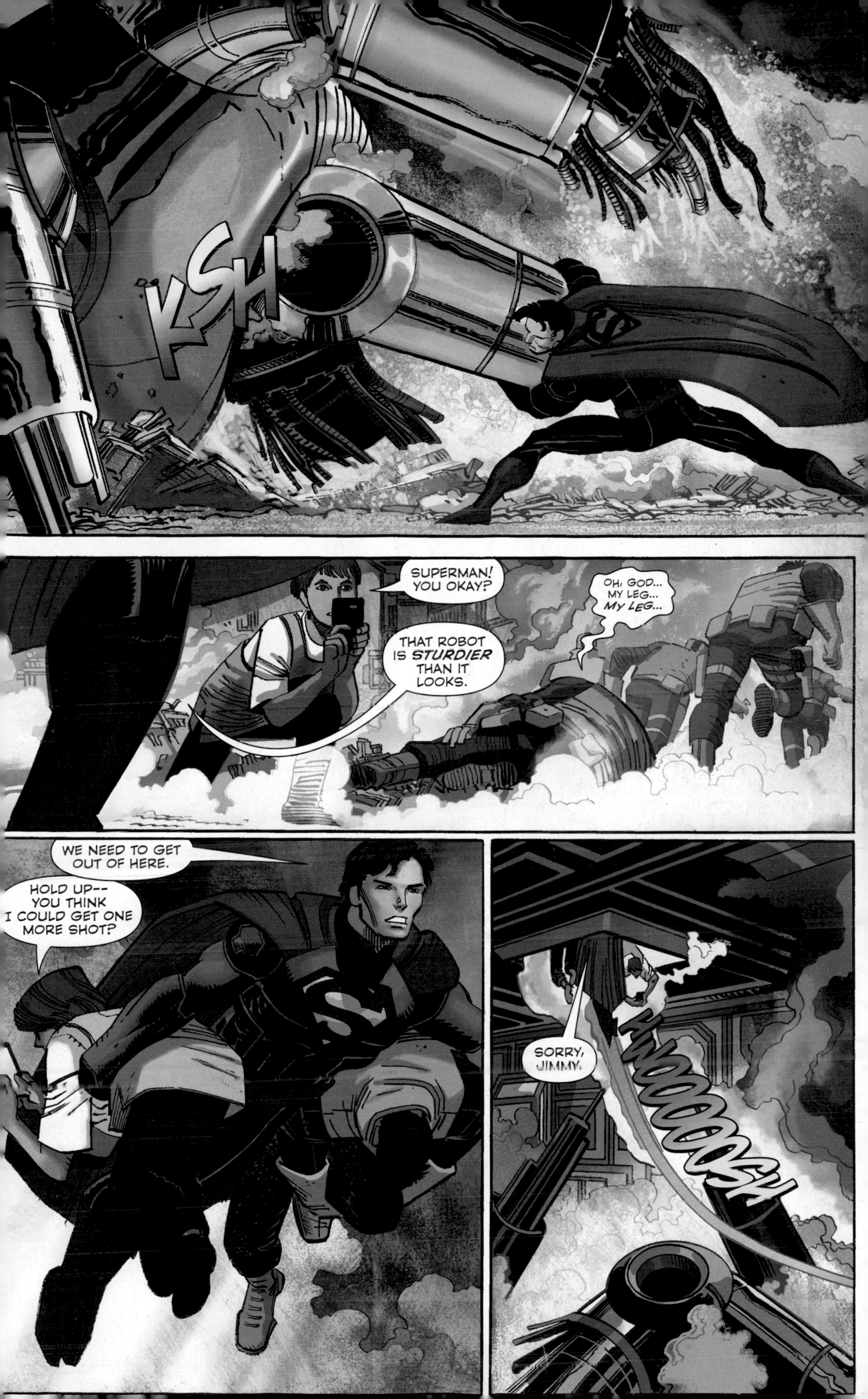
KSH
SUPERMAN! YOU OKAY?
OH, GOD... MY LEG... MY LEG...
THAT ROBOT IS STURDIER THAN IT LOOKS.
WE NEED TO GET OUT OF HERE.
HOLD UP-- YOU THINK I COULD GET ONE MORE SHOT?
SORRY, JIMMY.
WHOOOOOSH

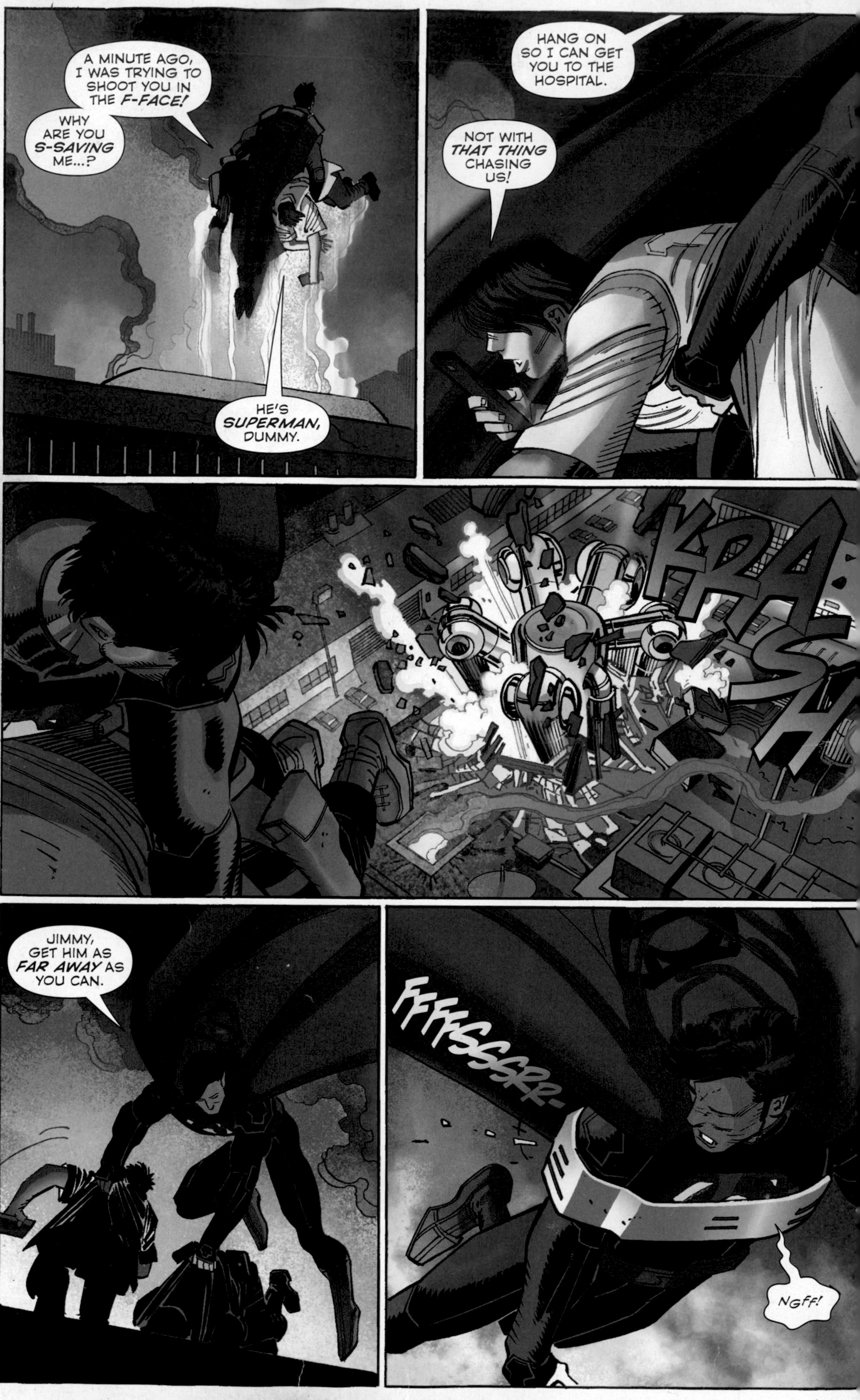
A MINUTE AGO, I WAS TRYING TO SHOOT YOU IN THE F-FACE!
WHY ARE YOU S-SAVING ME...?
HE'S SUPERMAN, DUMMY.
HANG ON SO I CAN GET YOU TO THE HOSPITAL.
NOT WITH THAT THING CHASING US!
KRASH
JIMMY, GET HIM AS FAR AWAY AS YOU CAN.
FFFSSSRR-
NGff!

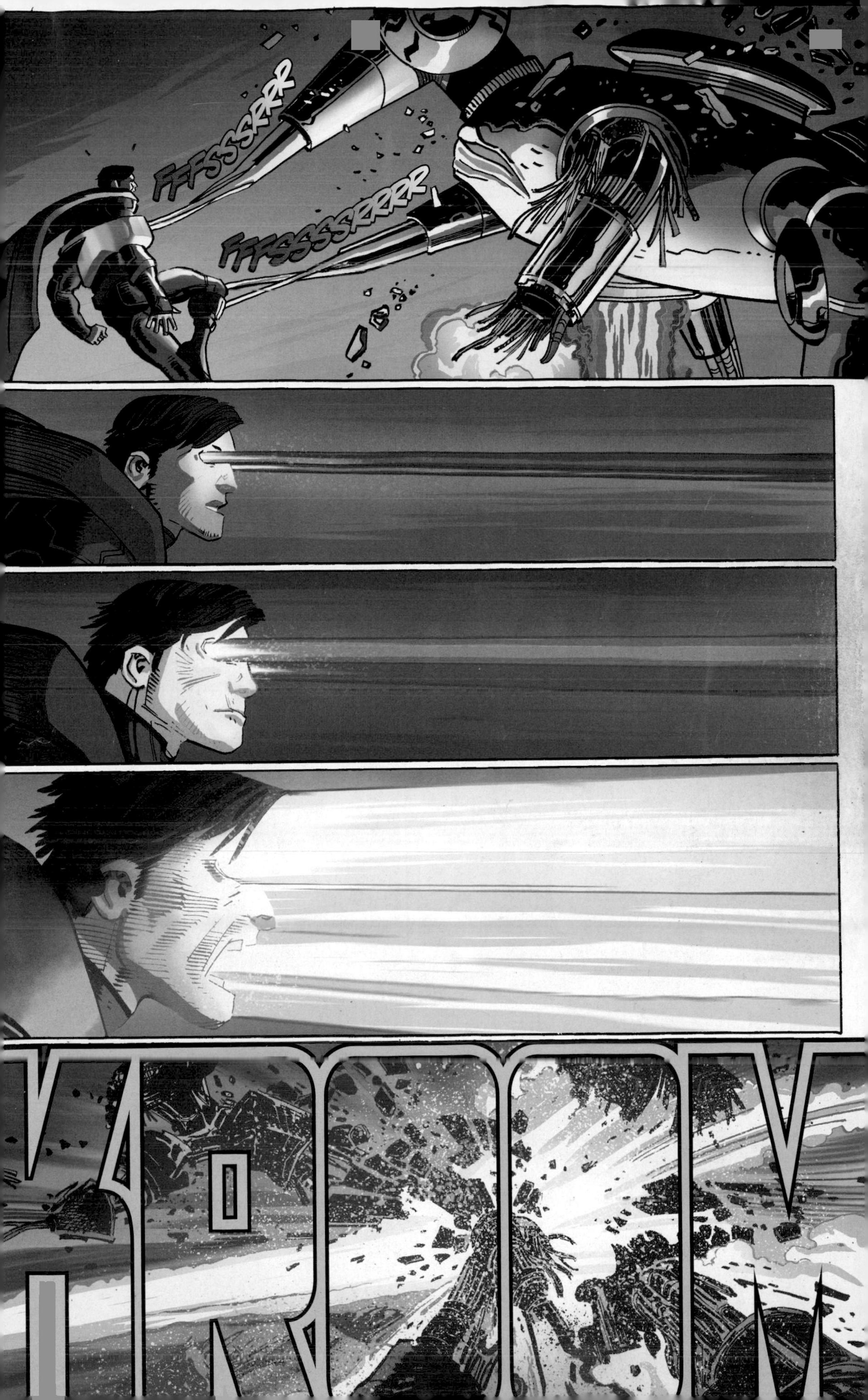
FFFSSSRRR
FFFSSSSRRRR
KROOM

CLARK, YOU GOTTA WARN A GUY BEFORE YOU DO THAT *SOLAR FLARE* THING! AND DON'T YOU NEED TO, I DON'T KNOW, *LIE DOWN* OR SOMETHING?

YOUR HEAD'S STILL SMOKING A LITTLE.

I'M OKAY. THE *JUSTICE LEAGUE* HELPED ME FIGURE OUT HOW TO KEEP MY FLARES SMALLER, MORE CONTAINED.

IT WON'T TAKE AS LONG FOR MY POWERS TO COME BACK.

BESIDES, WE REALLY NEED TO GET GOING ON THIS. THOSE PEOPLE NEED TO BE *STOPPED.*

WHAT PEOPLE? }sniff sniff{

AND WHAT'S THAT *SMELL?* YOU GUYS GO TO *KOREAN BARBEQUE* WITHOUT ME?

LOIS! WHAT ARE YOU DOING HERE?

MY *JOB.* THERE WAS A *HUGE EXPLOSION* IN *TECHNOLOGY PARK* ABOUT AN HOUR AGO--

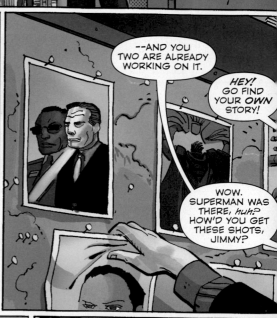

--AND YOU TWO ARE ALREADY WORKING ON IT.

HEY! GO FIND YOUR *OWN* STORY!

WOW. SUPERMAN WAS THERE, *huh?* HOW'D YOU GET THESE SHOTS, JIMMY?

ANONYMOUS TIP.

REALLY? THOSE ALMOST *NEVER* WORK OUT. THIS MAN WAS INVOLVED?

YEAH. YOU RECOGNIZE HIM?

YOU DON'T?

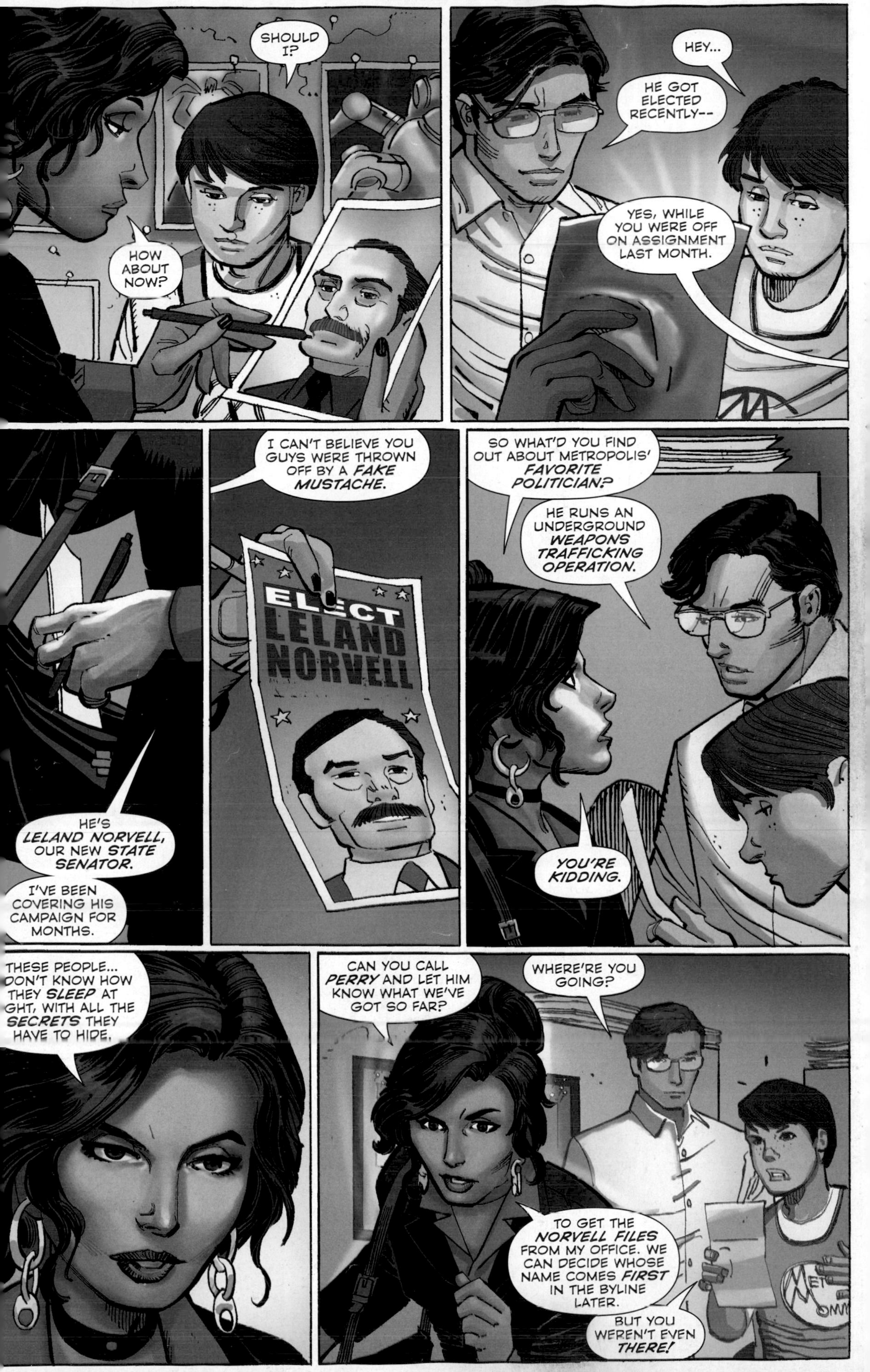
SHOULD I?
HOW ABOUT NOW?
HEY...
HE GOT ELECTED RECENTLY--
YES, WHILE YOU WERE OFF ON ASSIGNMENT LAST MONTH.
HE'S LELAND NORVELL, OUR NEW STATE SENATOR.
I'VE BEEN COVERING HIS CAMPAIGN FOR MONTHS.
I CAN'T BELIEVE YOU GUYS WERE THROWN OFF BY A FAKE MUSTACHE.
ELECT LELAND NORVELL
SO WHAT'D YOU FIND OUT ABOUT METROPOLIS' FAVORITE POLITICIAN?
HE RUNS AN UNDERGROUND WEAPONS TRAFFICKING OPERATION.
YOU'RE KIDDING.
THESE PEOPLE... DON'T KNOW HOW THEY SLEEP AT GHT, WITH ALL THE SECRETS THEY HAVE TO HIDE.
CAN YOU CALL PERRY AND LET HIM KNOW WHAT WE'VE GOT SO FAR?
WHERE'RE YOU GOING?
TO GET THE NORVELL FILES FROM MY OFFICE. WE CAN DECIDE WHOSE NAME COMES FIRST IN THE BYLINE LATER.
BUT YOU WEREN'T EVEN THERE!

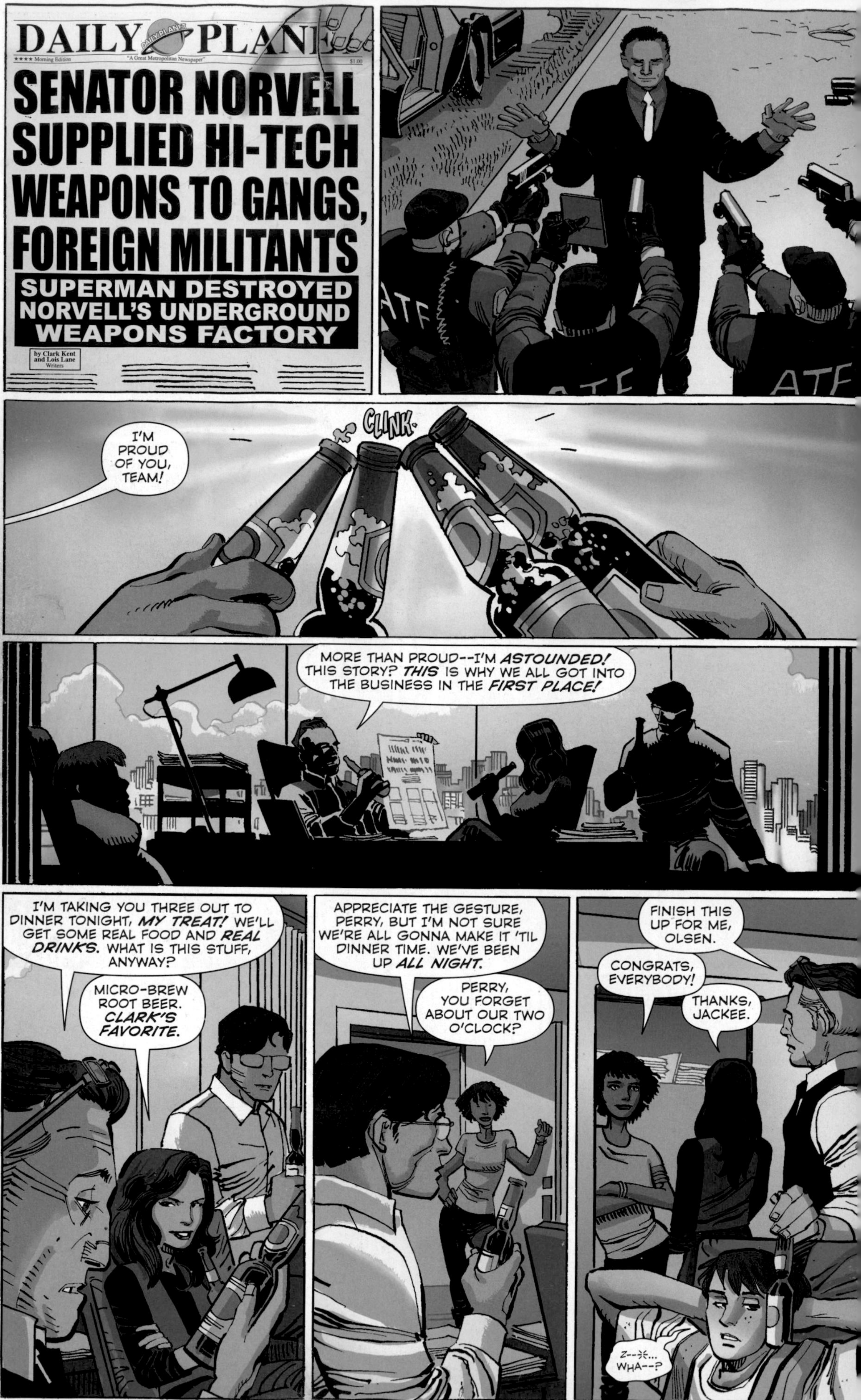

DAILY PLANET
DAILY PLANET
★★★★ Morning Edition
"A Great Metropolitan Newspaper"
$1.00
SENATOR NORVELL SUPPLIED HI-TECH WEAPONS TO GANGS, FOREIGN MILITANTS
SUPERMAN DESTROYED NORVELL'S UNDERGROUND WEAPONS FACTORY
by Clark Kent and Lois Lane Writers
ATF
ATF
ATF
CLINK
I'M PROUD OF YOU, TEAM!
MORE THAN PROUD--I'M ASTOUNDED! THIS STORY? THIS IS WHY WE ALL GOT INTO THE BUSINESS IN THE FIRST PLACE!
I'M TAKING YOU THREE OUT TO DINNER TONIGHT, MY TREAT! WE'LL GET SOME REAL FOOD AND REAL DRINKS. WHAT IS THIS STUFF, ANYWAY?
MICRO-BREW ROOT BEER. CLARK'S FAVORITE.
APPRECIATE THE GESTURE, PERRY, BUT I'M NOT SURE WE'RE ALL GONNA MAKE IT 'TIL DINNER TIME. WE'VE BEEN UP ALL NIGHT.
PERRY, YOU FORGET ABOUT OUR TWO O'CLOCK?
FINISH THIS UP FOR ME, OLSEN.
CONGRATS, EVERYBODY!
THANKS, JACKEE.
Z--✱... WHA--?

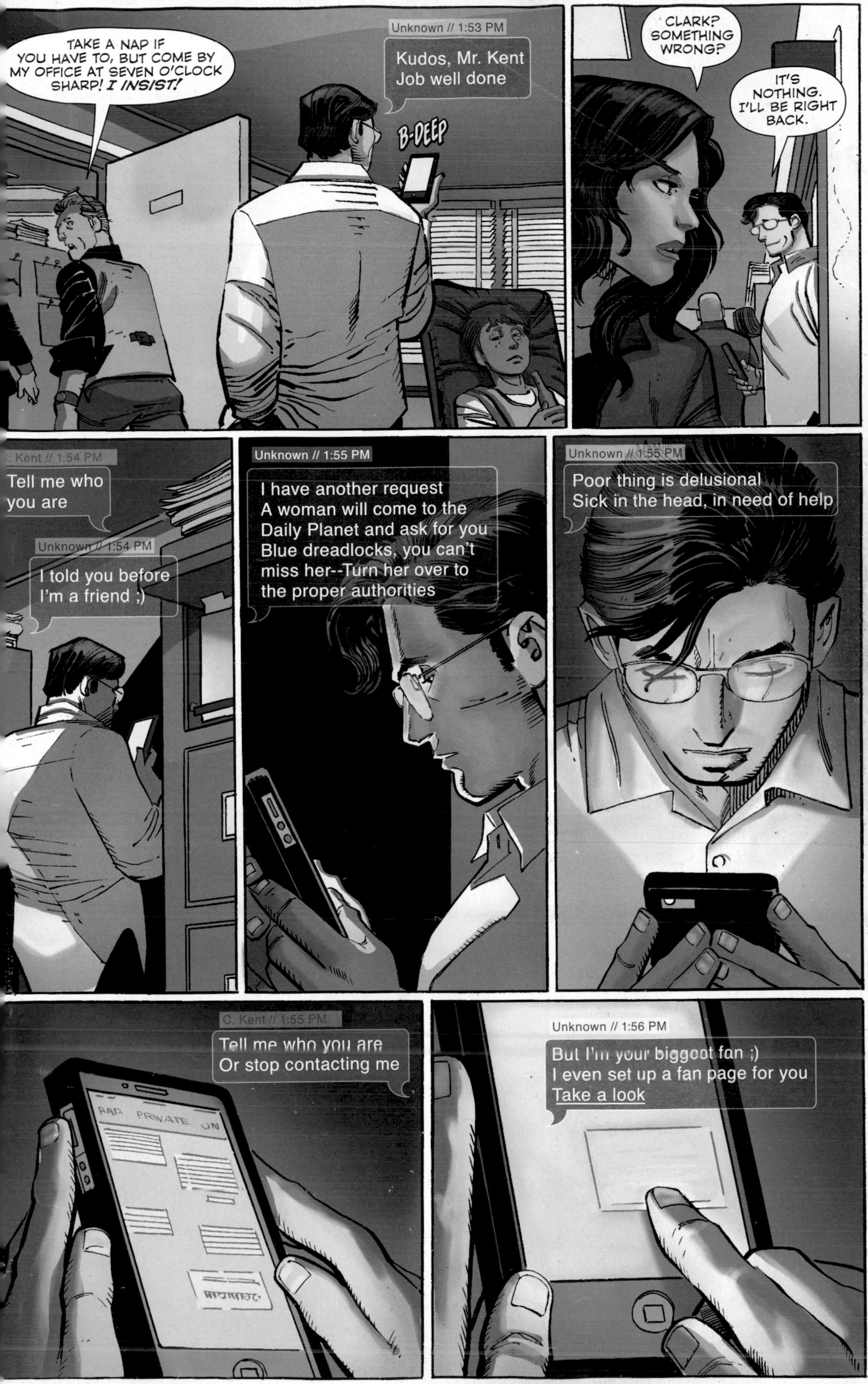
TAKE A NAP IF YOU HAVE TO, BUT COME BY MY OFFICE AT SEVEN O'CLOCK SHARP! *I INSIST!*
Unknown // 1:53 PM
Kudos, Mr. Kent
Job well done
B-DEEP
CLARK? SOMETHING WRONG?
IT'S NOTHING. I'LL BE RIGHT BACK.
Kent // 1:54 PM
Tell me who you are
Unknown // 1:54 PM
I told you before
I'm a friend ;)
Unknown // 1:55 PM
I have another request
A woman will come to the Daily Planet and ask for you
Blue dreadlocks, you can't miss her--Turn her over to the proper authorities
Unknown // 1:55 PM
Poor thing is delusional
Sick in the head, in need of help
C. Kent // 1:55 PM
Tell me who you are
Or stop contacting me
Unknown // 1:56 PM
But I'm your biggest fan ;)
I even set up a fan page for you
Take a look

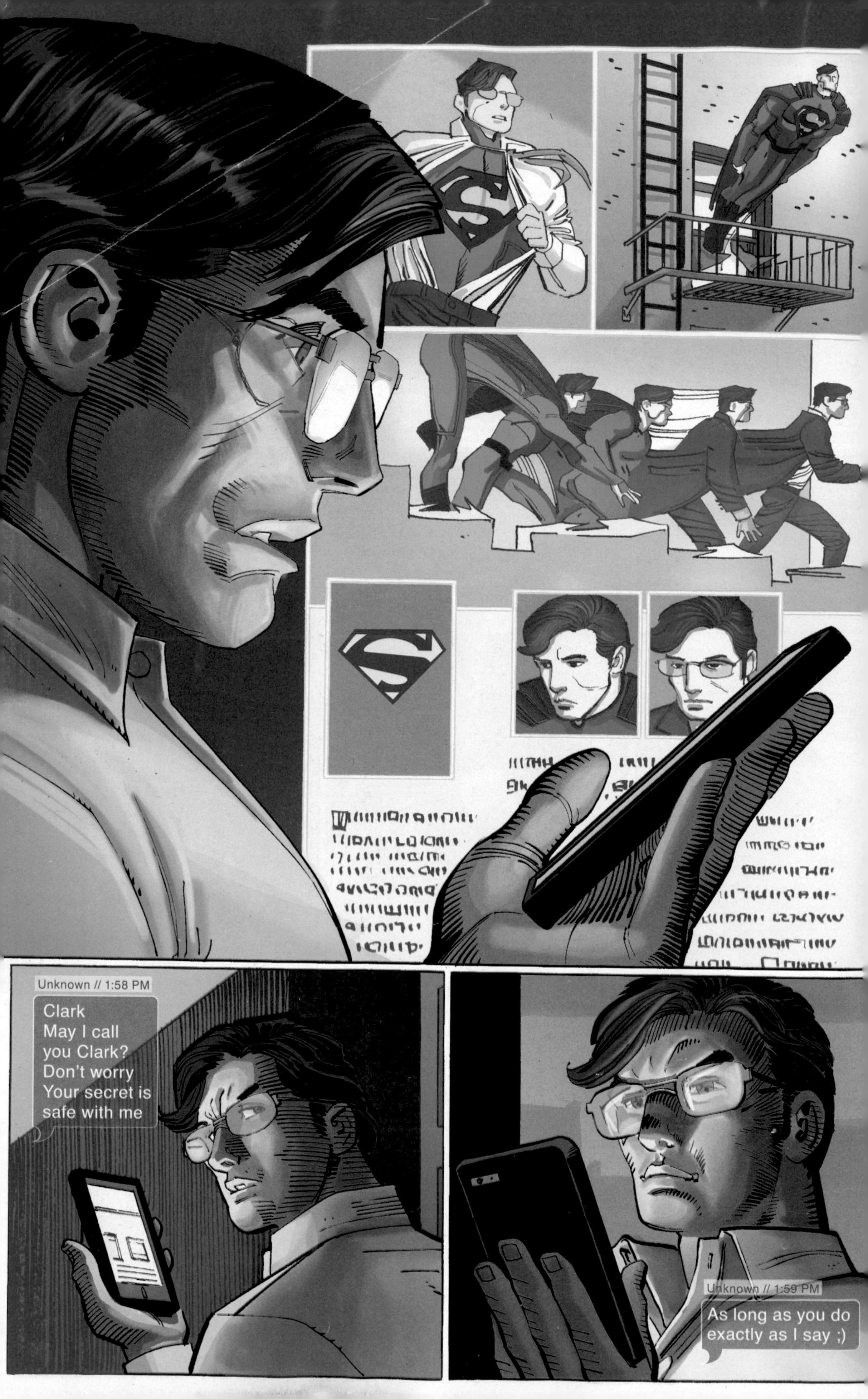

Unknown // 1:58 PM
Clark
May I call
you Clark?
Don't worry
Your secret is
safe with me
Unknown // 1:59 PM
As long as you do
exactly as I say ;)

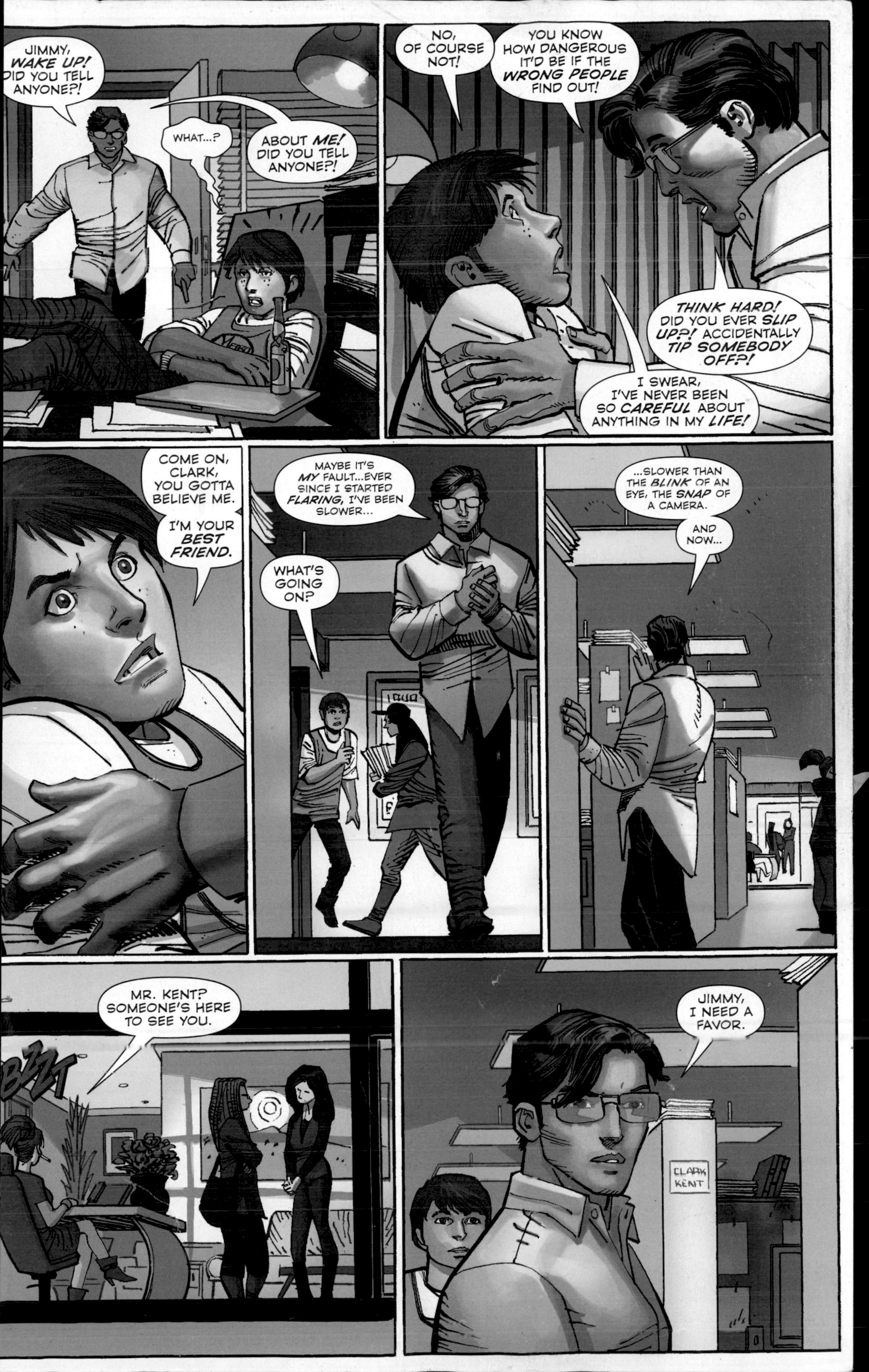
JIMMY, WAKE UP! DID YOU TELL ANYONE?!
WHAT...?
ABOUT ME! DID YOU TELL ANYONE?!
NO, OF COURSE NOT!
YOU KNOW HOW DANGEROUS IT'D BE IF THE WRONG PEOPLE FIND OUT!
THINK HARD! DID YOU EVER SLIP UP?! ACCIDENTALLY TIP SOMEBODY OFF?!
I SWEAR, I'VE NEVER BEEN SO CAREFUL ABOUT ANYTHING IN MY LIFE!
COME ON, CLARK, YOU GOTTA BELIEVE ME.
I'M YOUR BEST FRIEND.
MAYBE IT'S MY FAULT...EVER SINCE I STARTED FLARING, I'VE BEEN SLOWER...
WHAT'S GOING ON?
...SLOWER THAN THE BLINK OF AN EYE, THE SNAP OF A CAMERA.
AND NOW...
MR. KENT? SOMEONE'S HERE TO SEE YOU.
BZZZT
JIMMY, I NEED A FAVOR.
CLARK KENT

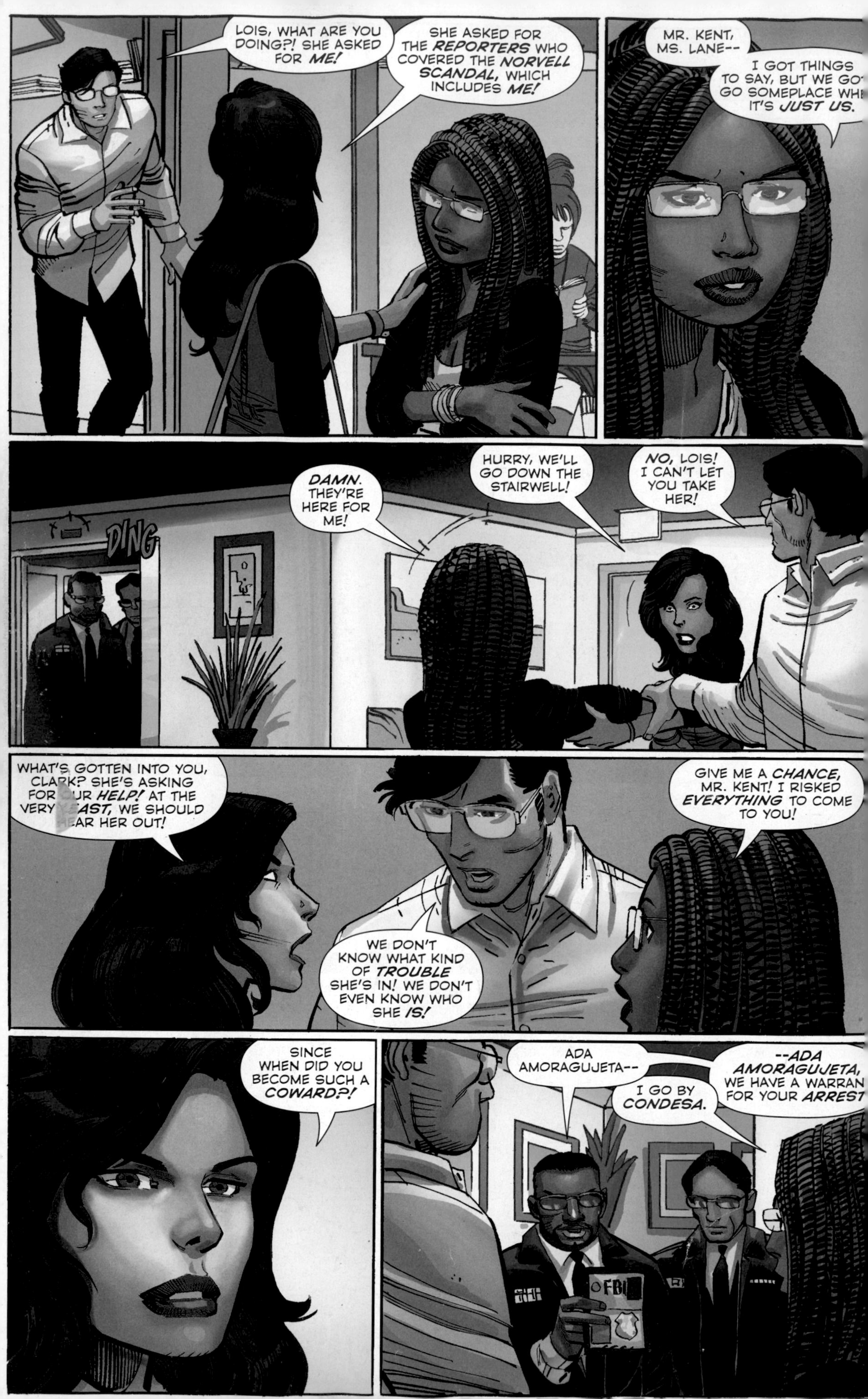
LOIS, WHAT ARE YOU DOING?! SHE ASKED FOR ME!
SHE ASKED FOR THE REPORTERS WHO COVERED THE NORVELL SCANDAL, WHICH INCLUDES ME!
MR. KENT, MS. LANE--
I GOT THINGS TO SAY, BUT WE GO SOMEPLACE WH IT'S JUST US.
DING
DAMN. THEY'RE HERE FOR ME!
HURRY, WE'LL GO DOWN THE STAIRWELL!
NO, LOIS! I CAN'T LET YOU TAKE HER!
WHAT'S GOTTEN INTO YOU, CLARK? SHE'S ASKING FOR OUR HELP! AT THE VERY LEAST, WE SHOULD HEAR HER OUT!
WE DON'T KNOW WHAT KIND OF TROUBLE SHE'S IN! WE DON'T EVEN KNOW WHO SHE IS!
GIVE ME A CHANCE, MR. KENT! I RISKED EVERYTHING TO COME TO YOU!
SINCE WHEN DID YOU BECOME SUCH A COWARD?!
ADA AMORAGUJETA--
I GO BY CONDESA.
--ADA AMORAGUJETA, WE HAVE A WARRAN FOR YOUR ARREST
FBI

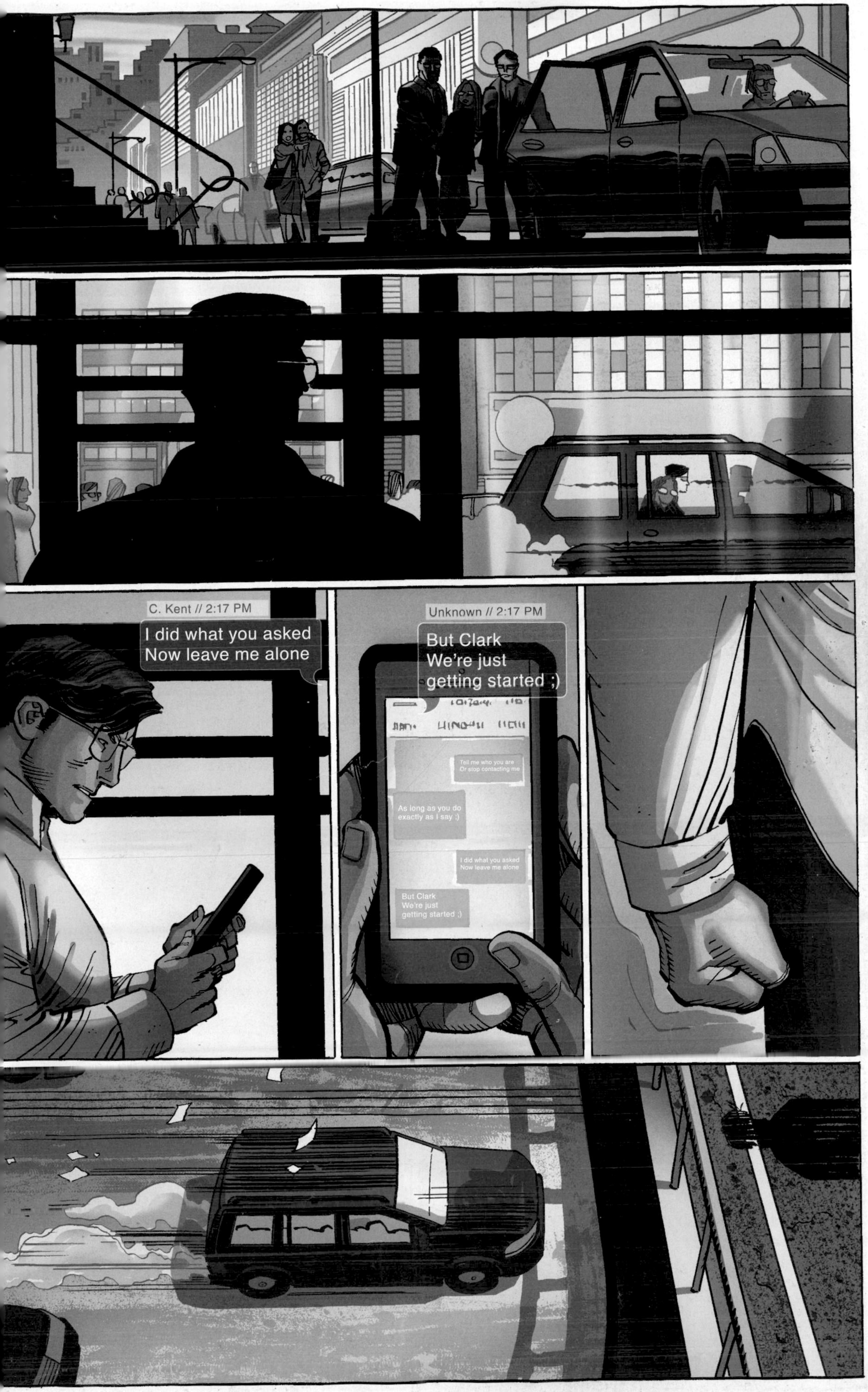
C. Kent // 2:17 PM
I did what you asked
Now leave me alone
Unknown // 2:17 PM
But Clark
We're just
getting started ;)
Tell me who you are
Or stop contacting me
As long as you do
exactly as I say :)
I did what you asked
Now leave me alone
But Clark
We're just
getting started ;)

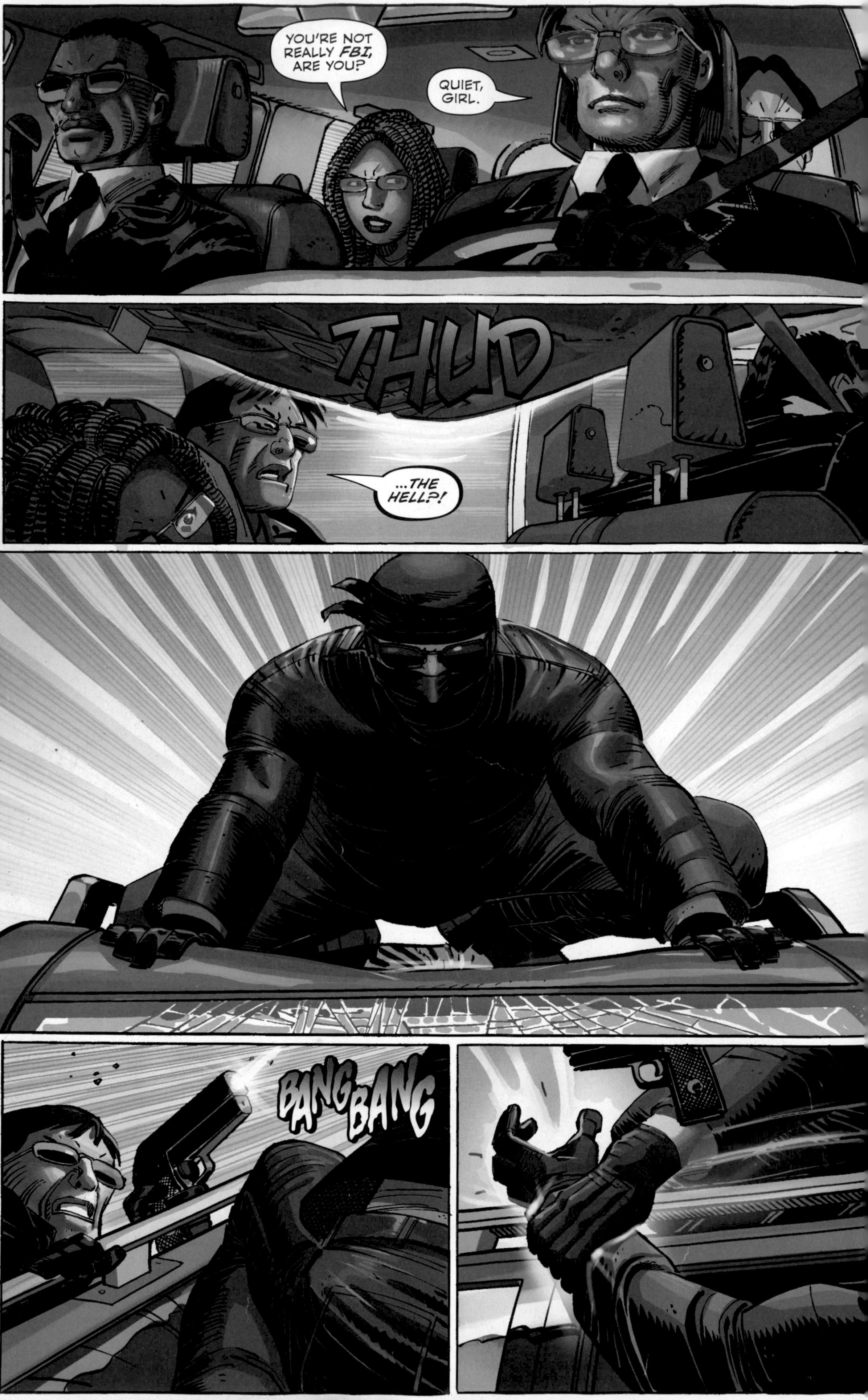
YOU'RE NOT REALLY FBI, ARE YOU?
QUIET, GIRL.
THUD
...THE HELL?!
BANG BANG

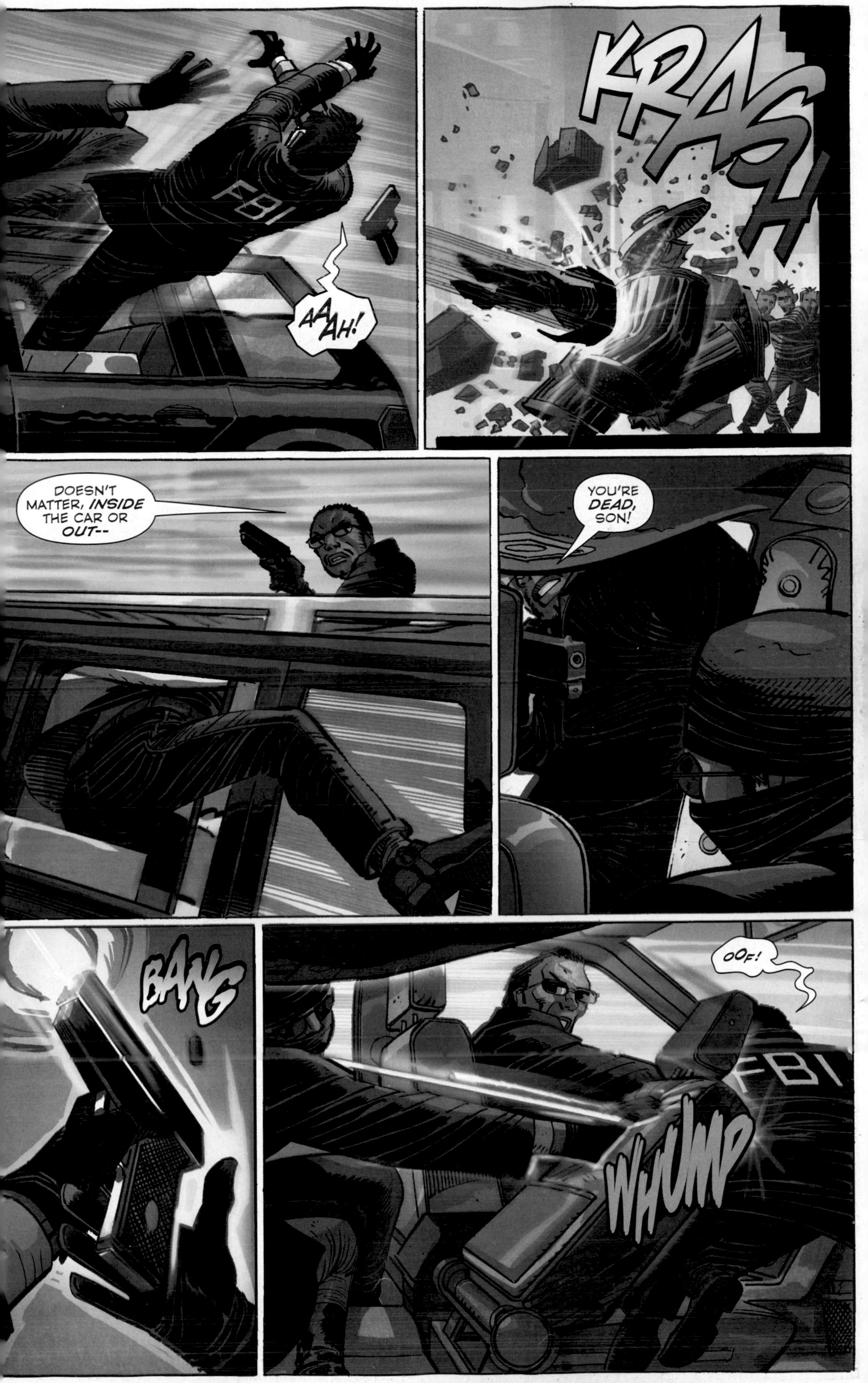
AAAH!
KRASH
DOESN'T MATTER, INSIDE THE CAR OR OUT--
YOU'RE DEAD, SON!
BANG
OOF!
WHUMP
FBI
FBI
FBI

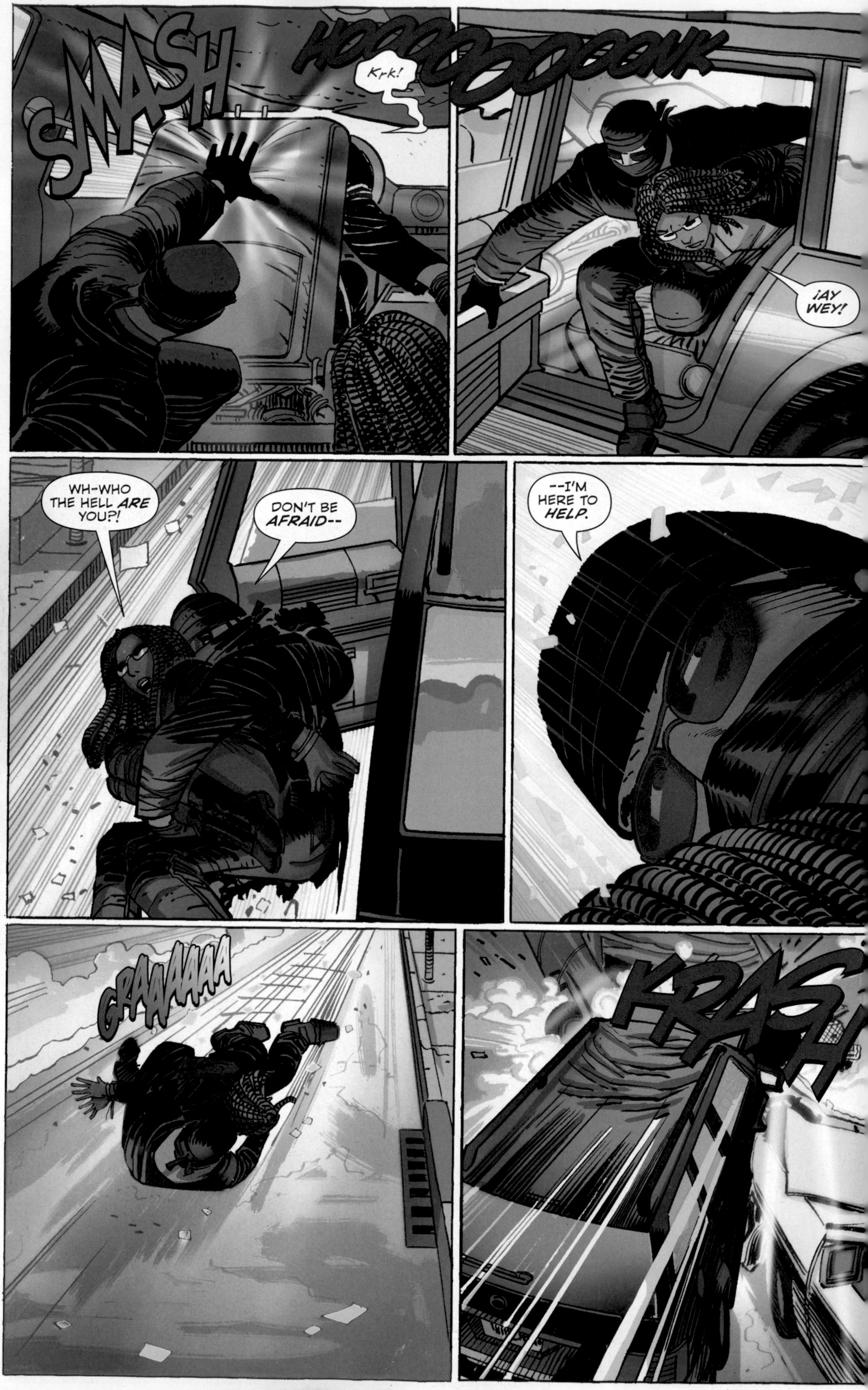
SMASH
HOOOOOOOOONK
Krk!
¡AY WEY!
WH-WHO THE HELL ARE YOU?!
DON'T BE AFRAID--
--I'M HERE TO HELP.
GRAAAAAA
KRASH

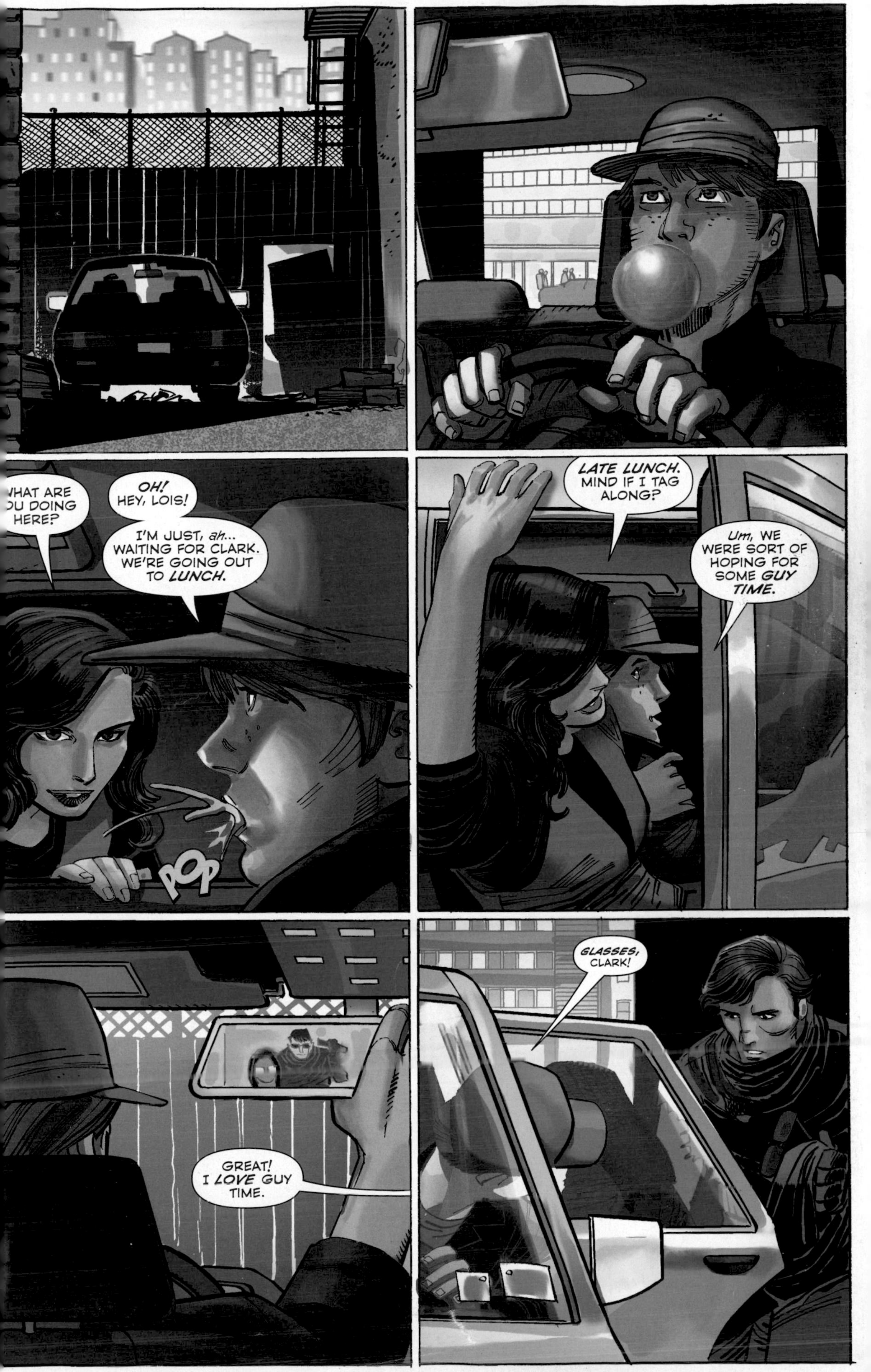
WHAT ARE
OU DOING
HERE?
OH!
HEY, LOIS!
I'M JUST, ah...
WAITING FOR CLARK.
WE'RE GOING OUT
TO LUNCH.
POP
LATE LUNCH.
MIND IF I TAG
ALONG?
Um, WE
WERE SORT OF
HOPING FOR
SOME GUY
TIME.
GREAT!
I LOVE GUY
TIME.
GLASSES,
CLARK!

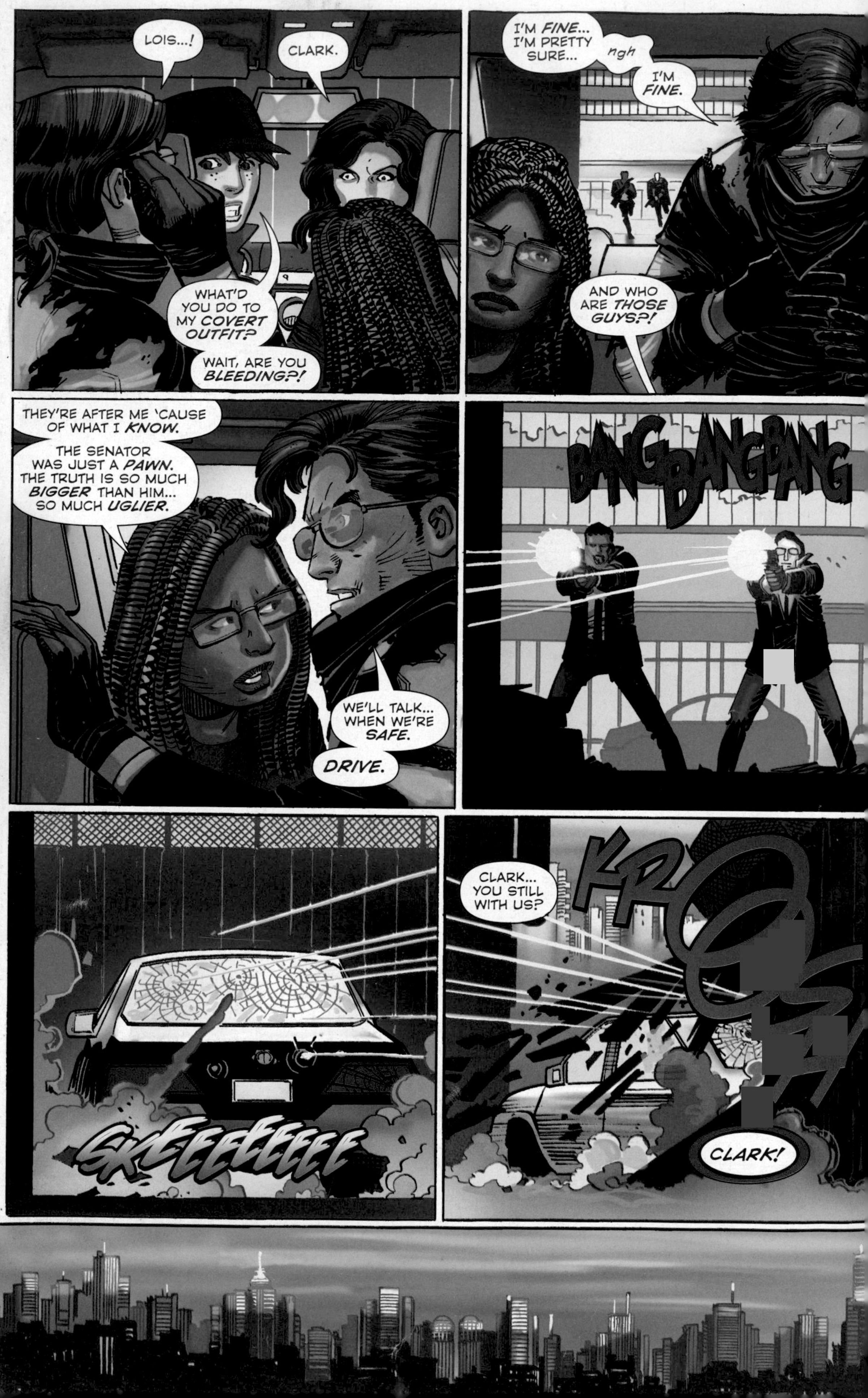
LOIS...!
CLARK.
WHAT'D YOU DO TO MY COVERT OUTFIT?
WAIT, ARE YOU BLEEDING?!
I'M FINE... I'M PRETTY SURE...
ngh
I'M FINE.
AND WHO ARE THOSE GUYS?!
THEY'RE AFTER ME 'CAUSE OF WHAT I KNOW.
THE SENATOR WAS JUST A PAWN. THE TRUTH IS SO MUCH BIGGER THAN HIM... SO MUCH UGLIER.
WE'LL TALK... WHEN WE'RE SAFE.
DRIVE.
BANGBANGBANG
SKEEEEEEEE
CLARK... YOU STILL WITH US?
CLARK!

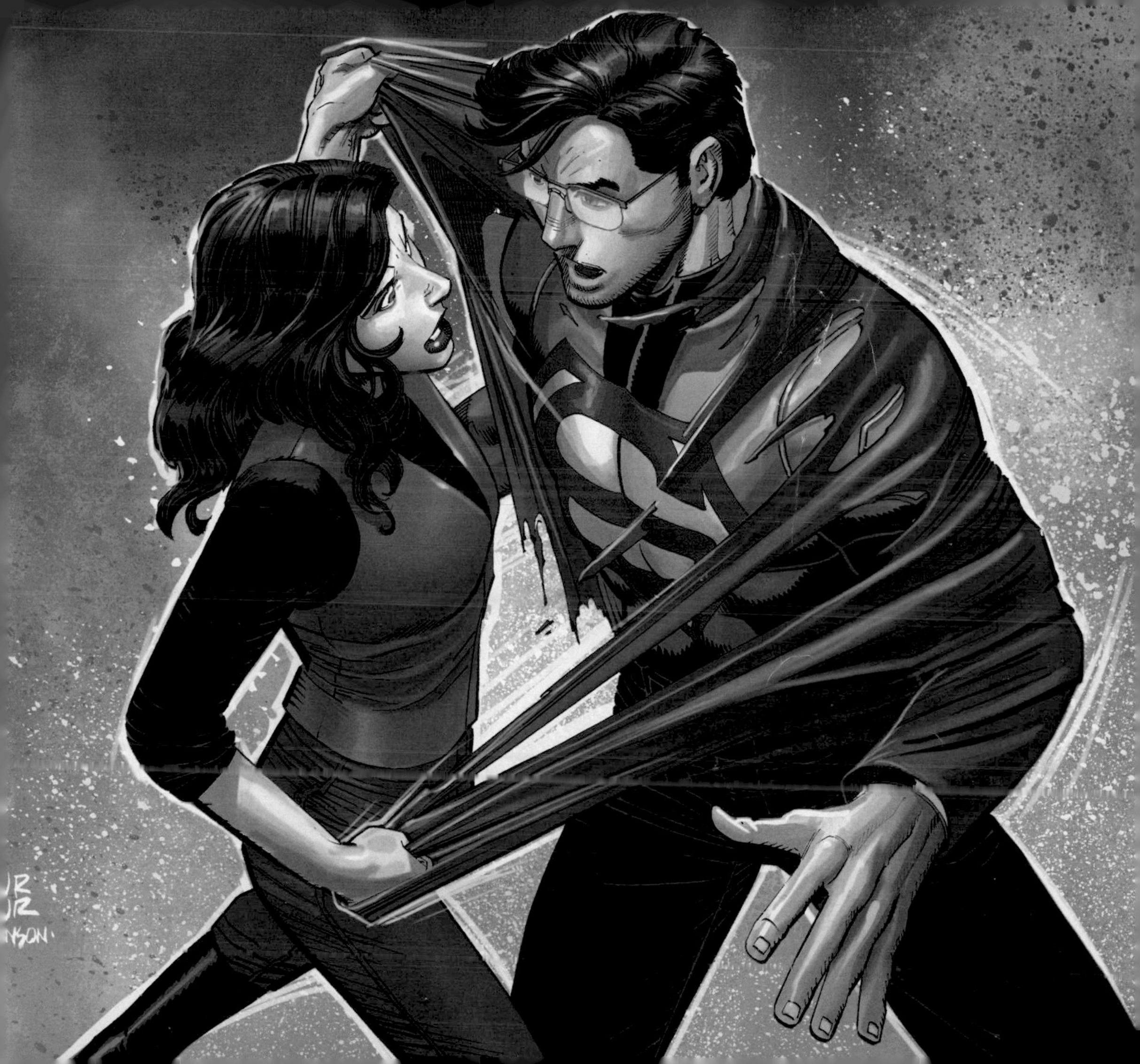

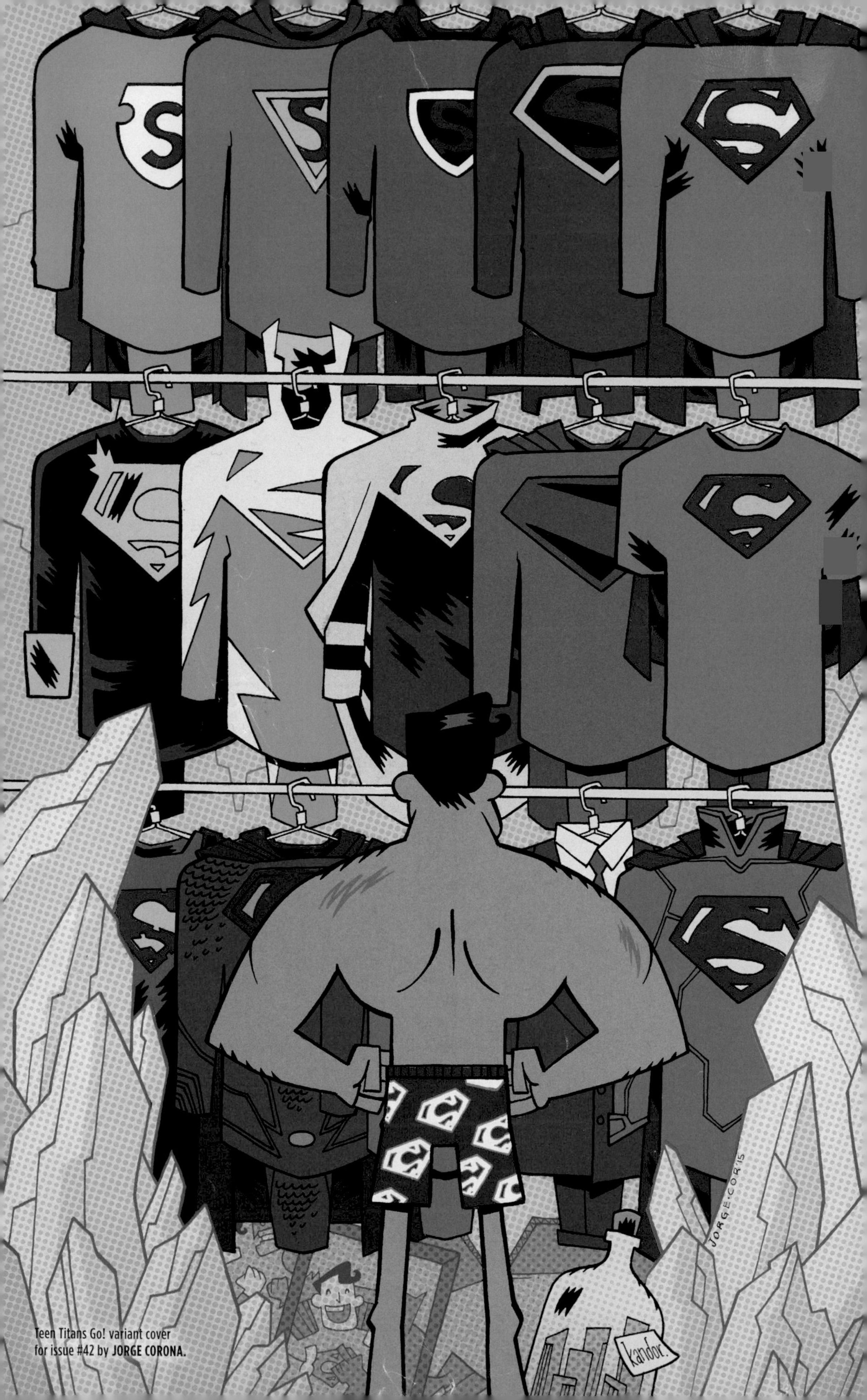
kandor.

Teen Titans Go! variant cover
for issue #42 by **JORGE CORONA.**

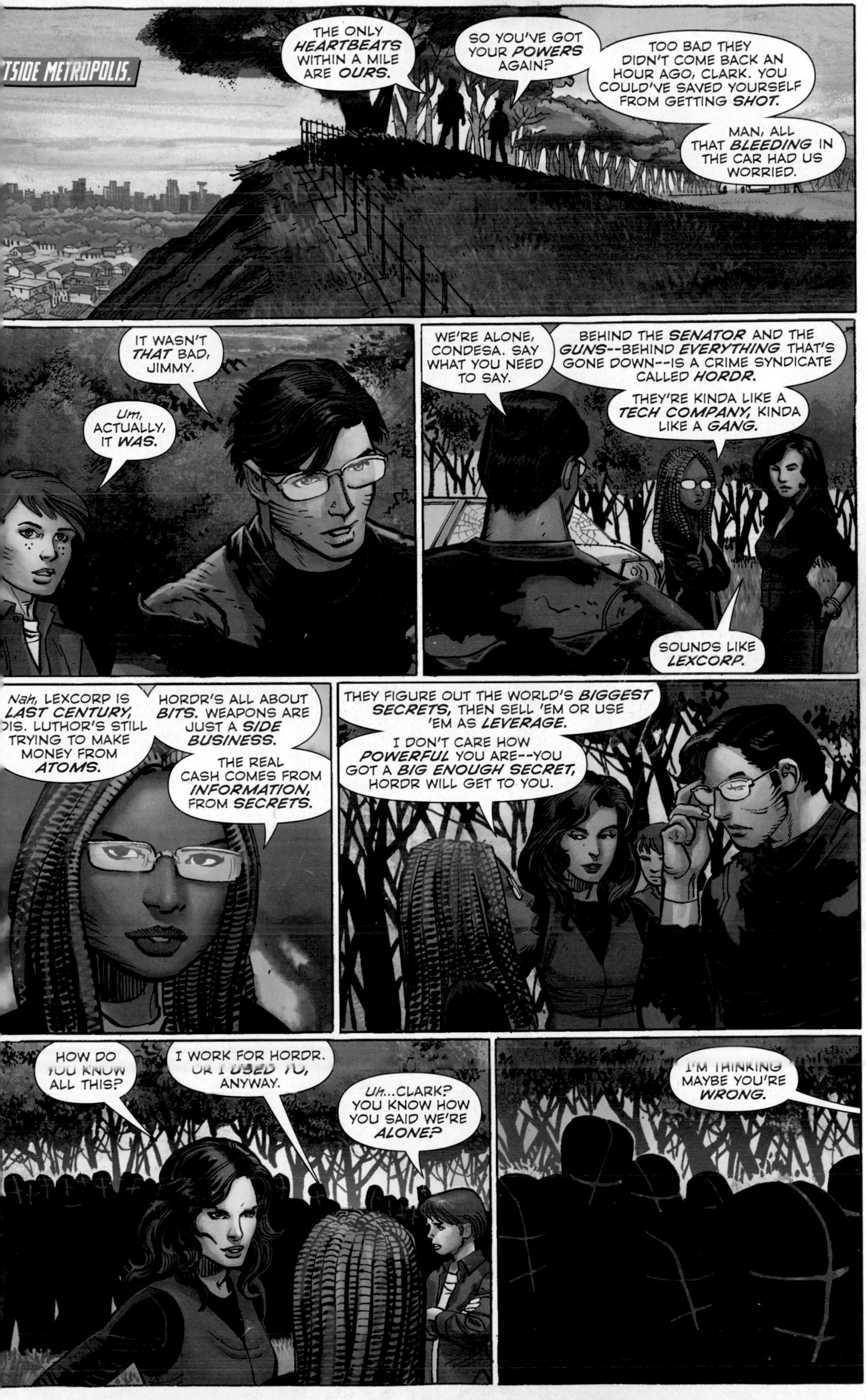

TSIDE METROPOLIS.
THE ONLY HEARTBEATS WITHIN A MILE ARE OURS.
SO YOU'VE GOT YOUR POWERS AGAIN?
TOO BAD THEY DIDN'T COME BACK AN HOUR AGO, CLARK. YOU COULD'VE SAVED YOURSELF FROM GETTING SHOT.
MAN, ALL THAT BLEEDING IN THE CAR HAD US WORRIED.
IT WASN'T THAT BAD, JIMMY.
Um, ACTUALLY, IT WAS.
WE'RE ALONE, CONDESA. SAY WHAT YOU NEED TO SAY.
BEHIND THE SENATOR AND THE GUNS--BEHIND EVERYTHING THAT'S GONE DOWN--IS A CRIME SYNDICATE CALLED HORDR.
THEY'RE KINDA LIKE A TECH COMPANY, KINDA LIKE A GANG.
SOUNDS LIKE LEXCORP.
Nah, LEXCORP IS LAST CENTURY, DIS. LUTHOR'S STILL TRYING TO MAKE MONEY FROM ATOMS.
HORDR'S ALL ABOUT BITS. WEAPONS ARE JUST A SIDE BUSINESS.
THE REAL CASH COMES FROM INFORMATION, FROM SECRETS.
THEY FIGURE OUT THE WORLD'S BIGGEST SECRETS, THEN SELL 'EM OR USE 'EM AS LEVERAGE.
I DON'T CARE HOW POWERFUL YOU ARE--YOU GOT A BIG ENOUGH SECRET, HORDR WILL GET TO YOU.
HOW DO YOU KNOW ALL THIS?
I WORK FOR HORDR. OR I USED TO, ANYWAY.
Uh...CLARK? YOU KNOW HOW YOU SAID WE'RE ALONE?
I'M THINKING MAYBE YOU'RE WRONG.

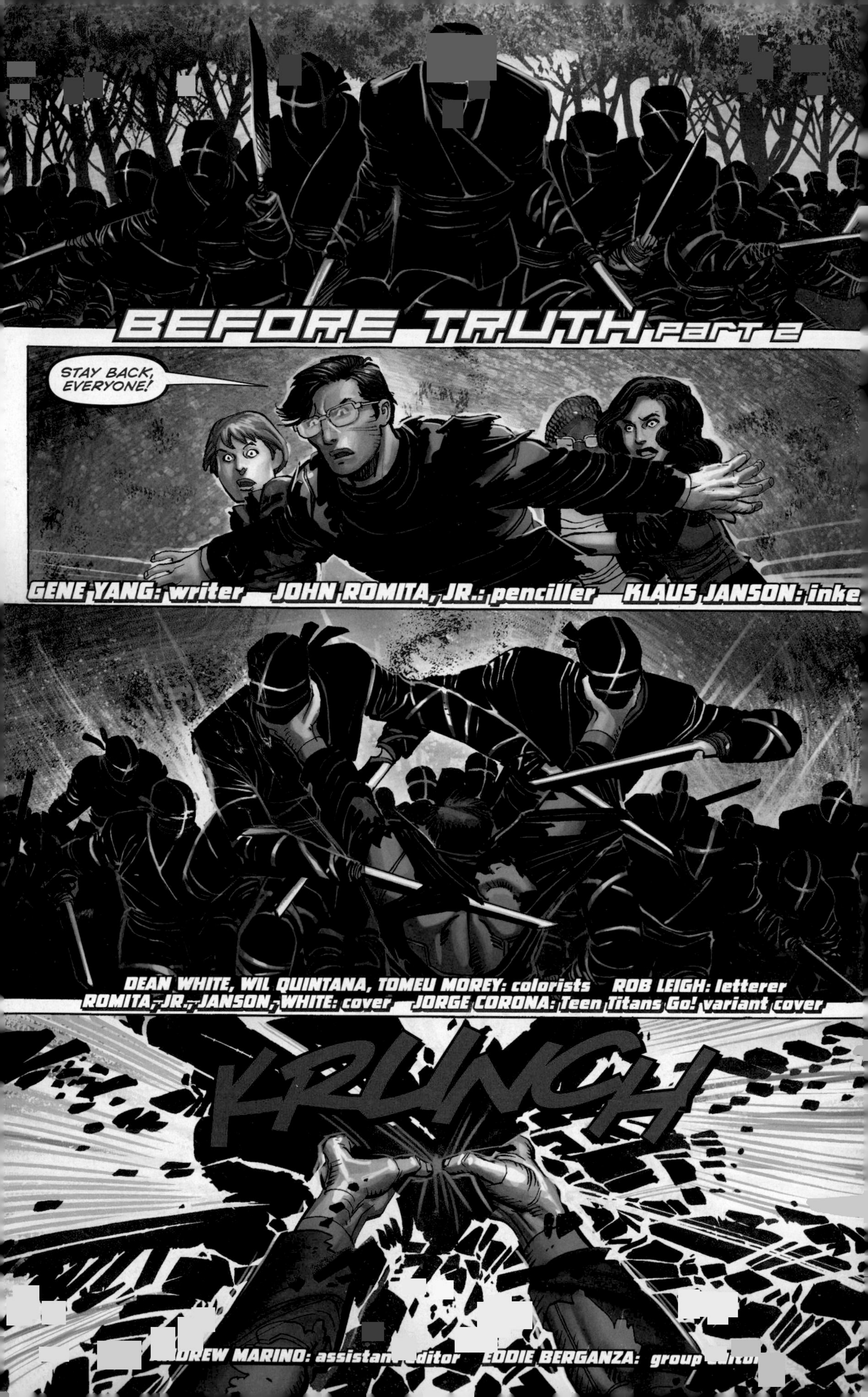
BEFORE TRUTH part 2
STAY BACK, EVERYONE!
GENE YANG: writer JOHN ROMITA, JR.: penciller KLAUS JANSON: inke
DEAN WHITE, WIL QUINTANA, TOMEU MOREY: colorists ROB LEIGH: letterer
ROMITA, JR., JANSON, WHITE: cover JORGE CORONA: Teen Titans Go! variant cover
KRUNCH
DREW MARINO: assistan ditor DDIE BERGANZA: group

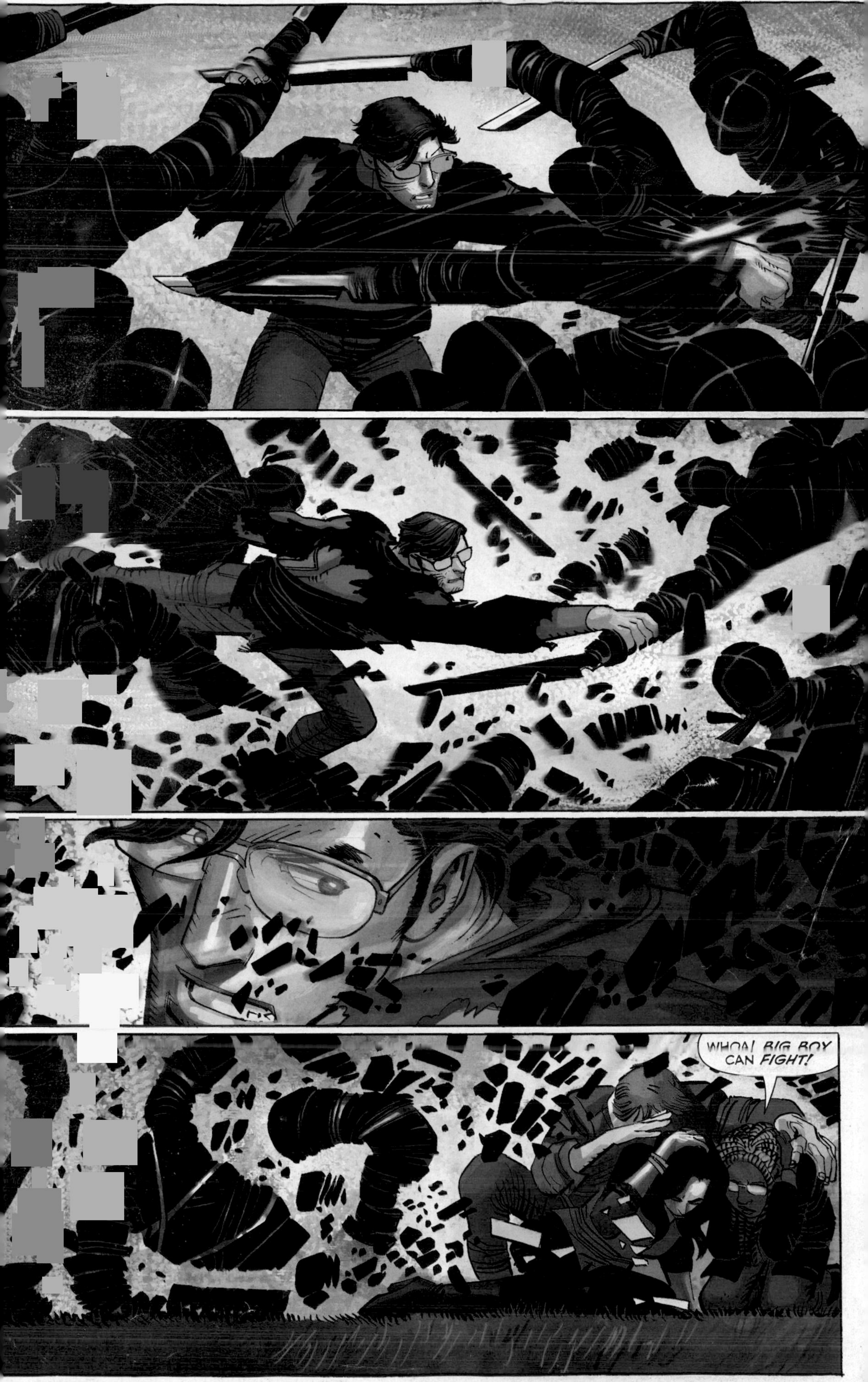
WHOA! BIG BOY CAN FIGHT!

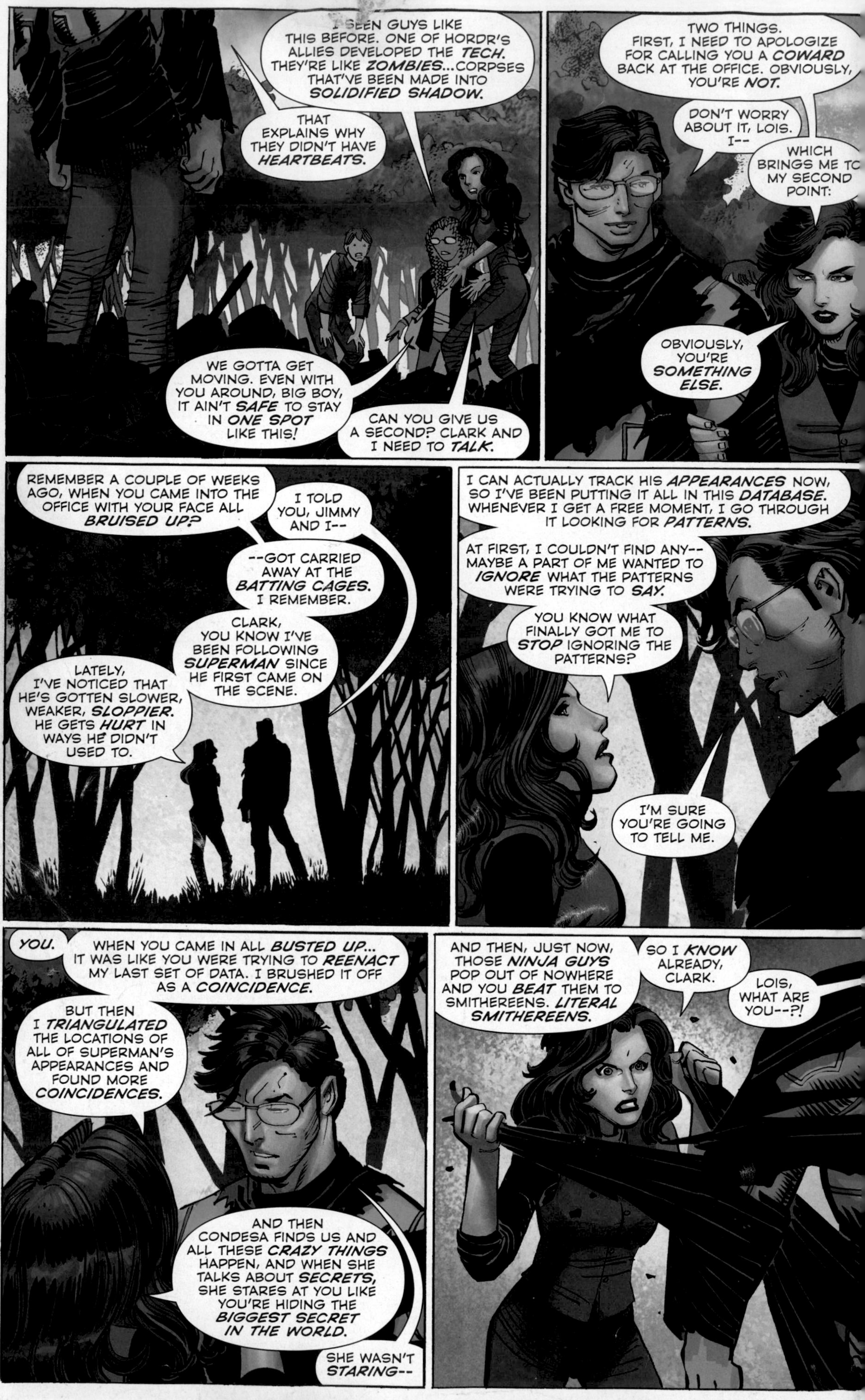
I SEEN GUYS LIKE THIS BEFORE. ONE OF HORDR'S ALLIES DEVELOPED THE TECH. THEY'RE LIKE ZOMBIES...CORPSES THAT'VE BEEN MADE INTO SOLIDIFIED SHADOW.
THAT EXPLAINS WHY THEY DIDN'T HAVE HEARTBEATS.
WE GOTTA GET MOVING. EVEN WITH YOU AROUND, BIG BOY, IT AIN'T SAFE TO STAY IN ONE SPOT LIKE THIS!
CAN YOU GIVE US A SECOND? CLARK AND I NEED TO TALK.
TWO THINGS. FIRST, I NEED TO APOLOGIZE FOR CALLING YOU A COWARD BACK AT THE OFFICE. OBVIOUSLY, YOU'RE NOT.
DON'T WORRY ABOUT IT, LOIS. I--
WHICH BRINGS ME TO MY SECOND POINT:
OBVIOUSLY, YOU'RE SOMETHING ELSE.
REMEMBER A COUPLE OF WEEKS AGO, WHEN YOU CAME INTO THE OFFICE WITH YOUR FACE ALL BRUISED UP?
I TOLD YOU, JIMMY AND I--
--GOT CARRIED AWAY AT THE BATTING CAGES. I REMEMBER.
CLARK, YOU KNOW I'VE BEEN FOLLOWING SUPERMAN SINCE HE FIRST CAME ON THE SCENE.
LATELY, I'VE NOTICED THAT HE'S GOTTEN SLOWER, WEAKER, SLOPPIER. HE GETS HURT IN WAYS HE DIDN'T USED TO.
I CAN ACTUALLY TRACK HIS APPEARANCES NOW, SO I'VE BEEN PUTTING IT ALL IN THIS DATABASE. WHENEVER I GET A FREE MOMENT, I GO THROUGH IT LOOKING FOR PATTERNS.
AT FIRST, I COULDN'T FIND ANY-- MAYBE A PART OF ME WANTED TO IGNORE WHAT THE PATTERNS WERE TRYING TO SAY.
YOU KNOW WHAT FINALLY GOT ME TO STOP IGNORING THE PATTERNS?
I'M SURE YOU'RE GOING TO TELL ME.
YOU.
WHEN YOU CAME IN ALL BUSTED UP... IT WAS LIKE YOU WERE TRYING TO REENACT MY LAST SET OF DATA. I BRUSHED IT OFF AS A COINCIDENCE.
BUT THEN I TRIANGULATED THE LOCATIONS OF ALL OF SUPERMAN'S APPEARANCES AND FOUND MORE COINCIDENCES.
AND THEN CONDESA FINDS US AND ALL THESE CRAZY THINGS HAPPEN, AND WHEN SHE TALKS ABOUT SECRETS, SHE STARES AT YOU LIKE YOU'RE HIDING THE BIGGEST SECRET IN THE WORLD.
SHE WASN'T STARING--
AND THEN, JUST NOW, THOSE NINJA GUYS POP OUT OF NOWHERE AND YOU BEAT THEM TO SMITHEREENS. LITERAL SMITHEREENS.
SO I KNOW ALREADY, CLARK.
LOIS, WHAT ARE YOU--?!

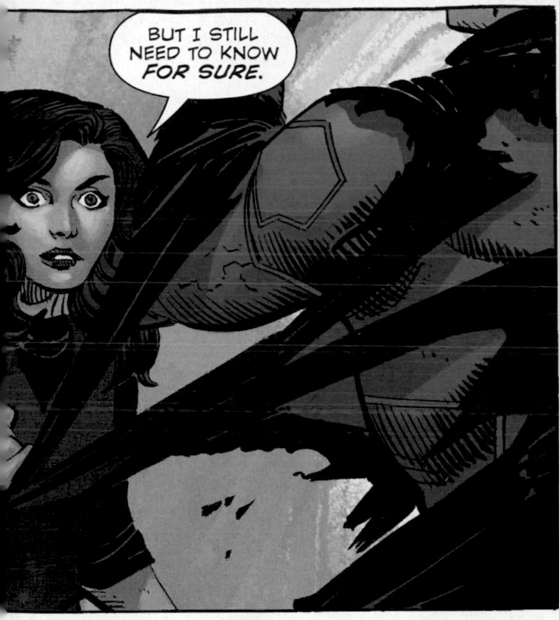
BUT I STILL
NEED TO KNOW
FOR SURE.

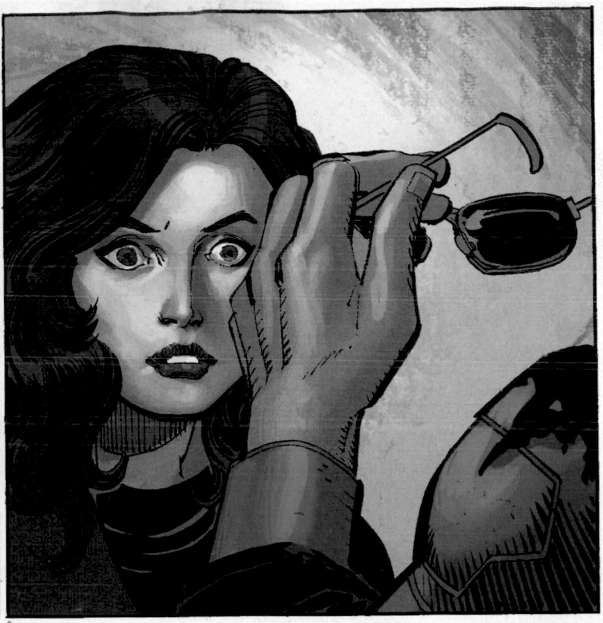

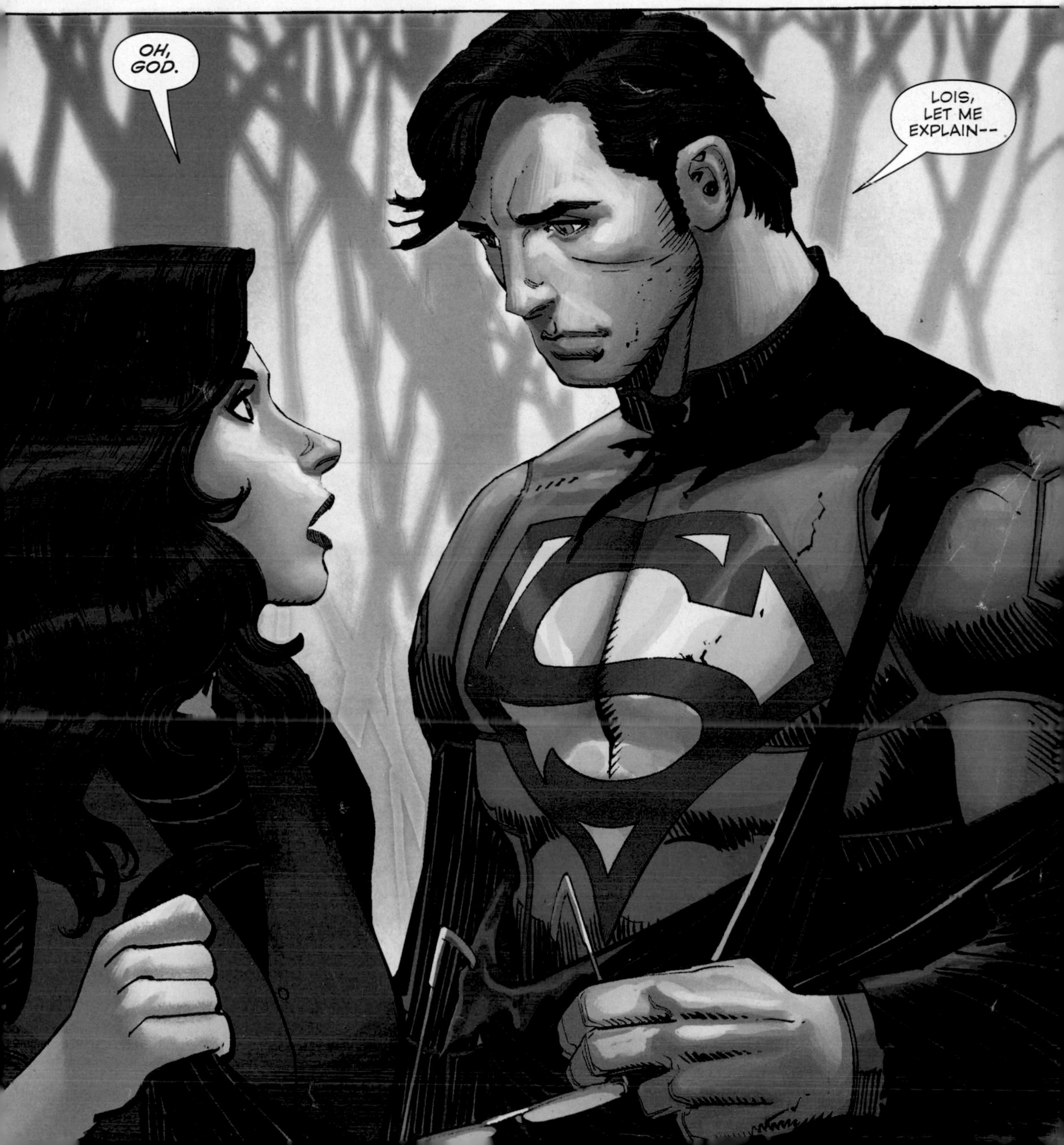
*OH,
GOD.*
LOIS,
LET ME
EXPLAIN--

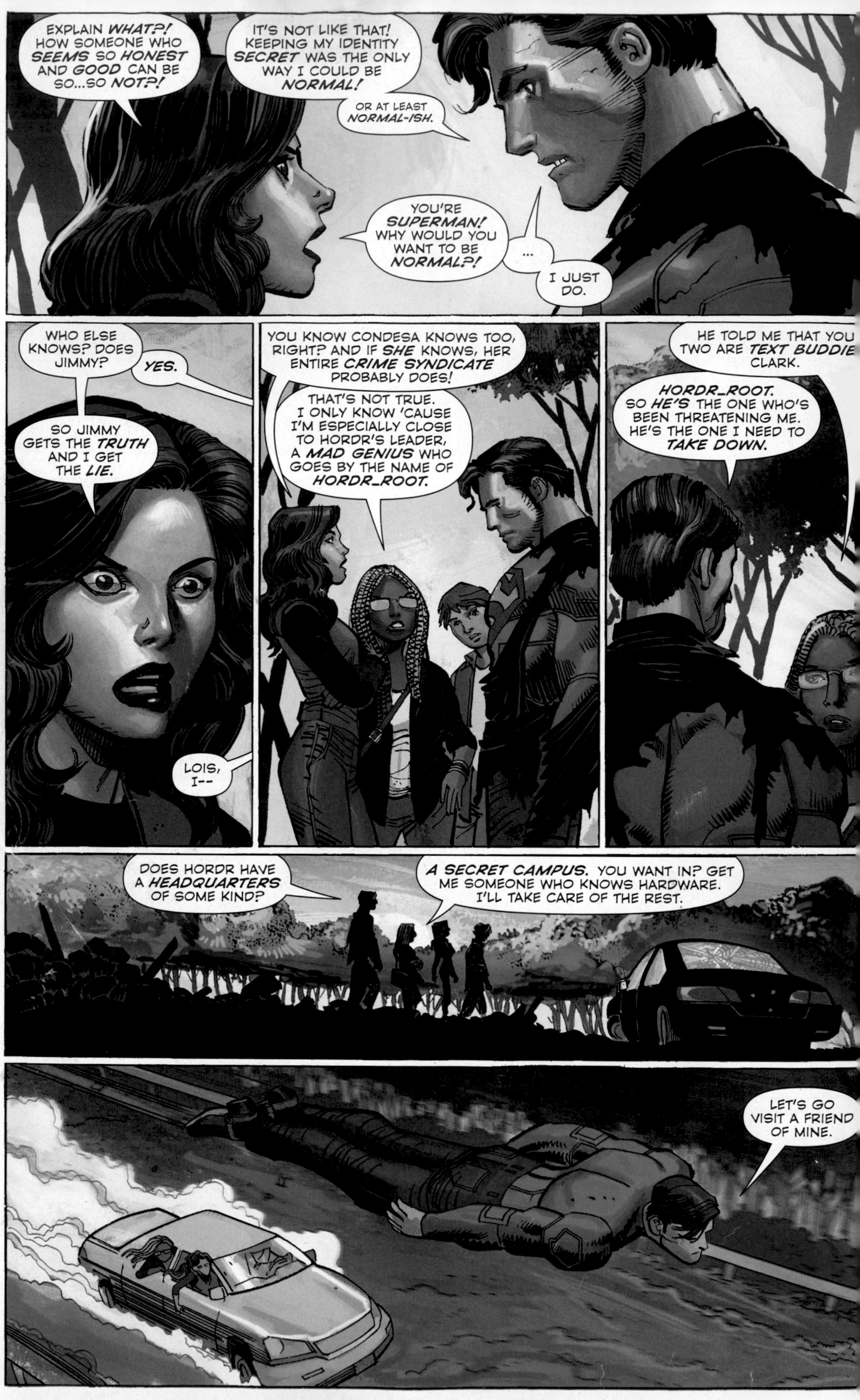
EXPLAIN WHAT?! HOW SOMEONE WHO SEEMS SO HONEST AND GOOD CAN BE SO...SO NOT?!
IT'S NOT LIKE THAT! KEEPING MY IDENTITY SECRET WAS THE ONLY WAY I COULD BE NORMAL!
OR AT LEAST NORMAL-ISH.
YOU'RE SUPERMAN! WHY WOULD YOU WANT TO BE NORMAL?!
...
I JUST DO.
WHO ELSE KNOWS? DOES JIMMY?
YES.
SO JIMMY GETS THE TRUTH AND I GET THE LIE.
LOIS, I--
YOU KNOW CONDESA KNOWS TOO, RIGHT? AND IF SHE KNOWS, HER ENTIRE CRIME SYNDICATE PROBABLY DOES!
THAT'S NOT TRUE. I ONLY KNOW 'CAUSE I'M ESPECIALLY CLOSE TO HORDR'S LEADER, A MAD GENIUS WHO GOES BY THE NAME OF HORDR_ROOT.
HE TOLD ME THAT YOU TWO ARE TEXT BUDDIE CLARK.
HORDR_ROOT. SO HE'S THE ONE WHO'S BEEN THREATENING ME. HE'S THE ONE I NEED TO TAKE DOWN.
DOES HORDR HAVE A HEADQUARTERS OF SOME KIND?
A SECRET CAMPUS. YOU WANT IN? GET ME SOMEONE WHO KNOWS HARDWARE. I'LL TAKE CARE OF THE REST.
LET'S GO VISIT A FRIEND OF MINE.

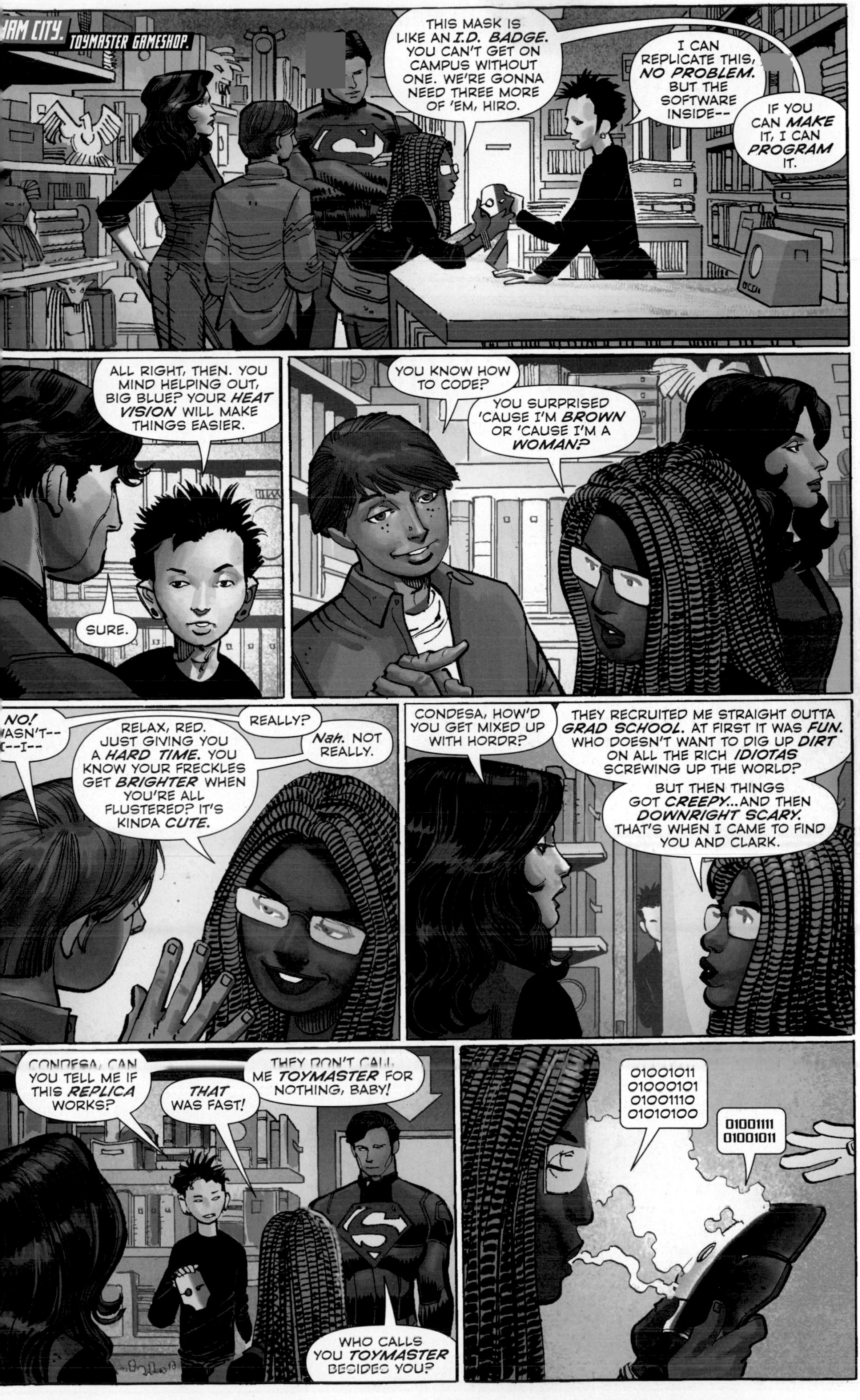
HAM CITY.
TOYMASTER GAMESHOP.
THIS MASK IS LIKE AN I.D. BADGE. YOU CAN'T GET ON CAMPUS WITHOUT ONE. WE'RE GONNA NEED THREE MORE OF 'EM, HIRO.
I CAN REPLICATE THIS, NO PROBLEM. BUT THE SOFTWARE INSIDE--
IF YOU CAN MAKE IT, I CAN PROGRAM IT.
ALL RIGHT, THEN. YOU MIND HELPING OUT, BIG BLUE? YOUR HEAT VISION WILL MAKE THINGS EASIER.
SURE.
YOU KNOW HOW TO CODE?
YOU SURPRISED 'CAUSE I'M BROWN OR 'CAUSE I'M A WOMAN?
NO!
ASN'T--
--I--
REALLY?
RELAX, RED. JUST GIVING YOU A HARD TIME. YOU KNOW YOUR FRECKLES GET BRIGHTER WHEN YOU'RE ALL FLUSTERED? IT'S KINDA CUTE.
Nah. NOT REALLY.
CONDESA, HOW'D YOU GET MIXED UP WITH HORDR?
THEY RECRUITED ME STRAIGHT OUTTA GRAD SCHOOL. AT FIRST IT WAS FUN. WHO DOESN'T WANT TO DIG UP DIRT ON ALL THE RICH IDIOTAS SCREWING UP THE WORLD?
BUT THEN THINGS GOT CREEPY...AND THEN DOWNRIGHT SCARY. THAT'S WHEN I CAME TO FIND YOU AND CLARK.
CONDESA, CAN YOU TELL ME IF THIS REPLICA WORKS?
THAT WAS FAST!
THEY DON'T CALL ME TOYMASTER FOR NOTHING, BABY!
WHO CALLS YOU TOYMASTER BESIDES YOU?
01001011 01000101 01001110 01010100
01001111 01001011

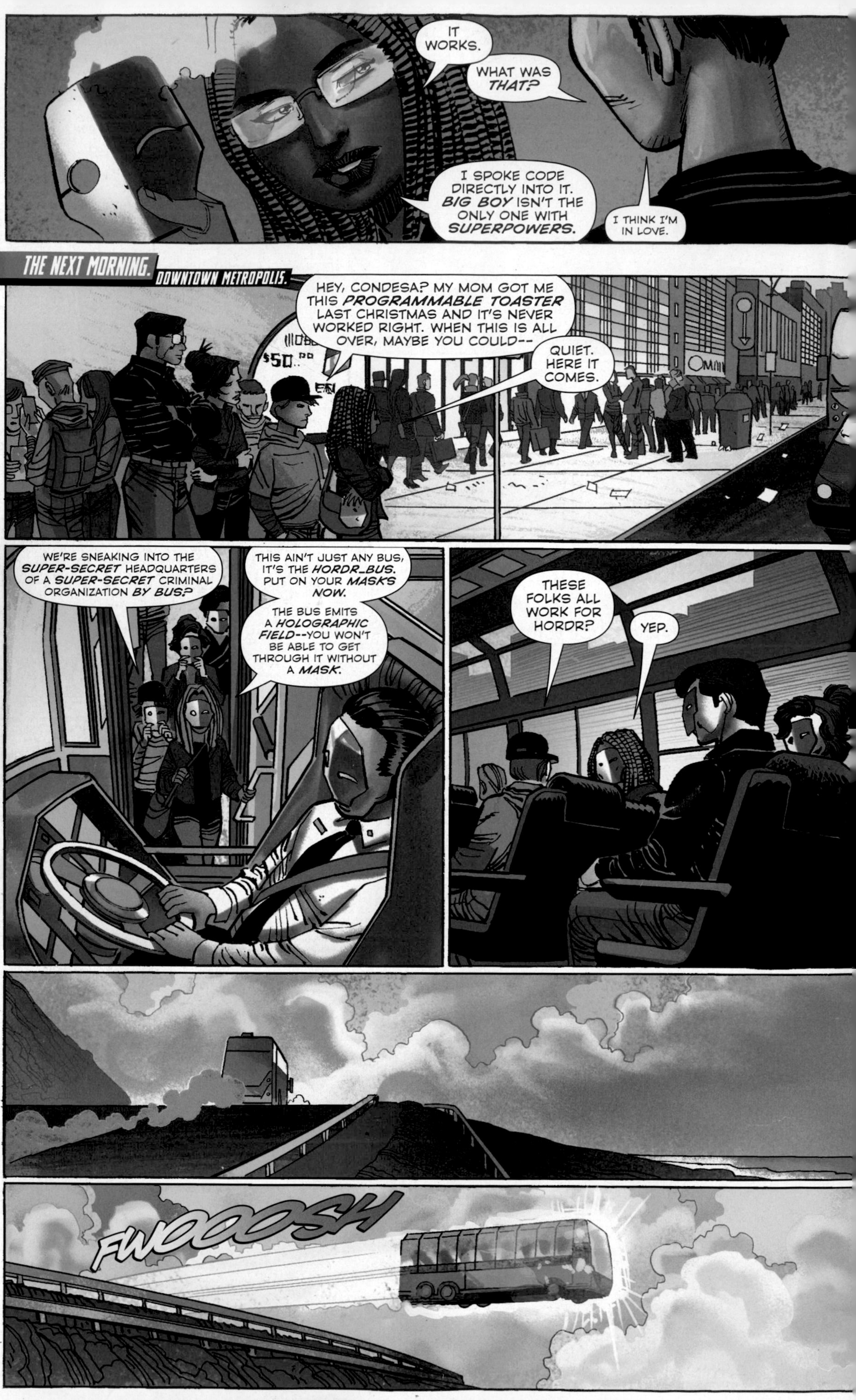
IT WORKS.
WHAT WAS THAT?
I SPOKE CODE DIRECTLY INTO IT. BIG BOY ISN'T THE ONLY ONE WITH SUPERPOWERS.
I THINK I'M IN LOVE.
THE NEXT MORNING.
DOWNTOWN METROPOLIS.
HEY, CONDESA? MY MOM GOT ME THIS PROGRAMMABLE TOASTER LAST CHRISTMAS AND IT'S NEVER WORKED RIGHT. WHEN THIS IS ALL OVER, MAYBE YOU COULD--
QUIET. HERE IT COMES.
WE'RE SNEAKING INTO THE SUPER-SECRET HEADQUARTERS OF A SUPER-SECRET CRIMINAL ORGANIZATION BY BUS?
THIS AIN'T JUST ANY BUS, IT'S THE HORDR_BUS. PUT ON YOUR MASKS NOW.
THE BUS EMITS A HOLOGRAPHIC FIELD--YOU WON'T BE ABLE TO GET THROUGH IT WITHOUT A MASK.
THESE FOLKS ALL WORK FOR HORDR?
YEP.
FWOOOSH

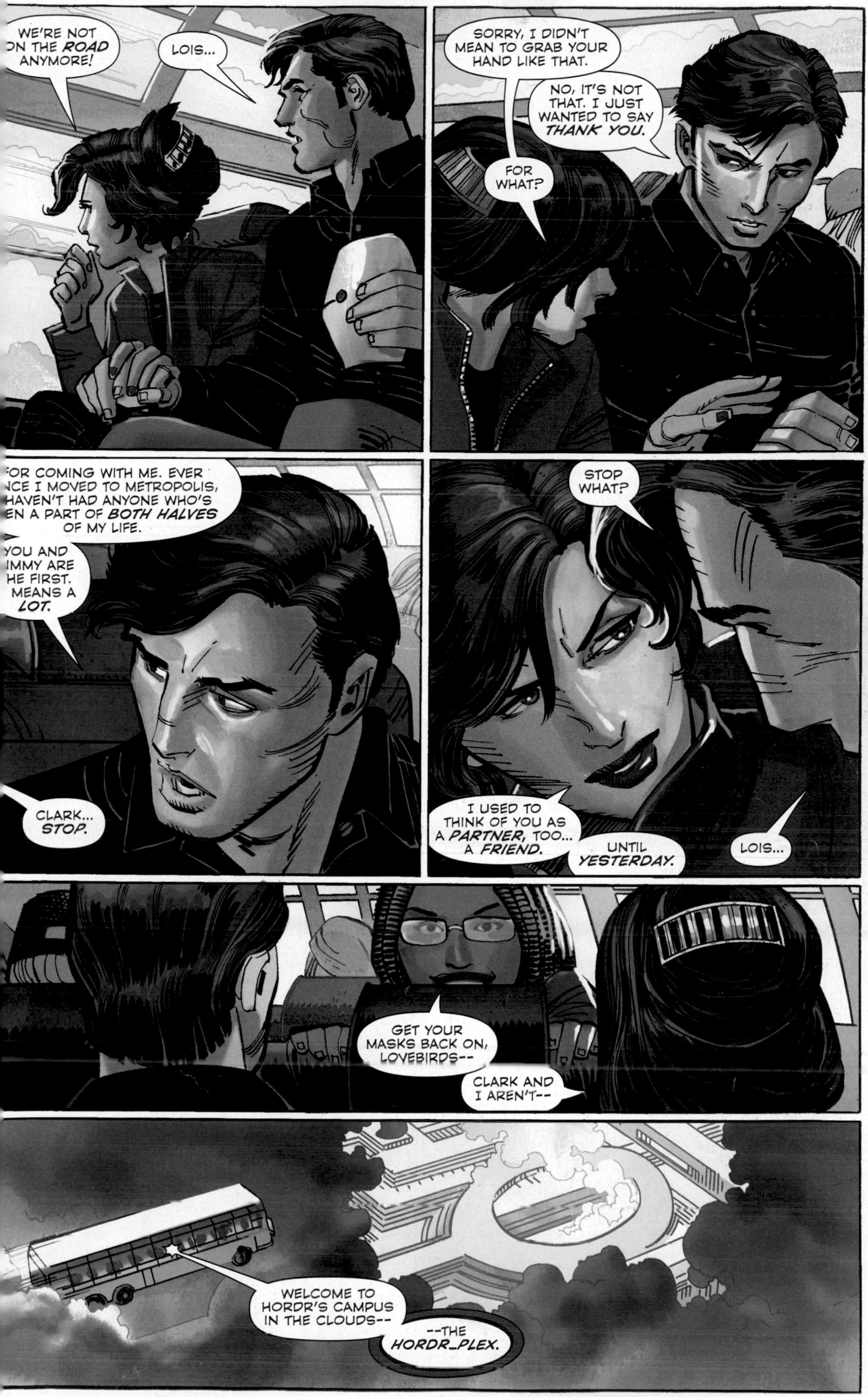
WE'RE NOT ON THE ROAD ANYMORE!
LOIS...
SORRY, I DIDN'T MEAN TO GRAB YOUR HAND LIKE THAT.
NO, IT'S NOT THAT. I JUST WANTED TO SAY THANK YOU.
FOR WHAT?
FOR COMING WITH ME. EVER NCE I MOVED TO METROPOLIS, HAVEN'T HAD ANYONE WHO'S EN A PART OF BOTH HALVES OF MY LIFE.
YOU AND IMMY ARE HE FIRST. MEANS A LOT.
CLARK... STOP.
STOP WHAT?
I USED TO THINK OF YOU AS A PARTNER, TOO... A FRIEND.
UNTIL YESTERDAY.
LOIS...
GET YOUR MASKS BACK ON, LOVEBIRDS--
CLARK AND I AREN'T--
WELCOME TO HORDR'S CAMPUS IN THE CLOUDS--
--THE HORDR_PLEX.

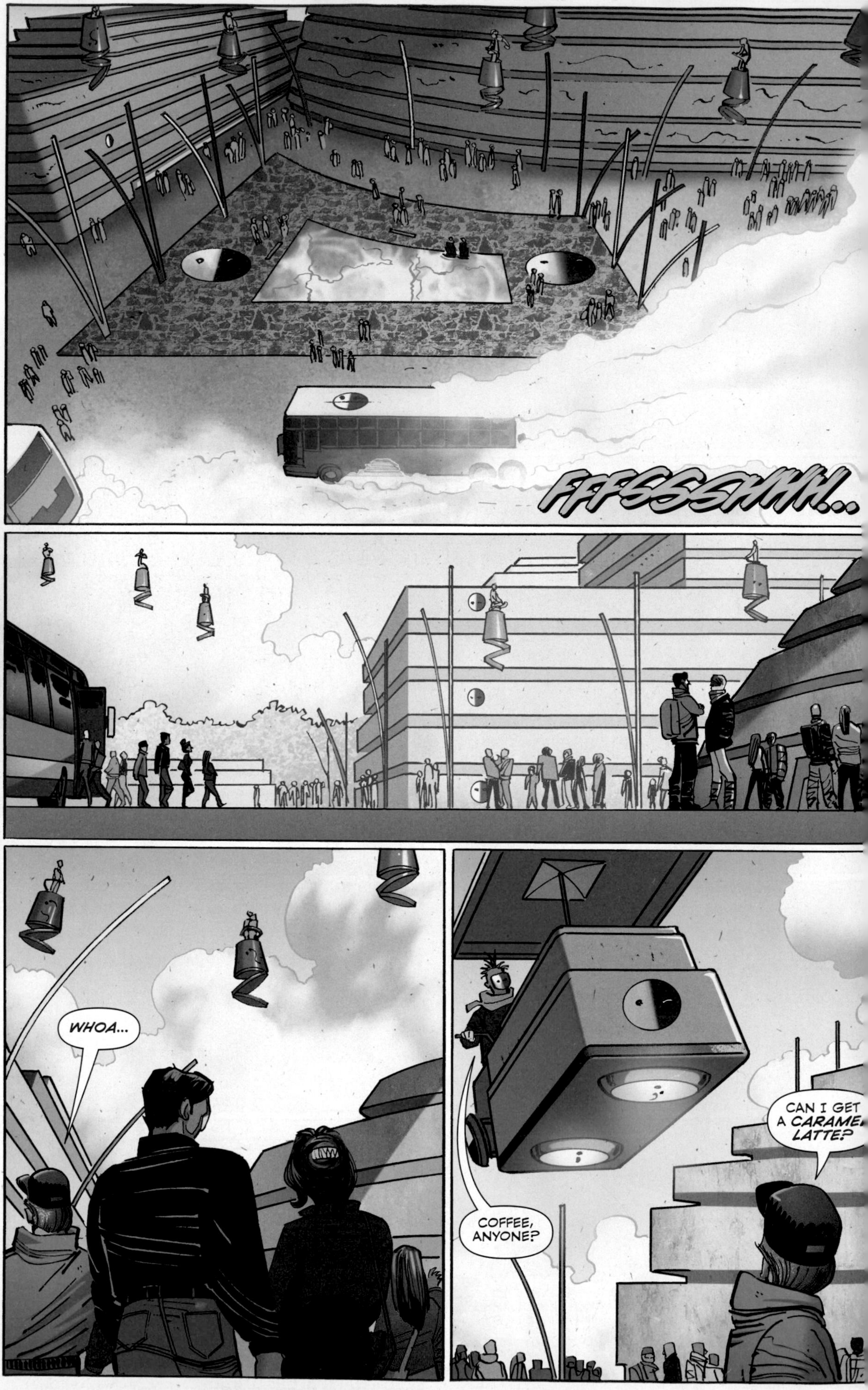
FFFSSSHHH...
WHOA...
COFFEE, ANYONE?
CAN I GET A CARAME LATTE?

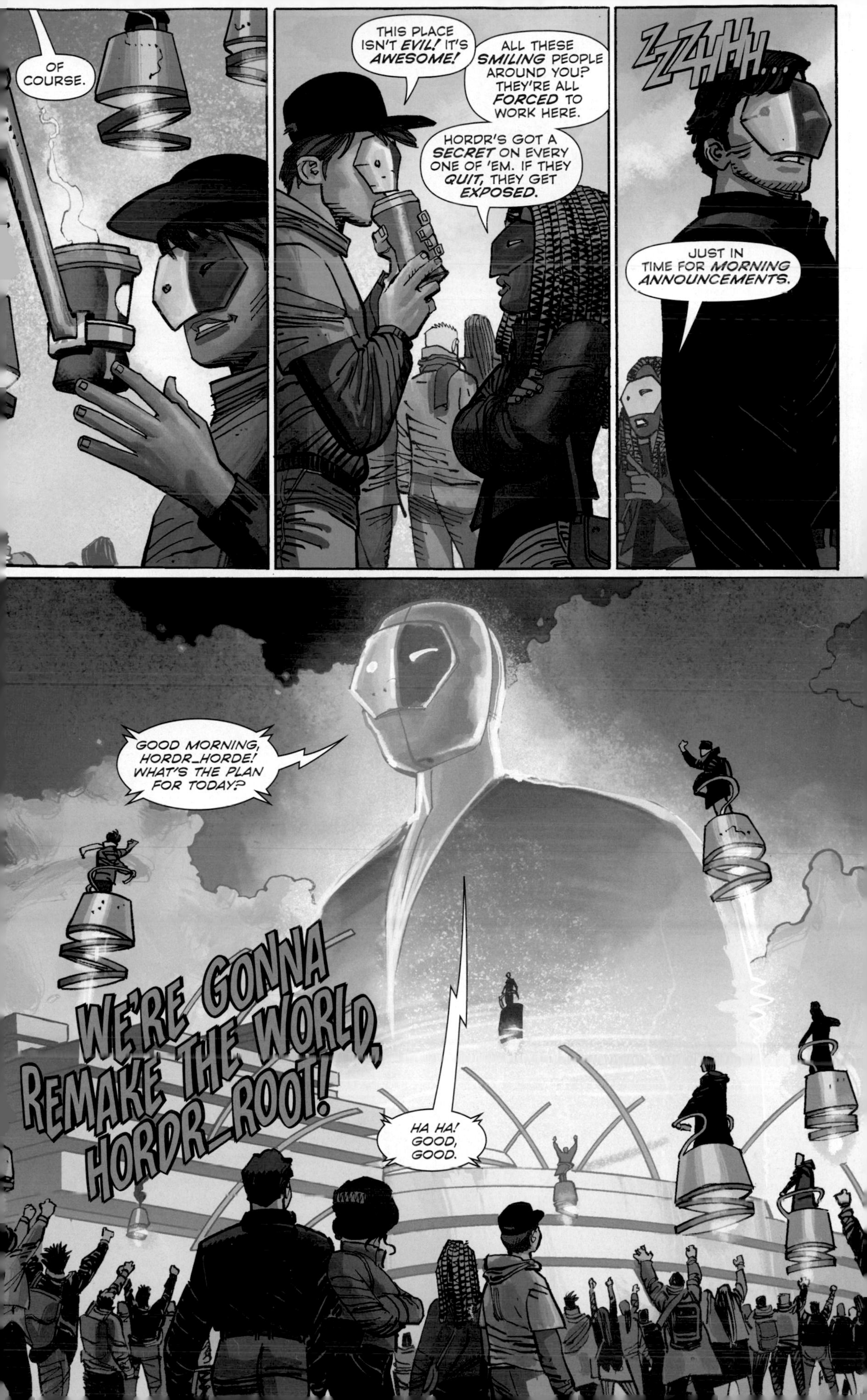

OF COURSE.
THIS PLACE ISN'T EVIL! IT'S AWESOME!
ALL THESE SMILING PEOPLE AROUND YOU? THEY'RE ALL FORCED TO WORK HERE.
HORDR'S GOT A SECRET ON EVERY ONE OF 'EM. IF THEY QUIT, THEY GET EXPOSED.
ZZZHHH...
JUST IN TIME FOR MORNING ANNOUNCEMENTS.
GOOD MORNING, HORDR_HORDE! WHAT'S THE PLAN FOR TODAY?
WE'RE GONNA REMAKE THE WORLD, HORDR_ROOT!
HA HA! GOOD, GOOD.

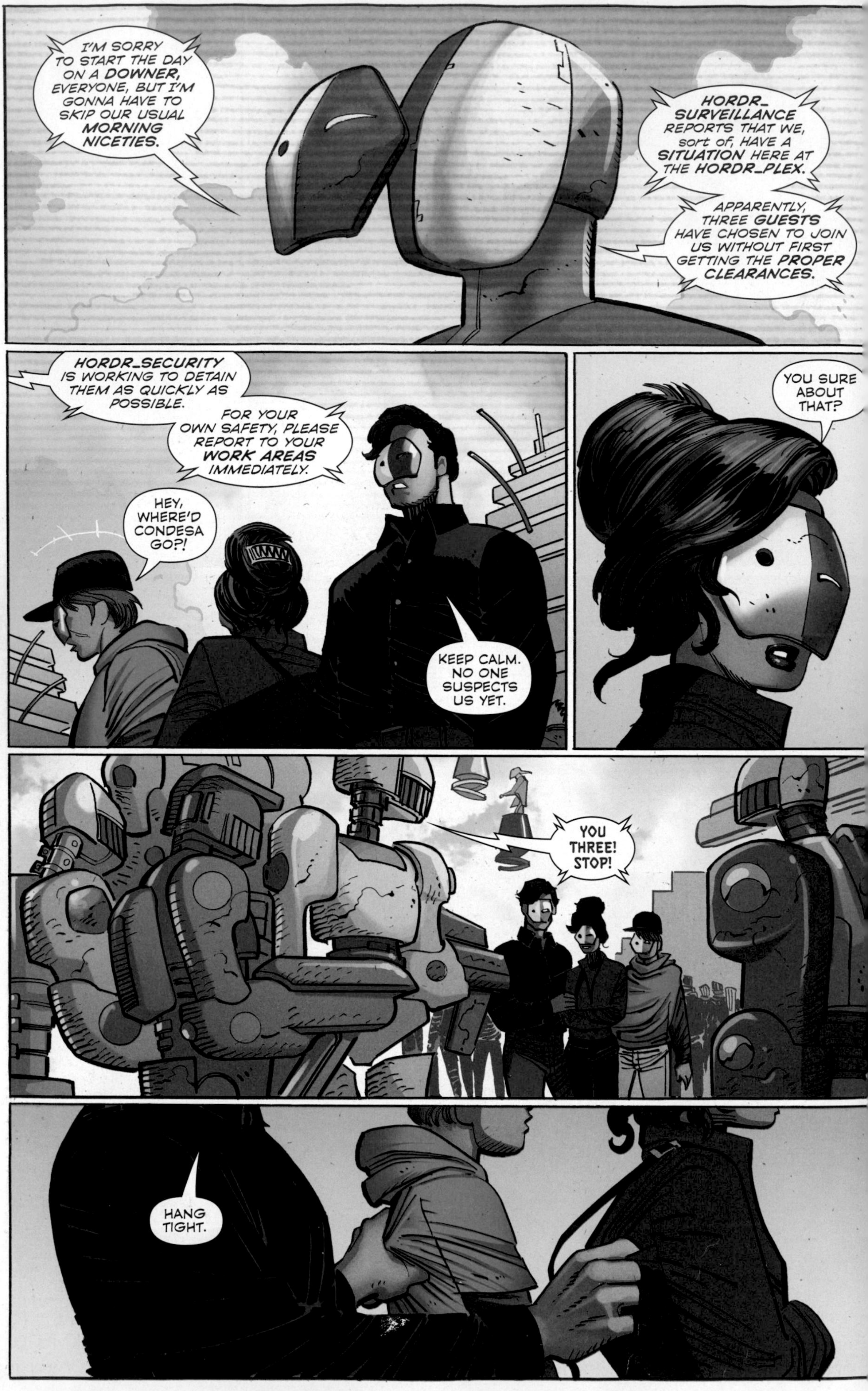
I'M SORRY TO START THE DAY ON A DOWNER, EVERYONE, BUT I'M GONNA HAVE TO SKIP OUR USUAL MORNING NICETIES.
HORDR_SURVEILLANCE REPORTS THAT WE, sort of, HAVE A SITUATION HERE AT THE HORDR_PLEX.
APPARENTLY, THREE GUESTS HAVE CHOSEN TO JOIN US WITHOUT FIRST GETTING THE PROPER CLEARANCES.
HORDR_SECURITY IS WORKING TO DETAIN THEM AS QUICKLY AS POSSIBLE.
FOR YOUR OWN SAFETY, PLEASE REPORT TO YOUR WORK AREAS IMMEDIATELY.
HEY, WHERE'D CONDESA GO?!
KEEP CALM. NO ONE SUSPECTS US YET.
YOU SURE ABOUT THAT?
YOU THREE! STOP!
HANG TIGHT.

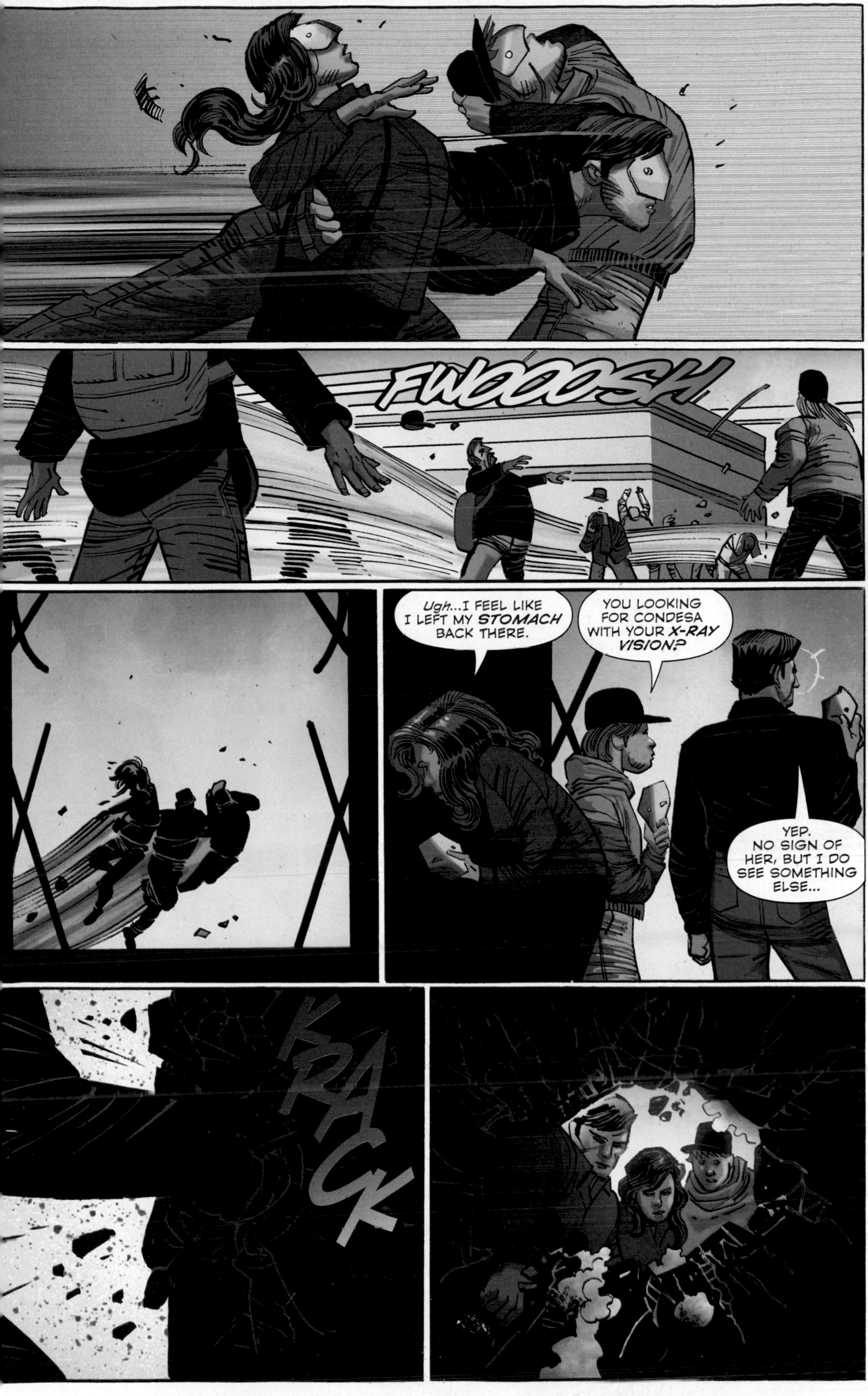
FWOOOSH
Ugh...I FEEL LIKE I LEFT MY STOMACH BACK THERE.
YOU LOOKING FOR CONDESA WITH YOUR X-RAY VISION?
YEP. NO SIGN OF HER, BUT I DO SEE SOMETHING ELSE...
KRACK

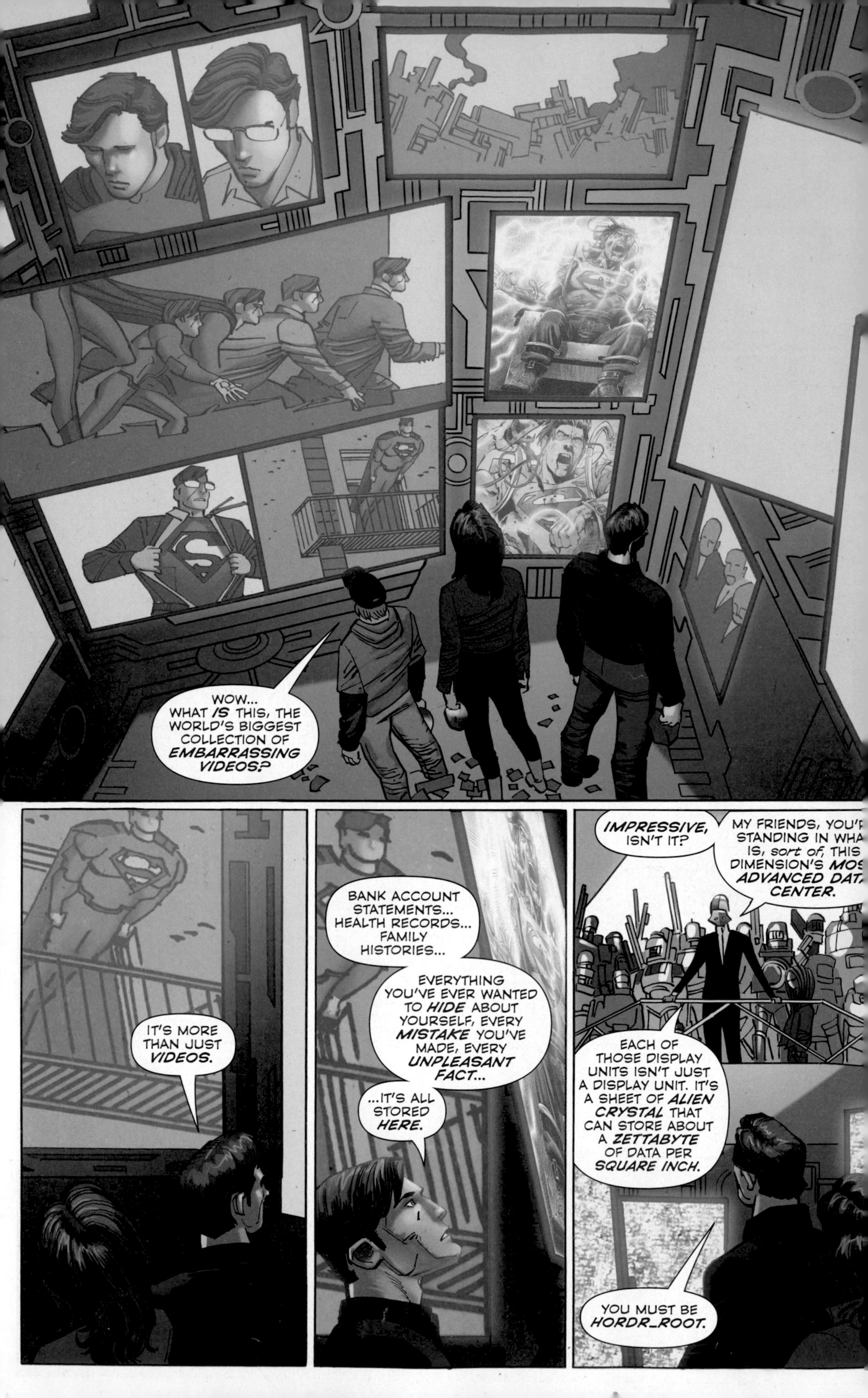
WOW... WHAT *IS* THIS, THE WORLD'S BIGGEST COLLECTION OF ***EMBARRASSING VIDEOS?***
IT'S MORE THAN JUST ***VIDEOS.***
BANK ACCOUNT STATEMENTS... HEALTH RECORDS... FAMILY HISTORIES...
EVERYTHING YOU'VE EVER WANTED TO ***HIDE*** ABOUT YOURSELF, EVERY ***MISTAKE*** YOU'VE MADE, EVERY ***UNPLEASANT FACT...***
...IT'S ALL STORED ***HERE.***
IMPRESSIVE, ISN'T IT?
MY FRIENDS, YOU'R STANDING IN WHA IS, *sort of,* THIS DIMENSION'S ***MOS ADVANCED DATA CENTER.***
EACH OF THOSE DISPLAY UNITS ISN'T JUST A DISPLAY UNIT. IT'S A SHEET OF ***ALIEN CRYSTAL*** THAT CAN STORE ABOUT A ***ZETTABYTE*** OF DATA PER ***SQUARE INCH.***
YOU MUST BE ***HORDR_ROOT.***

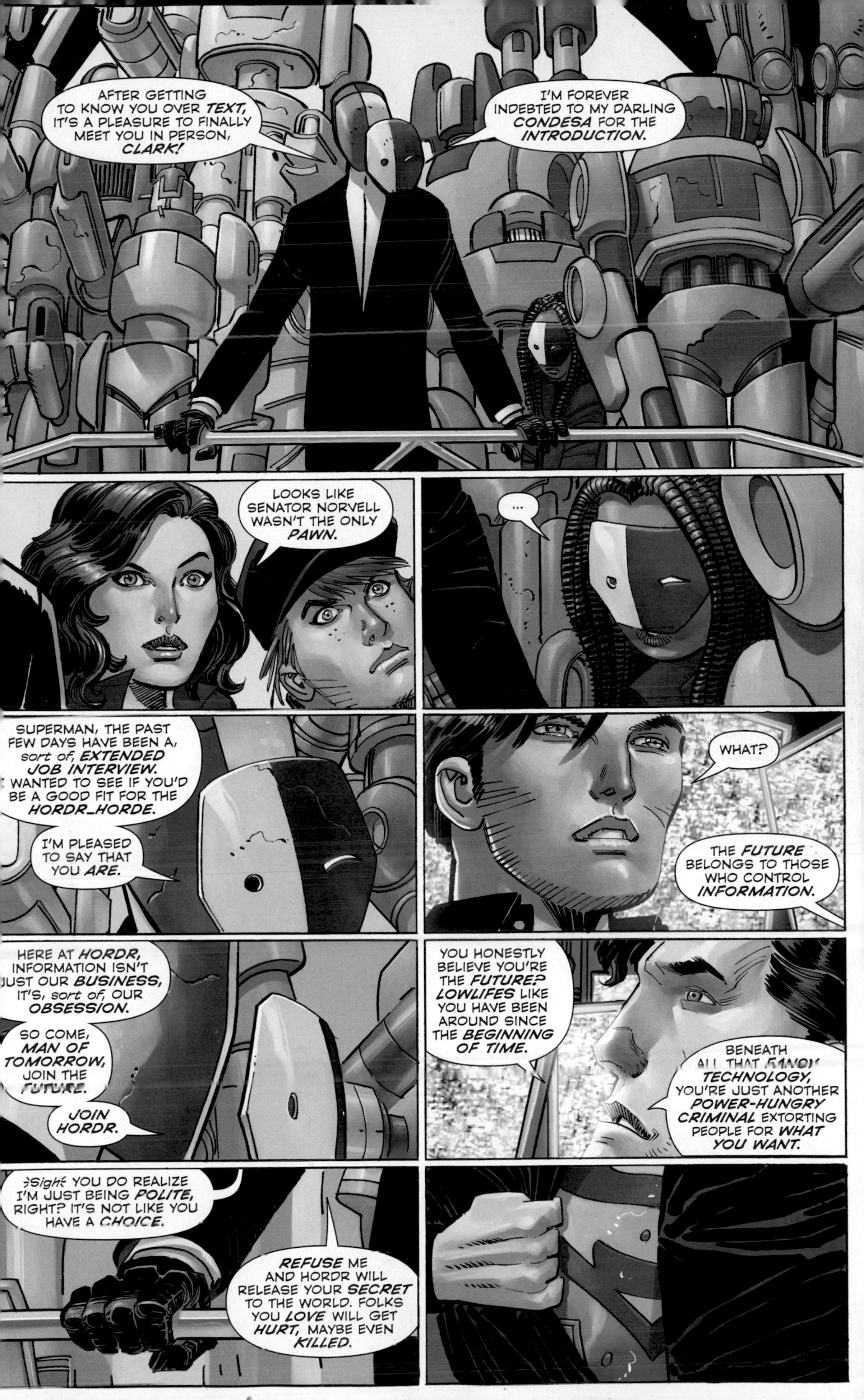
AFTER GETTING TO KNOW YOU OVER TEXT, IT'S A PLEASURE TO FINALLY MEET YOU IN PERSON, CLARK!
I'M FOREVER INDEBTED TO MY DARLING CONDESA FOR THE INTRODUCTION.
LOOKS LIKE SENATOR NORVELL WASN'T THE ONLY PAWN.
...
SUPERMAN, THE PAST FEW DAYS HAVE BEEN A, sort of, EXTENDED JOB INTERVIEW. WANTED TO SEE IF YOU'D BE A GOOD FIT FOR THE HORDR_HORDE.
I'M PLEASED TO SAY THAT YOU ARE.
WHAT?
THE FUTURE BELONGS TO THOSE WHO CONTROL INFORMATION.
HERE AT HORDR, INFORMATION ISN'T JUST OUR BUSINESS, IT'S, sort of, OUR OBSESSION.
SO COME, MAN OF TOMORROW, JOIN THE FUTURE.
JOIN HORDR.
YOU HONESTLY BELIEVE YOU'RE THE FUTURE? LOWLIFES LIKE YOU HAVE BEEN AROUND SINCE THE BEGINNING OF TIME.
BENEATH ALL THAT TECHNOLOGY, YOU'RE JUST ANOTHER POWER-HUNGRY CRIMINAL EXTORTING PEOPLE FOR WHAT YOU WANT.
Sigh YOU DO REALIZE I'M JUST BEING POLITE, RIGHT? IT'S NOT LIKE YOU HAVE A CHOICE.
REFUSE ME AND HORDR WILL RELEASE YOUR SECRET TO THE WORLD. FOLKS YOU LOVE WILL GET HURT, MAYBE EVEN KILLED.

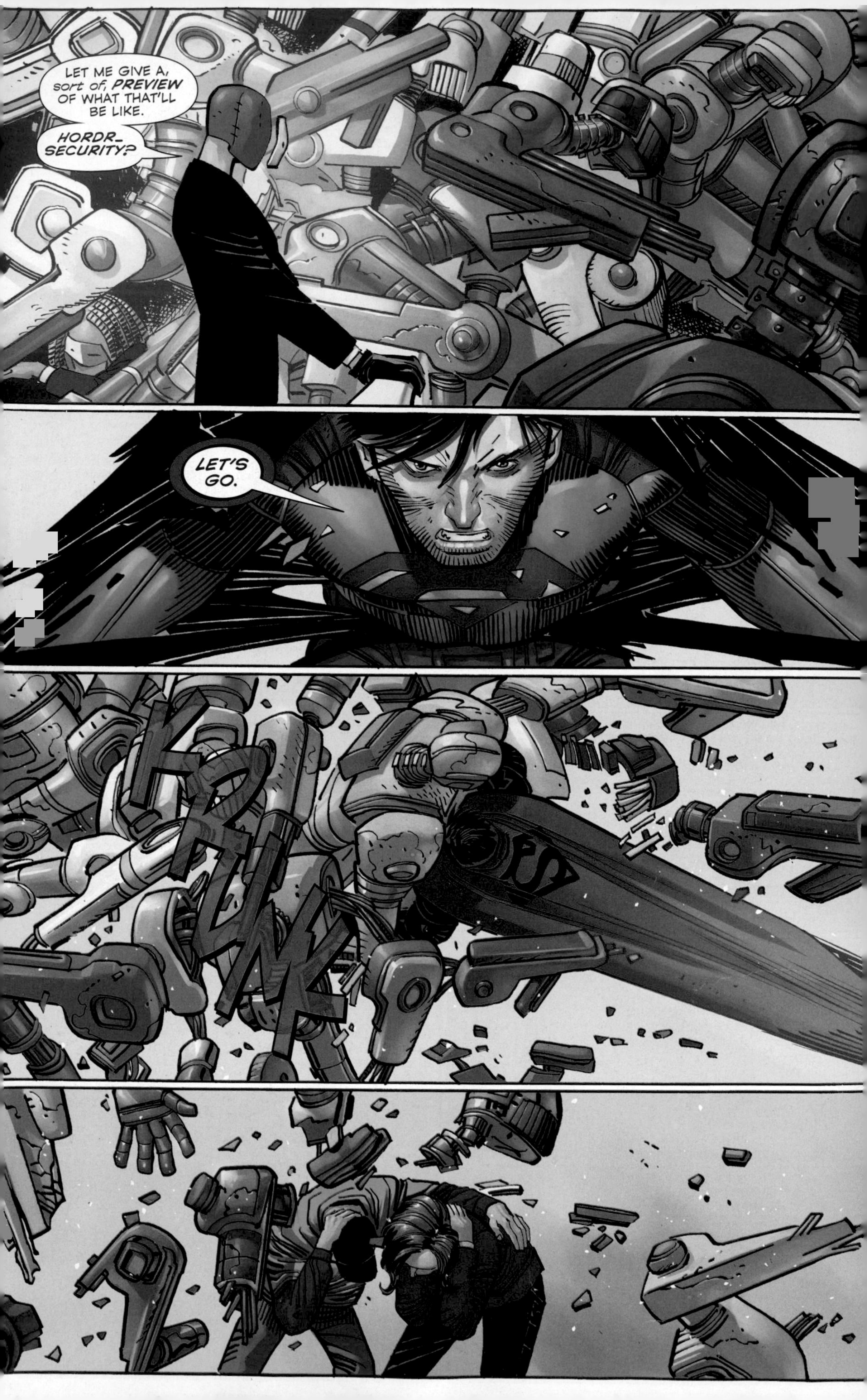
LET ME GIVE A, sort of, PREVIEW OF WHAT THAT'LL BE LIKE.
HORDR_ SECURITY?
LET'S GO.
KRUNK

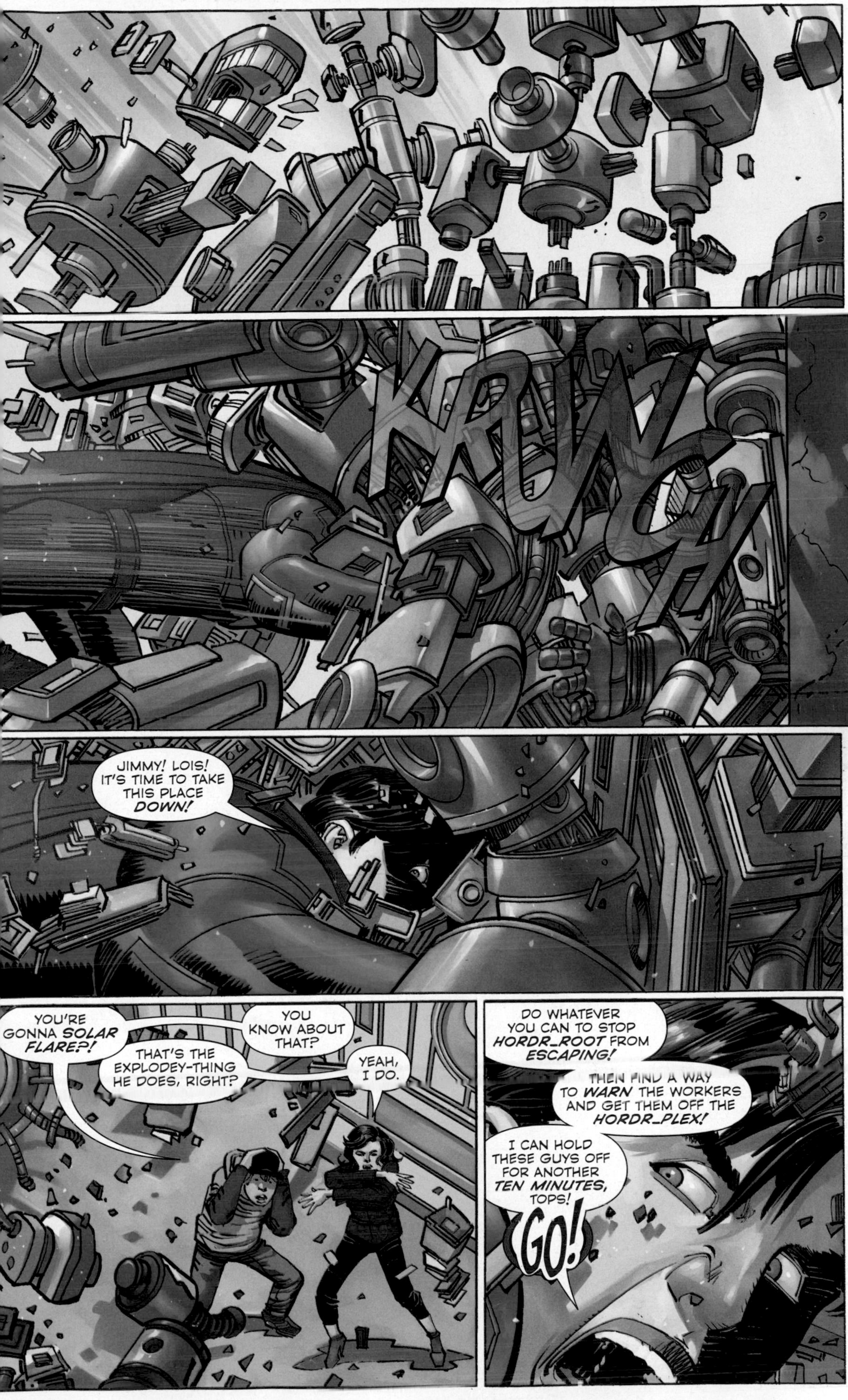
KRUNCH
JIMMY! LOIS! IT'S TIME TO TAKE THIS PLACE DOWN!
YOU'RE GONNA SOLAR FLARE?!
YOU KNOW ABOUT THAT?
THAT'S THE EXPLODEY-THING HE DOES, RIGHT?
YEAH, I DO.
DO WHATEVER YOU CAN TO STOP HORDR_ROOT FROM ESCAPING!
THEN FIND A WAY TO WARN THE WORKERS AND GET THEM OFF THE HORDR_PLEX!
I CAN HOLD THESE GUYS OFF FOR ANOTHER TEN MINUTES, TOPS!
GO!

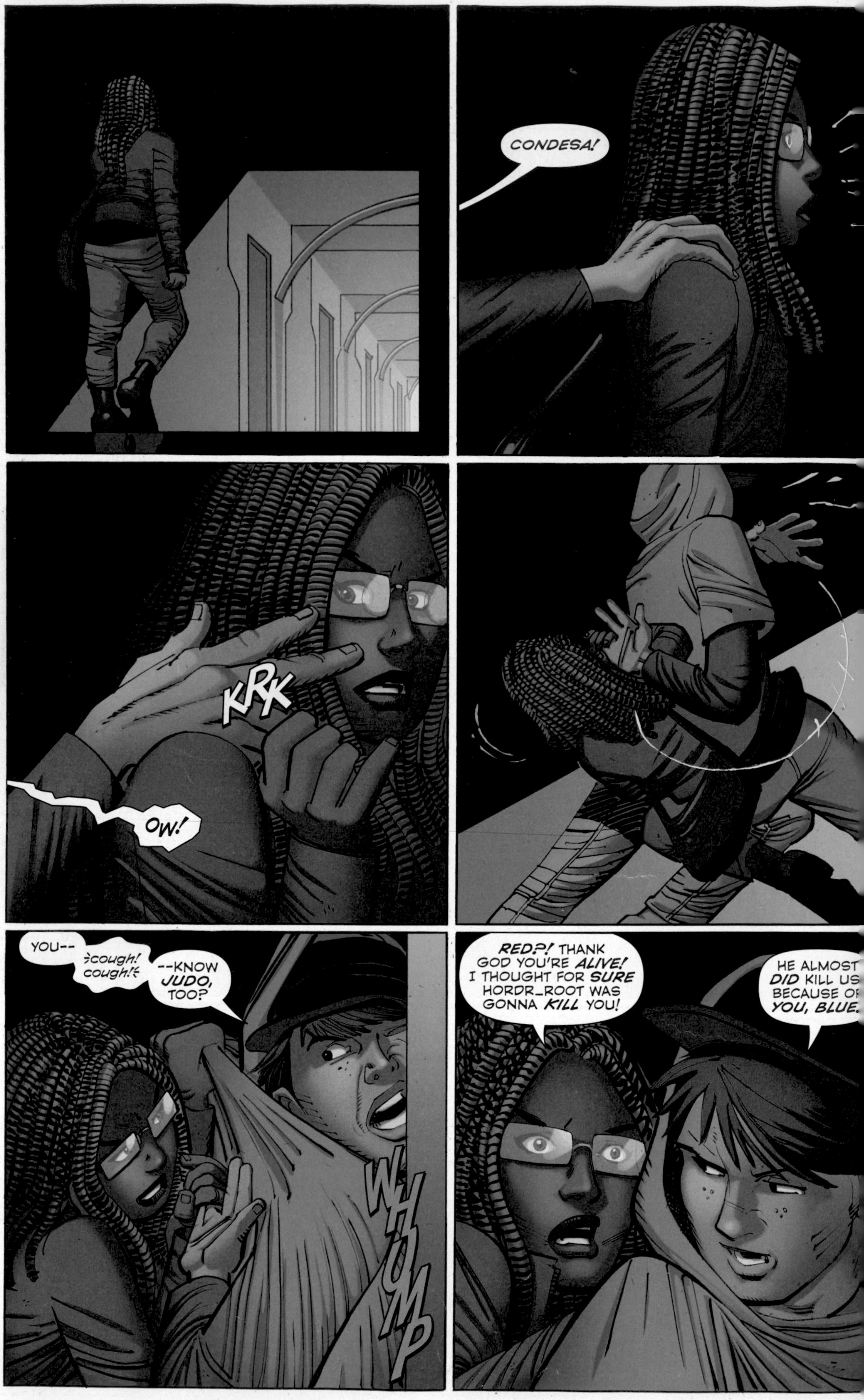
CONDESA!
KRK
OW!
YOU--
cough! cough!
--KNOW JUDO, TOO?
WHUMP
RED?! THANK GOD YOU'RE ALIVE! I THOUGHT FOR SURE HORDR_ROOT WAS GONNA KILL YOU!
HE ALMOST DID KILL US BECAUSE OF YOU, BLUE.

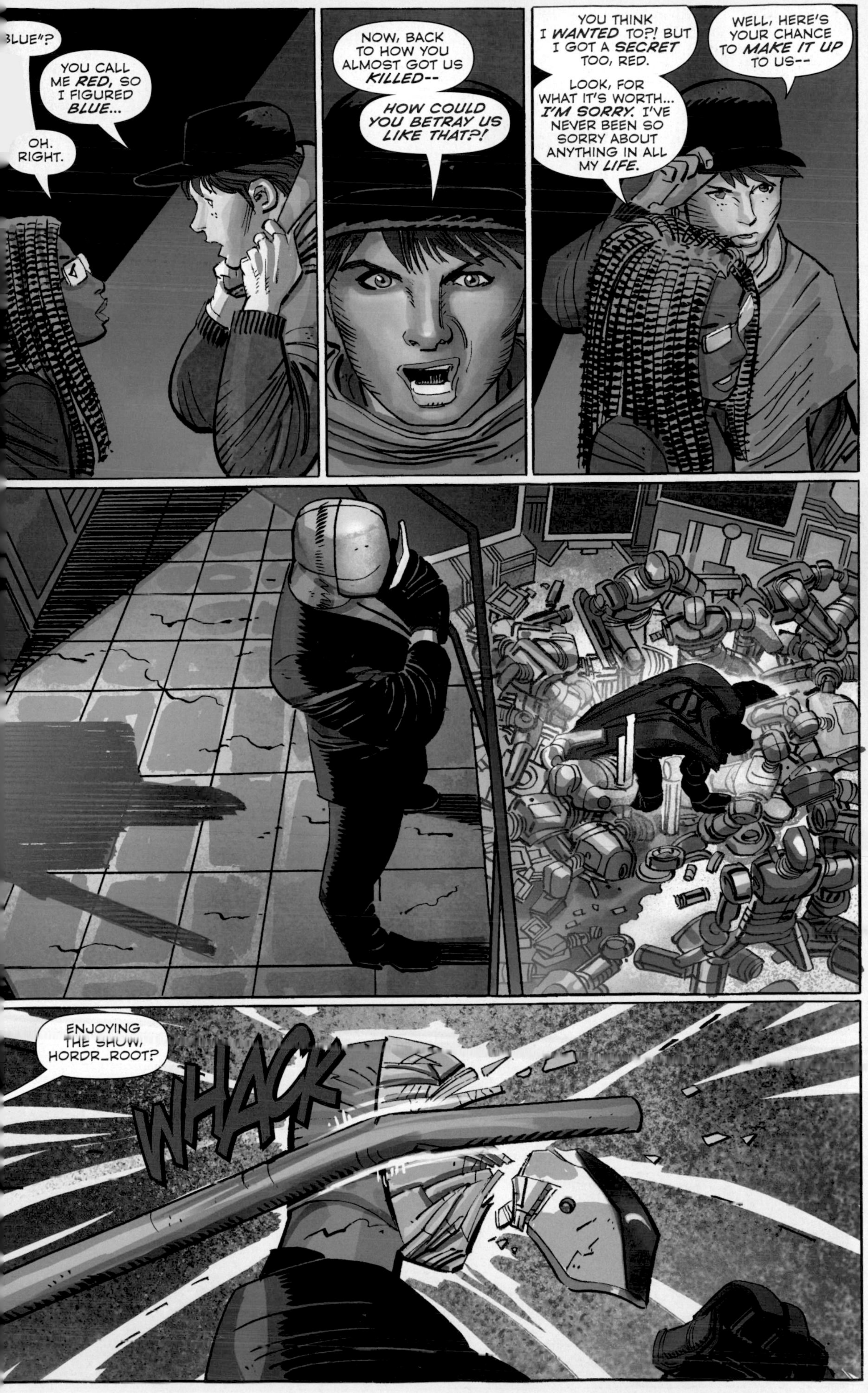
"BLUE"?
YOU CALL ME RED, SO I FIGURED BLUE...
OH. RIGHT.
NOW, BACK TO HOW YOU ALMOST GOT US KILLED--
HOW COULD YOU BETRAY US LIKE THAT?!
YOU THINK I WANTED TO?! BUT I GOT A SECRET TOO, RED.
LOOK, FOR WHAT IT'S WORTH... I'M SORRY. I'VE NEVER BEEN SO SORRY ABOUT ANYTHING IN ALL MY LIFE.
WELL, HERE'S YOUR CHANCE TO MAKE IT UP TO US--
ENJOYING THE SHOW, HORDR_ROOT?
WHACK

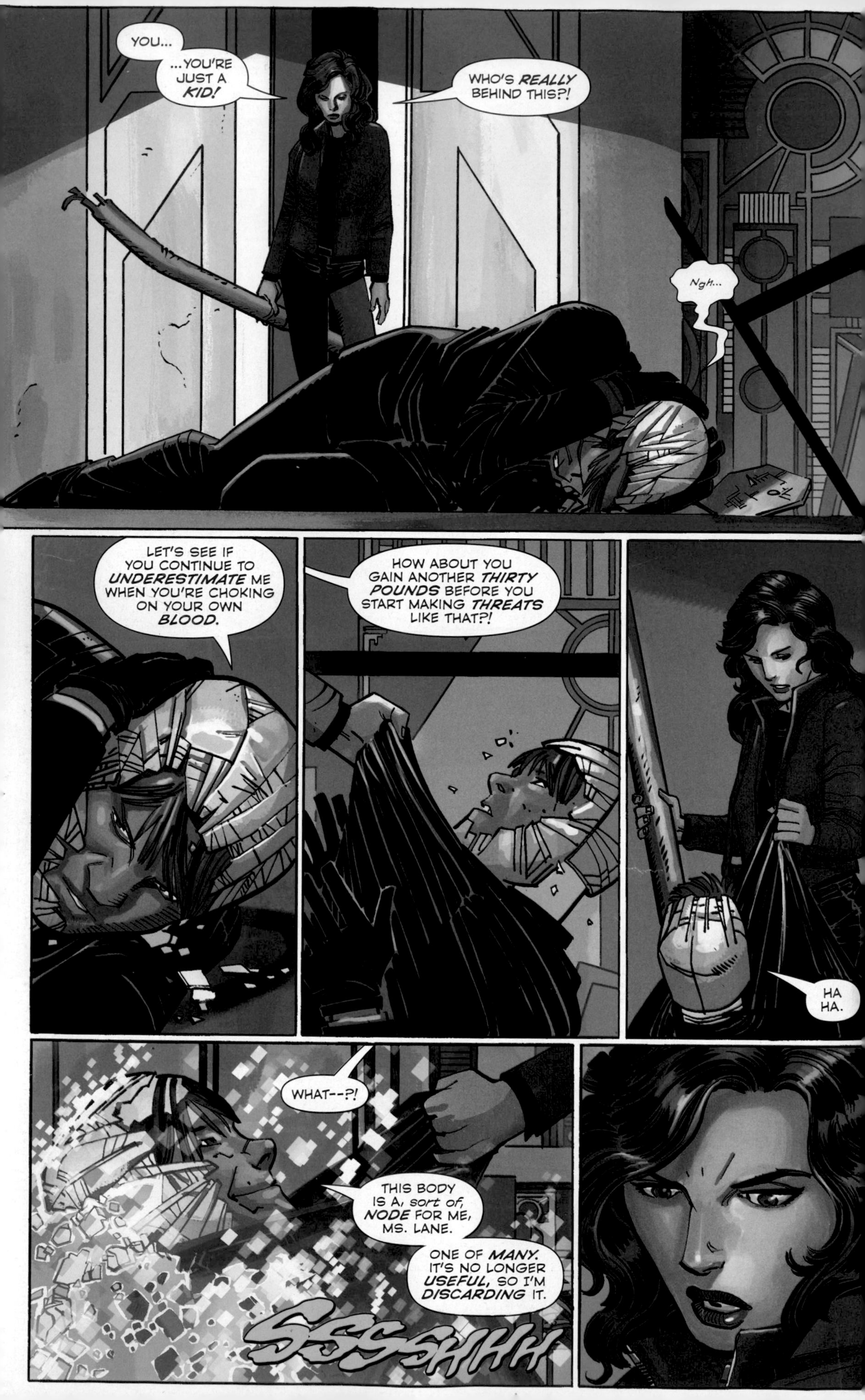
YOU... ...YOU'RE JUST A KID!
WHO'S REALLY BEHIND THIS?!
Ngh...
LET'S SEE IF YOU CONTINUE TO UNDERESTIMATE ME WHEN YOU'RE CHOKING ON YOUR OWN BLOOD.
HOW ABOUT YOU GAIN ANOTHER THIRTY POUNDS BEFORE YOU START MAKING THREATS LIKE THAT?!
HA HA.
WHAT--?!
THIS BODY IS A, sort of, NODE FOR ME, MS. LANE.
ONE OF MANY. IT'S NO LONGER USEFUL, SO I'M DISCARDING IT.
SSSSHHH

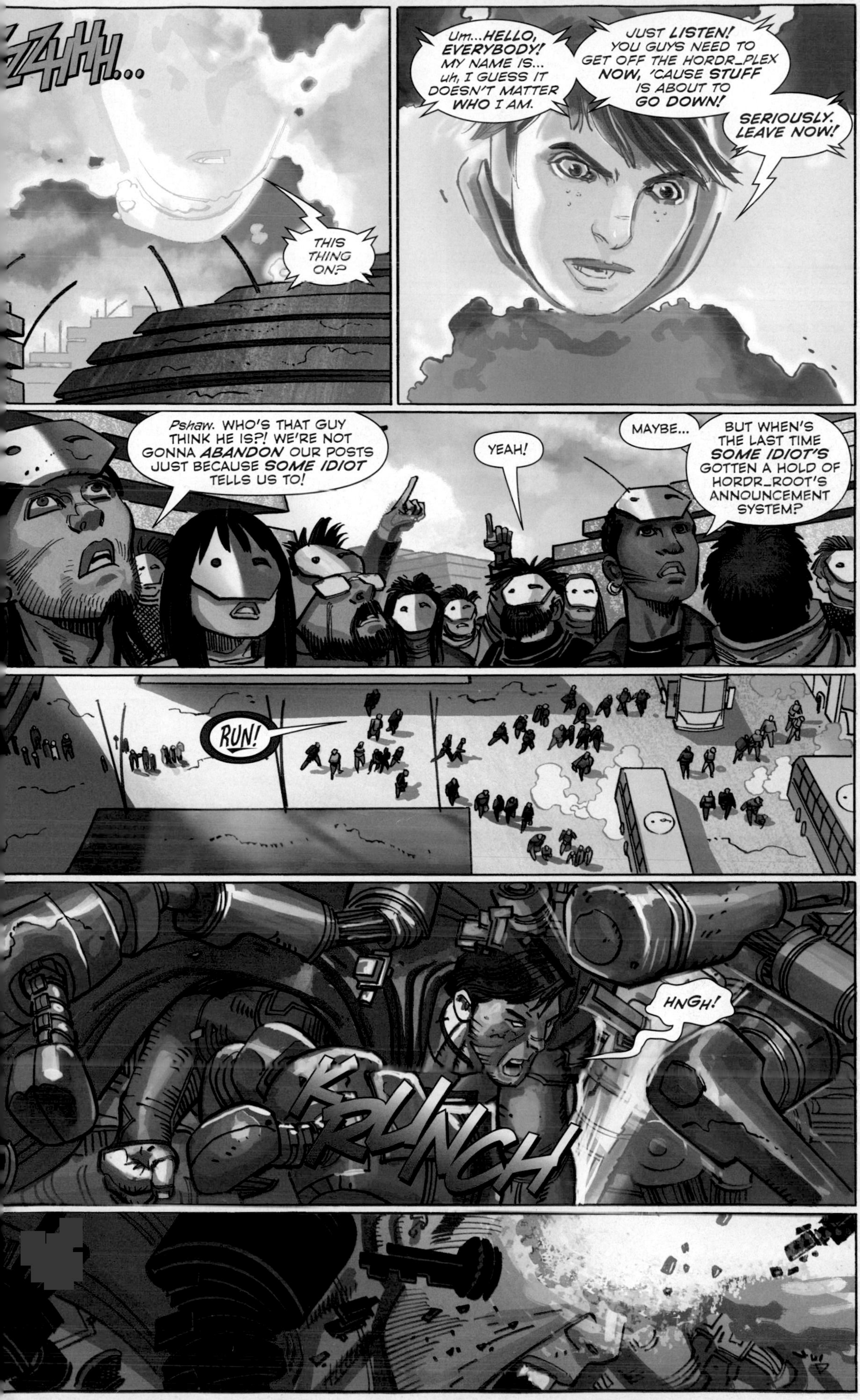
ZZHHH...
THIS THING ON?
Um...HELLO, EVERYBODY! MY NAME IS... uh, I GUESS IT DOESN'T MATTER WHO I AM.
JUST LISTEN! YOU GUYS NEED TO GET OFF THE HORDR_PLEX NOW, 'CAUSE STUFF IS ABOUT TO GO DOWN!
SERIOUSLY. LEAVE NOW!
Pshaw. WHO'S THAT GUY THINK HE IS?! WE'RE NOT GONNA ABANDON OUR POSTS JUST BECAUSE SOME IDIOT TELLS US TO!
YEAH!
MAYBE...
BUT WHEN'S THE LAST TIME SOME IDIOT'S GOTTEN A HOLD OF HORDR_ROOT'S ANNOUNCEMENT SYSTEM?
RUN!
HNGH!
KRUNCH

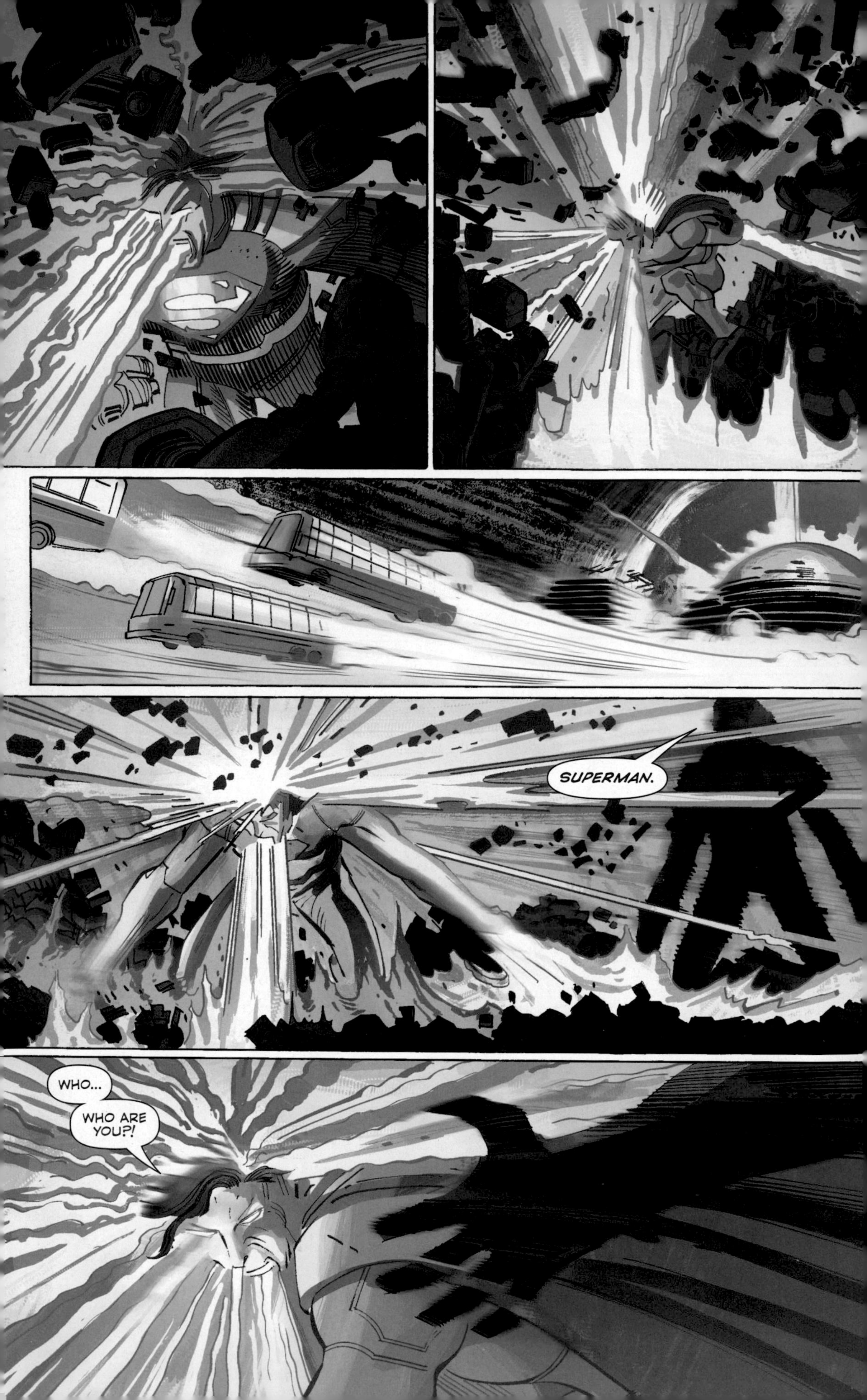
SUPERMAN.
WHO...
WHO ARE YOU?!

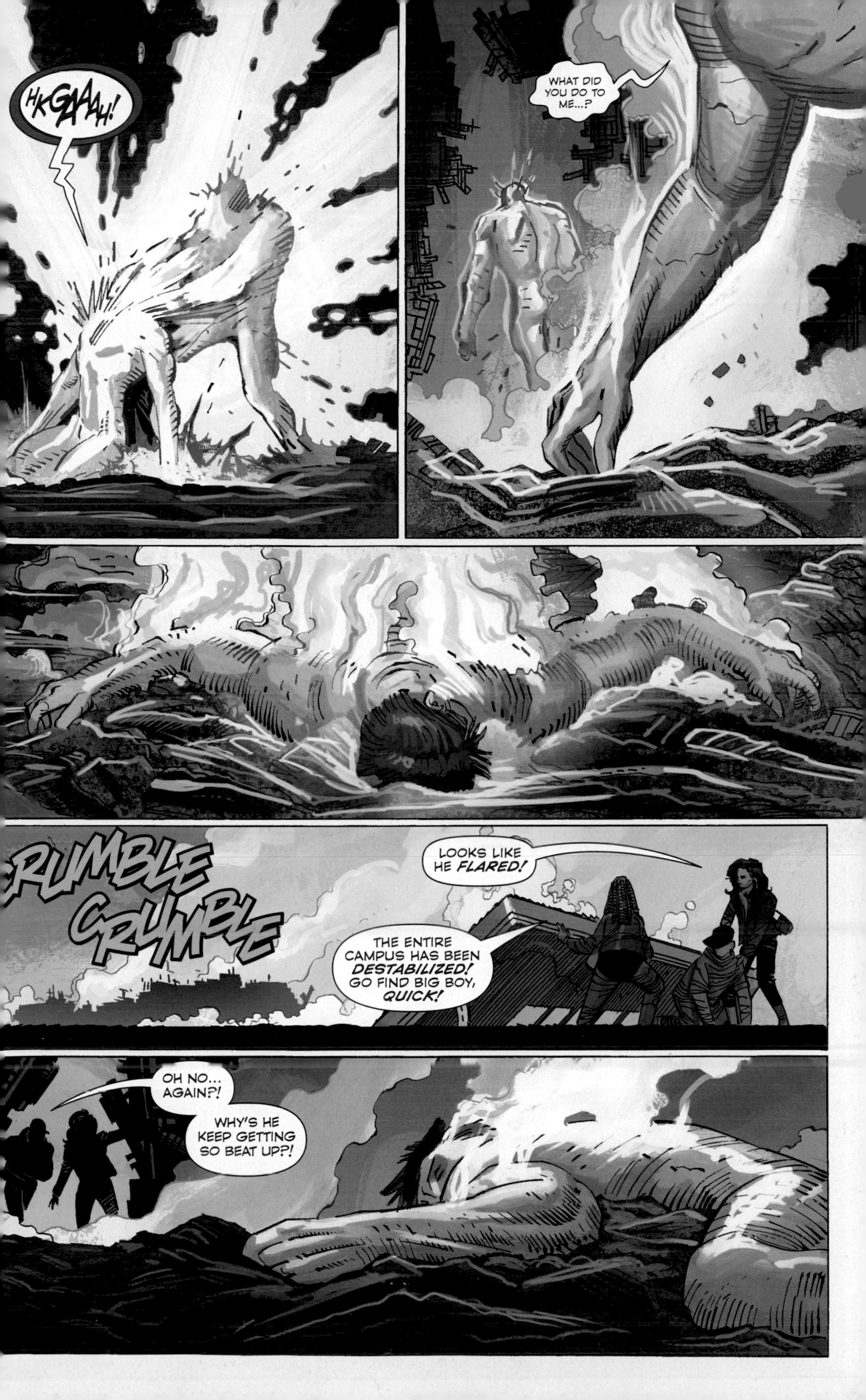
HKGAAAAH!
WHAT DID YOU DO TO ME...?
RUMBLE CRUMBLE
LOOKS LIKE HE FLARED!
THE ENTIRE CAMPUS HAS BEEN DESTABILIZED! GO FIND BIG BOY, QUICK!
OH NO... AGAIN?!
WHY'S HE KEEP GETTING SO BEAT UP?!

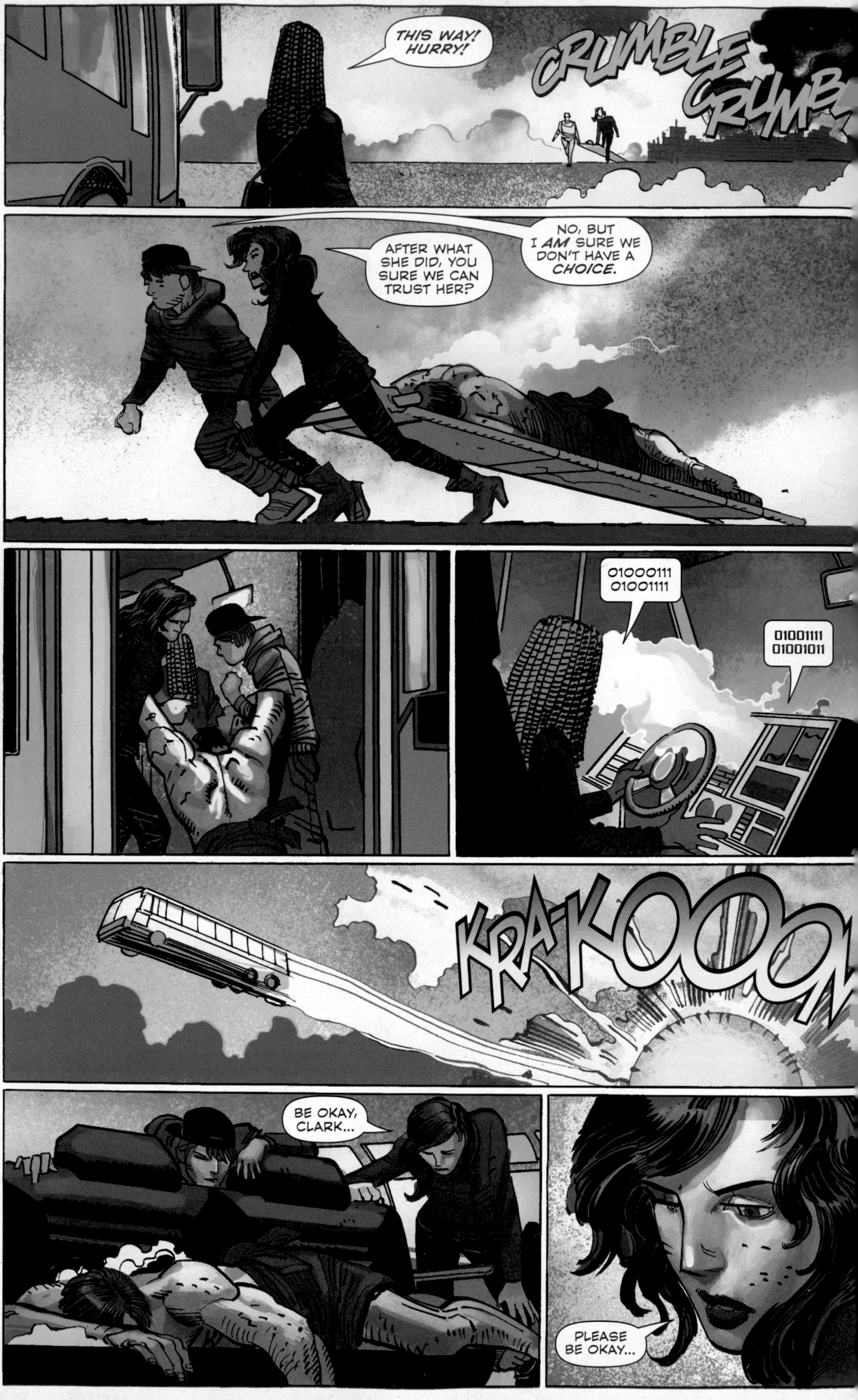
THIS WAY! HURRY!
CRUMBLE CRUMB
AFTER WHAT SHE DID, YOU SURE WE CAN TRUST HER?
NO, BUT I AM SURE WE DON'T HAVE A CHOICE.
01000111 01001111
01001111 01001011
KRA-KOOOO
BE OKAY, CLARK...
PLEASE BE OKAY...

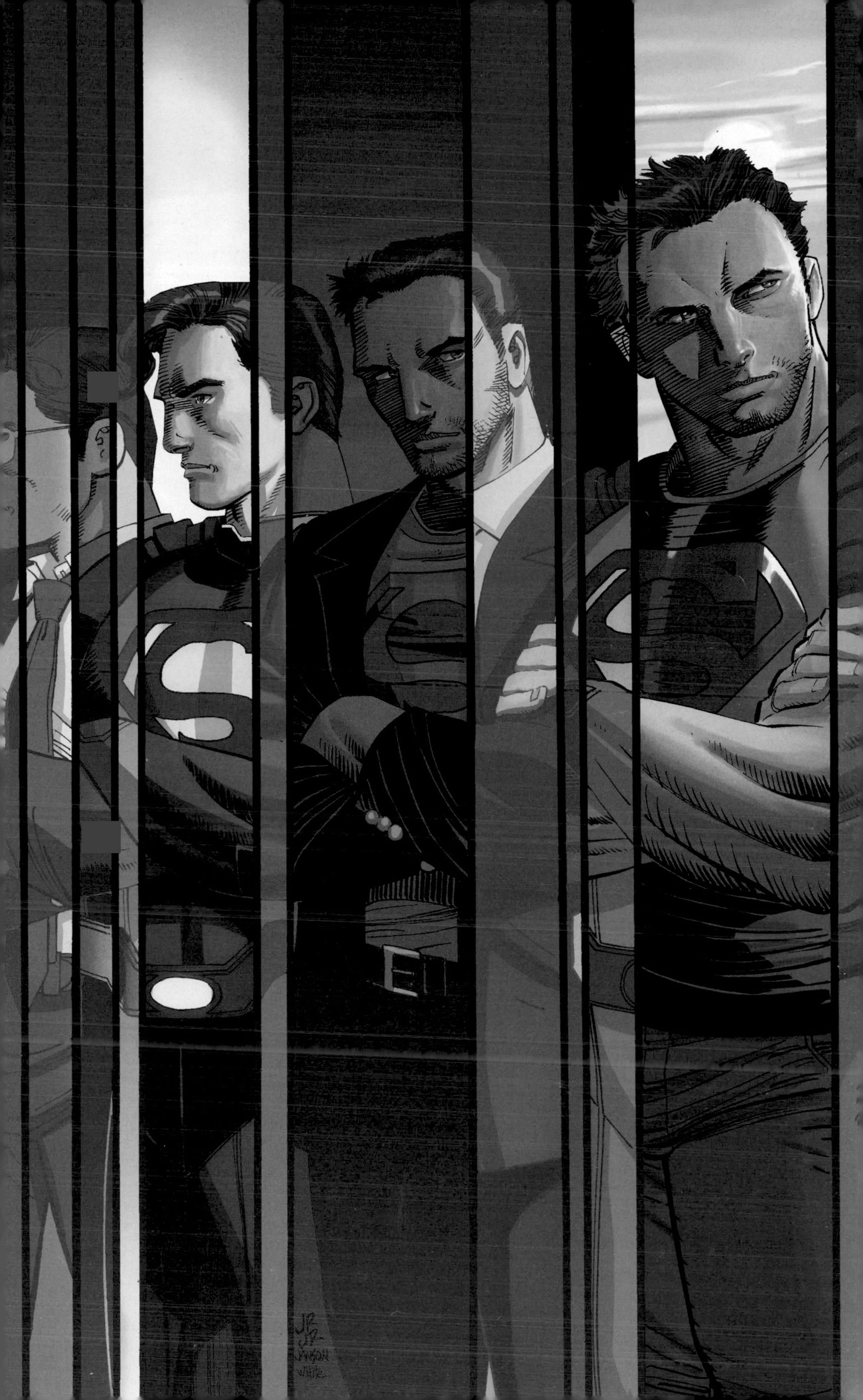

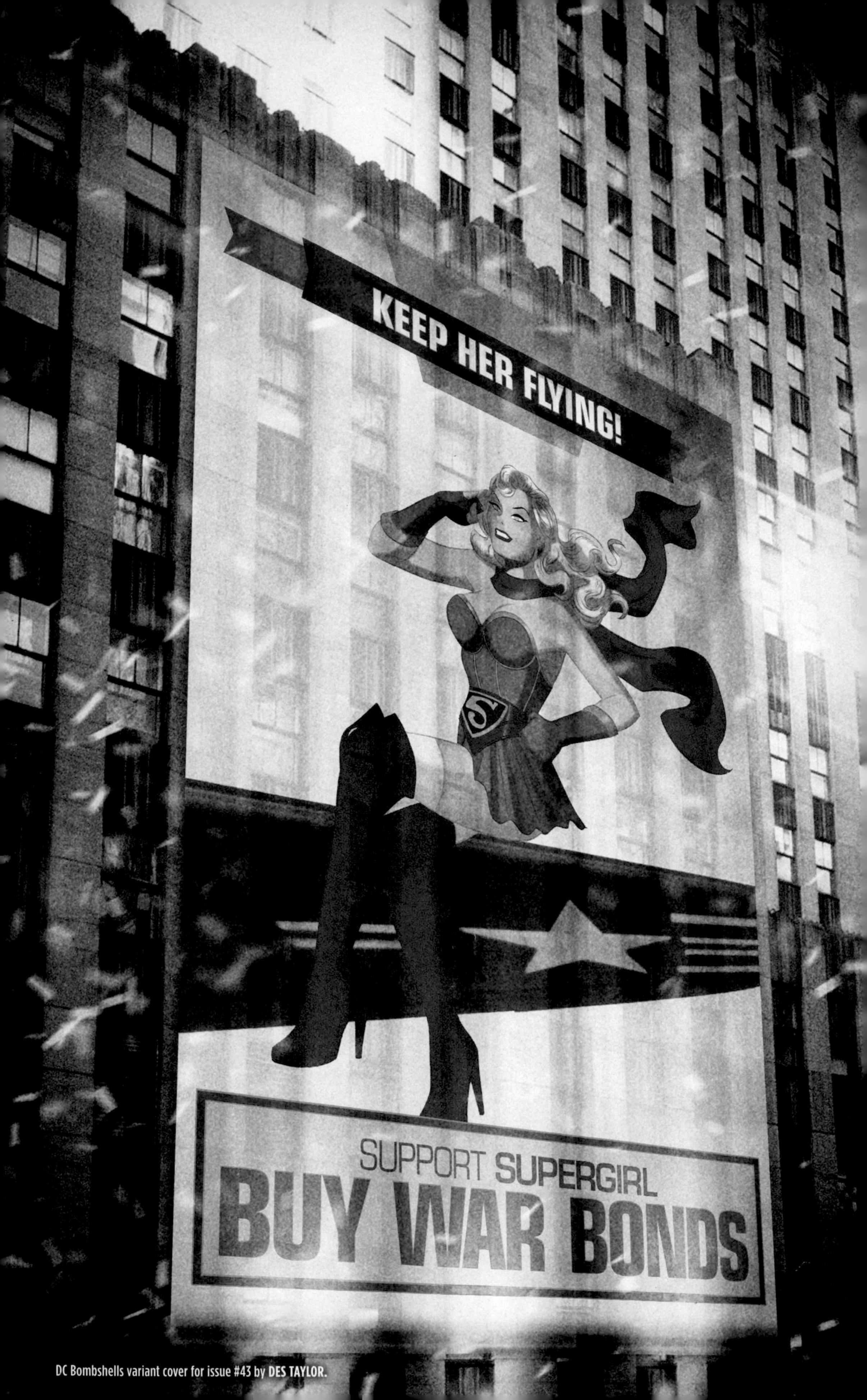
KEEP HER FLYING!
S
SUPPORT SUPERGIRL
BUY WAR BONDS

DC Bombshells variant cover for issue #43 by **DES TAYLOR.**

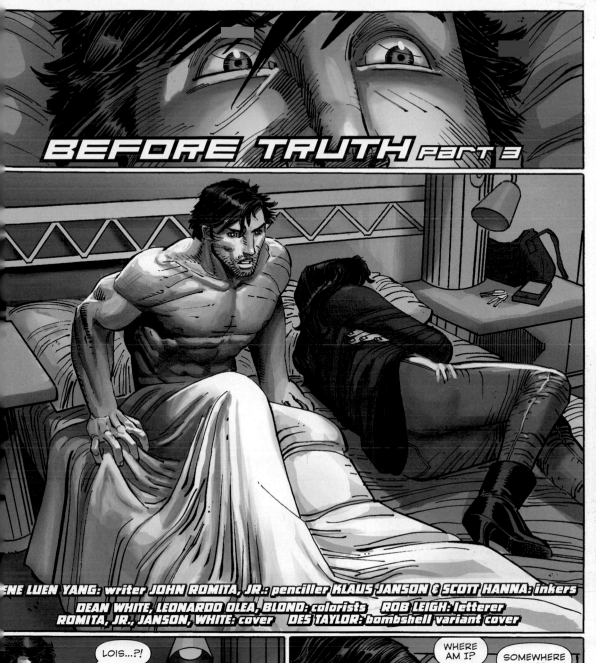

BEFORE TRUTH part 3

ENE LUEN YANG: writer JOHN ROMITA, JR.: penciller KLAUS JANSON & SCOTT HANNA: inkers

DEAN WHITE, LEONARDO OLEA, BLOND: colorists ROB LEIGH: letterer
ROMITA, JR., JANSON, WHITE: cover DES TAYLOR: bombshell variant cover

LOIS...?!

CLARK!

ANDREW MARINO: assistant editor

WHERE AM I?

SOMEWHERE SAFE.

EDDIE BERGANZA: group editor

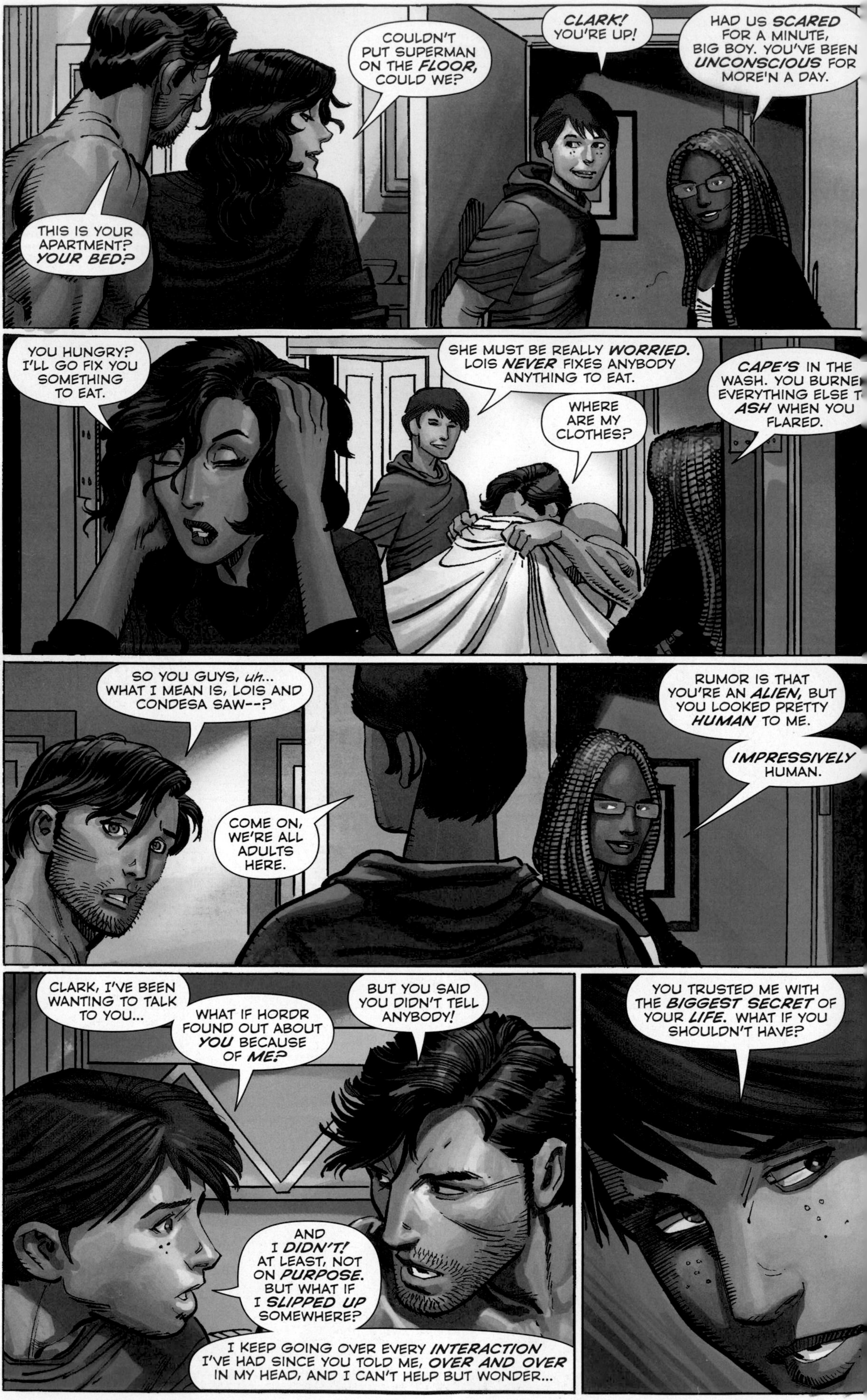
THIS IS YOUR APARTMENT? YOUR BED?
COULDN'T PUT SUPERMAN ON THE FLOOR, COULD WE?
CLARK! YOU'RE UP!
HAD US SCARED FOR A MINUTE, BIG BOY. YOU'VE BEEN UNCONSCIOUS FOR MORE'N A DAY.
YOU HUNGRY? I'LL GO FIX YOU SOMETHING TO EAT.
SHE MUST BE REALLY WORRIED. LOIS NEVER FIXES ANYBODY ANYTHING TO EAT.
WHERE ARE MY CLOTHES?
CAPE'S IN THE WASH. YOU BURNE EVERYTHING ELSE T ASH WHEN YOU FLARED.
SO YOU GUYS, uh... WHAT I MEAN IS, LOIS AND CONDESA SAW--?
COME ON, WE'RE ALL ADULTS HERE.
RUMOR IS THAT YOU'RE AN ALIEN, BUT YOU LOOKED PRETTY HUMAN TO ME.
IMPRESSIVELY HUMAN.
CLARK, I'VE BEEN WANTING TO TALK TO YOU...
WHAT IF HORDR FOUND OUT ABOUT YOU BECAUSE OF ME?
BUT YOU SAID YOU DIDN'T TELL ANYBODY!
AND I DIDN'T! AT LEAST, NOT ON PURPOSE. BUT WHAT IF I SLIPPED UP SOMEWHERE?
I KEEP GOING OVER EVERY INTERACTION I'VE HAD SINCE YOU TOLD ME, OVER AND OVER IN MY HEAD, AND I CAN'T HELP BUT WONDER...
YOU TRUSTED ME WITH THE BIGGEST SECRET OF YOUR LIFE. WHAT IF YOU SHOULDN'T HAVE?

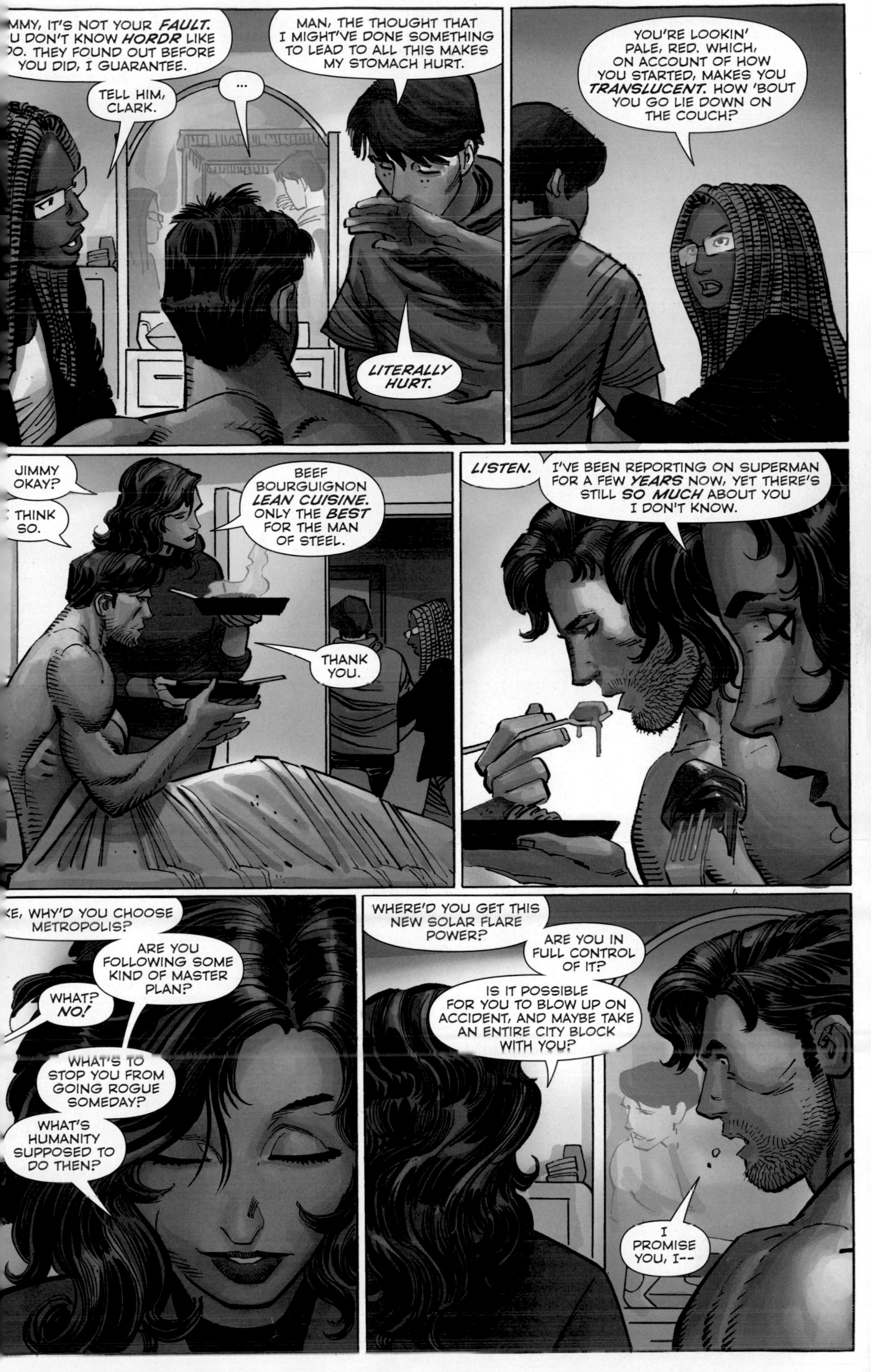
MMY, IT'S NOT YOUR FAULT. U DON'T KNOW HORDR LIKE O. THEY FOUND OUT BEFORE YOU DID, I GUARANTEE.
TELL HIM, CLARK.
...
MAN, THE THOUGHT THAT I MIGHT'VE DONE SOMETHING TO LEAD TO ALL THIS MAKES MY STOMACH HURT.
LITERALLY HURT.
YOU'RE LOOKIN' PALE, RED. WHICH, ON ACCOUNT OF HOW YOU STARTED, MAKES YOU TRANSLUCENT. HOW 'BOUT YOU GO LIE DOWN ON THE COUCH?
JIMMY OKAY?
THINK SO.
BEEF BOURGUIGNON LEAN CUISINE. ONLY THE BEST FOR THE MAN OF STEEL.
THANK YOU.
LISTEN.
I'VE BEEN REPORTING ON SUPERMAN FOR A FEW YEARS NOW, YET THERE'S STILL SO MUCH ABOUT YOU I DON'T KNOW.
E, WHY'D YOU CHOOSE METROPOLIS?
ARE YOU FOLLOWING SOME KIND OF MASTER PLAN?
WHAT? NO!
WHAT'S TO STOP YOU FROM GOING ROGUE SOMEDAY?
WHAT'S HUMANITY SUPPOSED TO DO THEN?
WHERE'D YOU GET THIS NEW SOLAR FLARE POWER?
ARE YOU IN FULL CONTROL OF IT?
IS IT POSSIBLE FOR YOU TO BLOW UP ON ACCIDENT, AND MAYBE TAKE AN ENTIRE CITY BLOCK WITH YOU?
I PROMISE YOU, I--

THESE ARE QUESTIONS THE *PUBLIC* NEEDS ANSWERED, DON'T YOU THINK?

QUESTIONS *I* NEED ANSWERED.

LOIS...

BUT THEN... BACK IN HORDR'S *DATA CENTER*, I SAW THIS *VIDEO* OF YOU-- *CAPE* YOU, NOT *GLASSES* YOU.

IT WAS FROM A FE YEARS AGO. YOU WERE STILL WEARIN THAT GOOFY *BRIG BLUE T-SHIRT.*

THEY HAD YOU STRAPPED TO AN *ELECTRIC CHAIR.*

I REMEMBER.

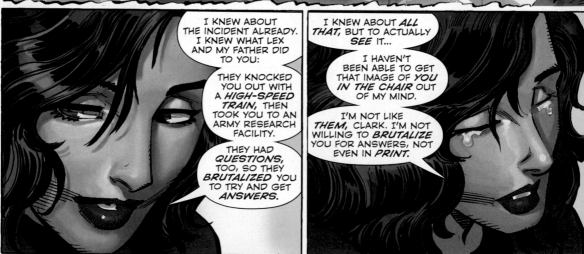

I KNEW ABOUT THE INCIDENT ALREADY. I KNEW WHAT LEX AND MY FATHER DID TO YOU:

THEY KNOCKED YOU OUT WITH A *HIGH-SPEED TRAIN,* THEN TOOK YOU TO AN ARMY RESEARCH FACILITY.

THEY HAD *QUESTIONS,* TOO, SO THEY *BRUTALIZED* YOU TO TRY AND GET *ANSWERS.*

I KNEW ABOUT *ALL THAT,* BUT TO ACTUALLY *SEE* IT...

I HAVEN'T BEEN ABLE TO GET THAT IMAGE OF *YOU IN THE CHAIR* OUT OF MY MIND.

I'M NOT LIKE *THEM,* CLARK. I'M NOT WILLING TO *BRUTALIZE* YOU FOR ANSWERS, NOT EVEN IN *PRINT.*

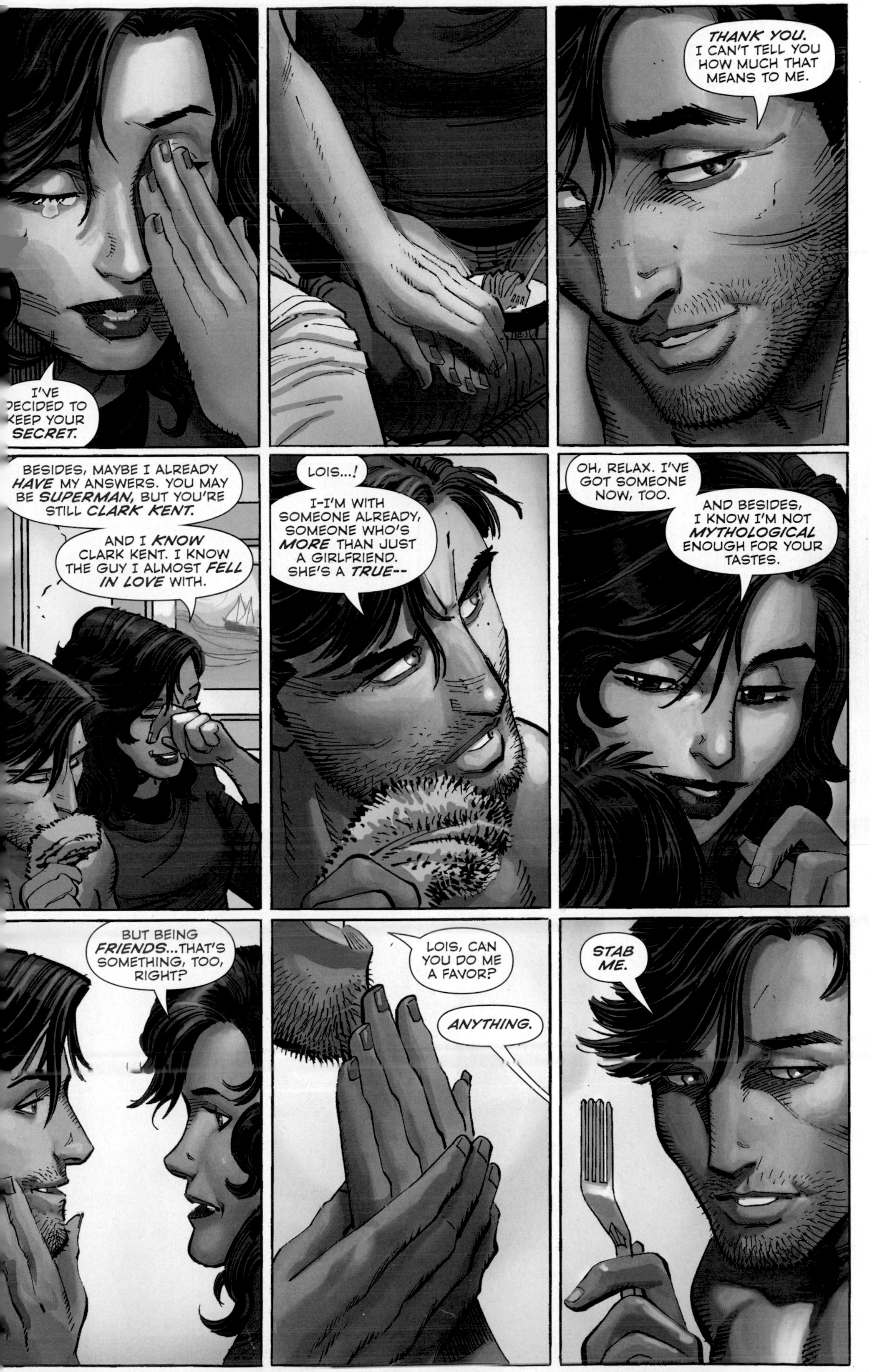
I'VE DECIDED TO KEEP YOUR SECRET.
THANK YOU. I CAN'T TELL YOU HOW MUCH THAT MEANS TO ME.
BESIDES, MAYBE I ALREADY HAVE MY ANSWERS. YOU MAY BE SUPERMAN, BUT YOU'RE STILL CLARK KENT.
AND I KNOW CLARK KENT. I KNOW THE GUY I ALMOST FELL IN LOVE WITH.
LOIS...!
I-I'M WITH SOMEONE ALREADY, SOMEONE WHO'S MORE THAN JUST A GIRLFRIEND. SHE'S A TRUE--
OH, RELAX. I'VE GOT SOMEONE NOW, TOO.
AND BESIDES, I KNOW I'M NOT MYTHOLOGICAL ENOUGH FOR YOUR TASTES.
BUT BEING FRIENDS...THAT'S SOMETHING, TOO, RIGHT?
LOIS, CAN YOU DO ME A FAVOR?
ANYTHING.
STAB ME.

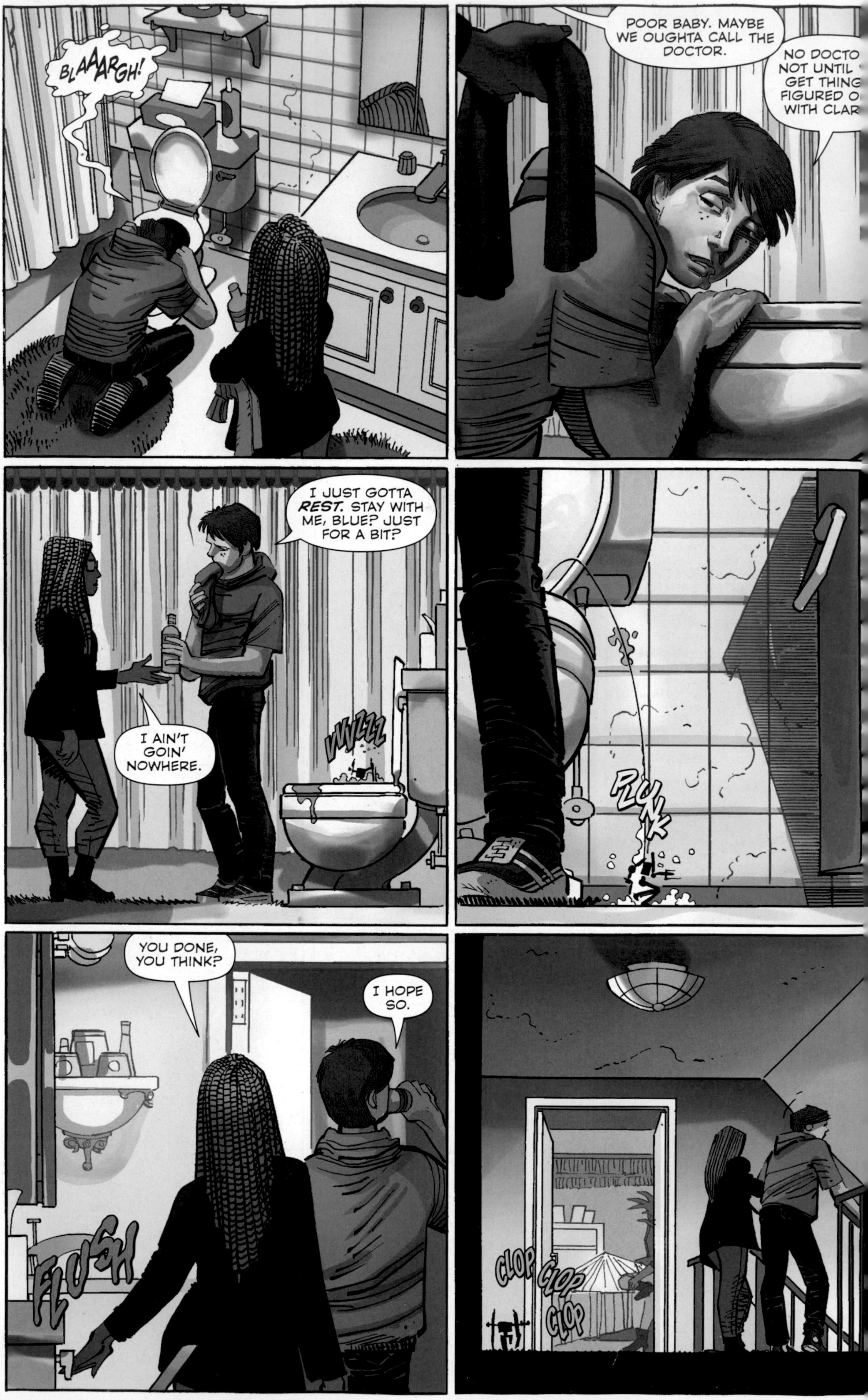
BLAAARGH!
POOR BABY. MAYBE WE OUGHTA CALL THE DOCTOR.
NO DOCTO NOT UNTIL GET THING FIGURED O WITH CLAR
I JUST GOTTA *REST.* STAY WITH ME, BLUE? JUST FOR A BIT?
I AIN'T GOIN' NOWHERE.
VVVZZZ
PLUNK
YOU DONE, YOU THINK?
I HOPE SO.
FLUSH
CLOP
CLOP
CLOP

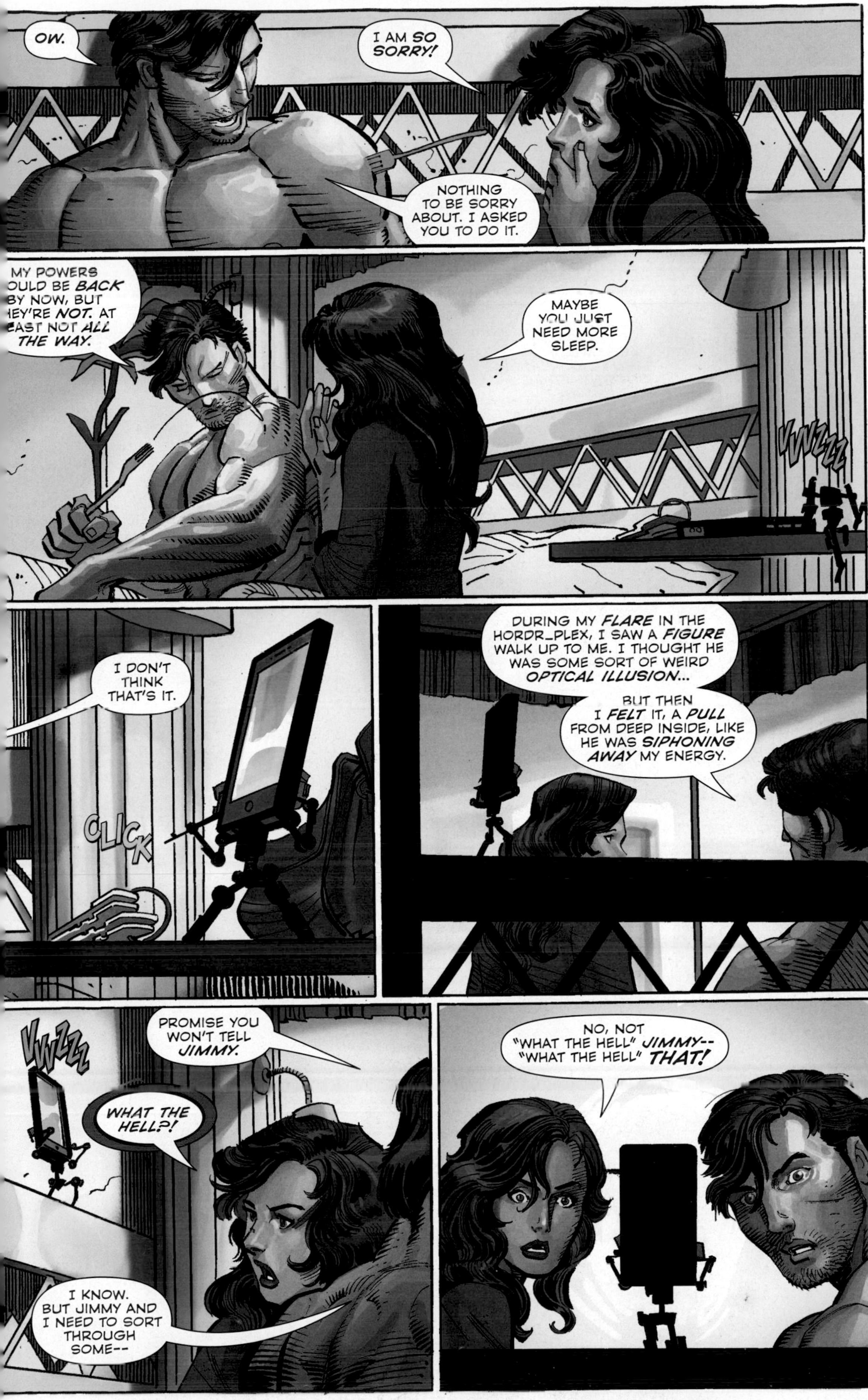
OW.
I AM SO SORRY!
NOTHING TO BE SORRY ABOUT. I ASKED YOU TO DO IT.
MY POWERS OULD BE BACK BY NOW, BUT HEY'RE NOT. AT EAST NOT ALL THE WAY.
MAYBE YOU JUST NEED MORE SLEEP.
VVVZZZ
I DON'T THINK THAT'S IT.
CLICK
DURING MY FLARE IN THE HORDR_PLEX, I SAW A FIGURE WALK UP TO ME. I THOUGHT HE WAS SOME SORT OF WEIRD OPTICAL ILLUSION...
BUT THEN I FELT IT, A PULL FROM DEEP INSIDE, LIKE HE WAS SIPHONING AWAY MY ENERGY.
VVVZZZ
PROMISE YOU WON'T TELL JIMMY.
I KNOW. BUT JIMMY AND I NEED TO SORT THROUGH SOME--
WHAT THE HELL?!
NO, NOT "WHAT THE HELL" JIMMY-- "WHAT THE HELL" THAT!

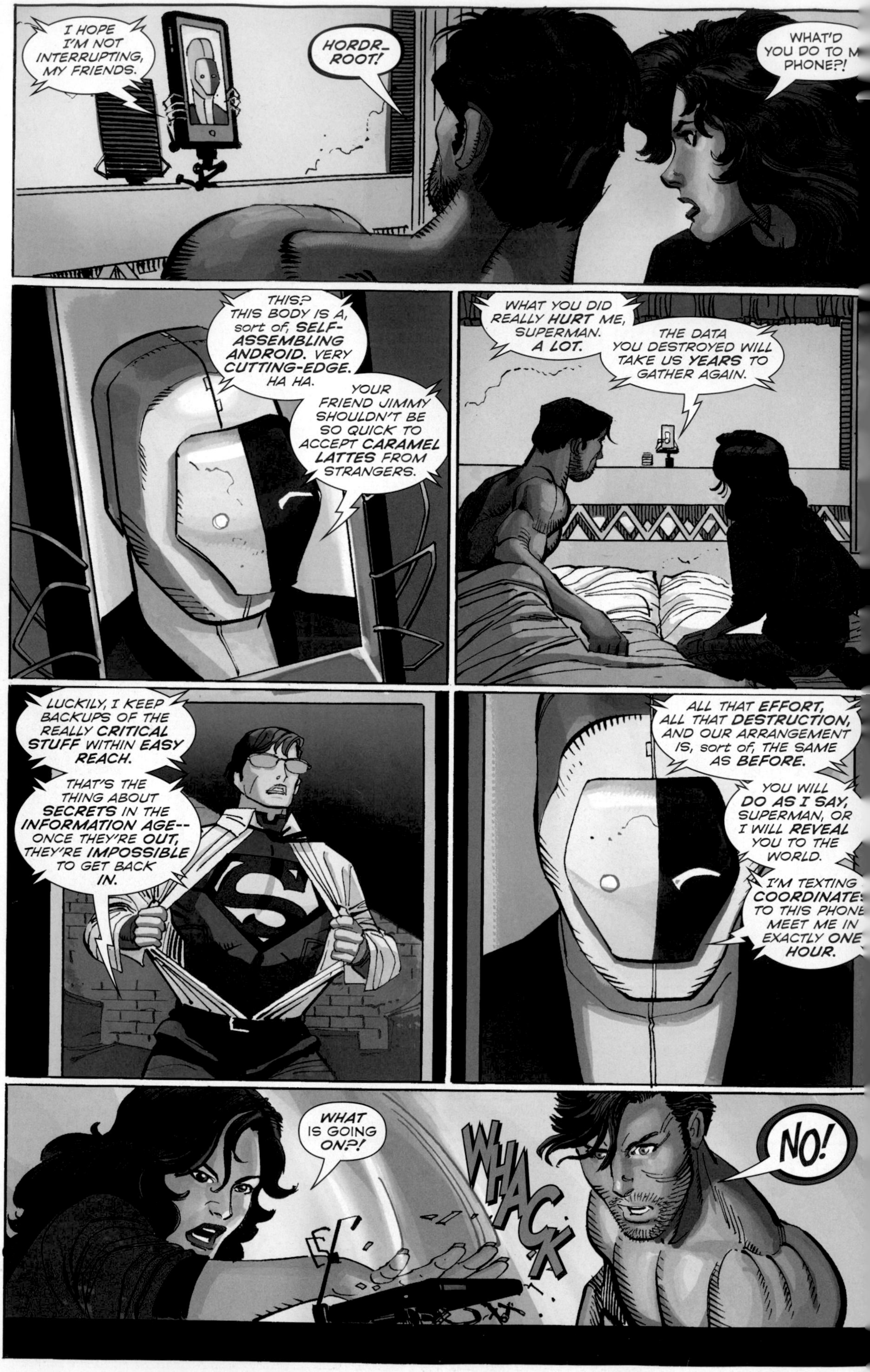
I HOPE I'M NOT INTERRUPTING, MY FRIENDS.
HORDR-ROOT!
WHAT'D YOU DO TO M PHONE?!
THIS? THIS BODY IS A, sort of, SELF-ASSEMBLING ANDROID. VERY CUTTING-EDGE. HA HA.
YOUR FRIEND JIMMY SHOULDN'T BE SO QUICK TO ACCEPT CARAMEL LATTES FROM STRANGERS.
WHAT YOU DID REALLY HURT ME, SUPERMAN. A LOT.
THE DATA YOU DESTROYED WILL TAKE US YEARS TO GATHER AGAIN.
LUCKILY, I KEEP BACKUPS OF THE REALLY CRITICAL STUFF WITHIN EASY REACH.
THAT'S THE THING ABOUT SECRETS IN THE INFORMATION AGE-- ONCE THEY'RE OUT, THEY'RE IMPOSSIBLE TO GET BACK IN.
ALL THAT EFFORT, ALL THAT DESTRUCTION, AND OUR ARRANGEMENT IS, sort of, THE SAME AS BEFORE.
YOU WILL DO AS I SAY, SUPERMAN, OR I WILL REVEAL YOU TO THE WORLD.
I'M TEXTING COORDINATES TO THIS PHONE MEET ME IN EXACTLY ONE HOUR.
WHAT IS GOING ON?!
WHACK
NO!

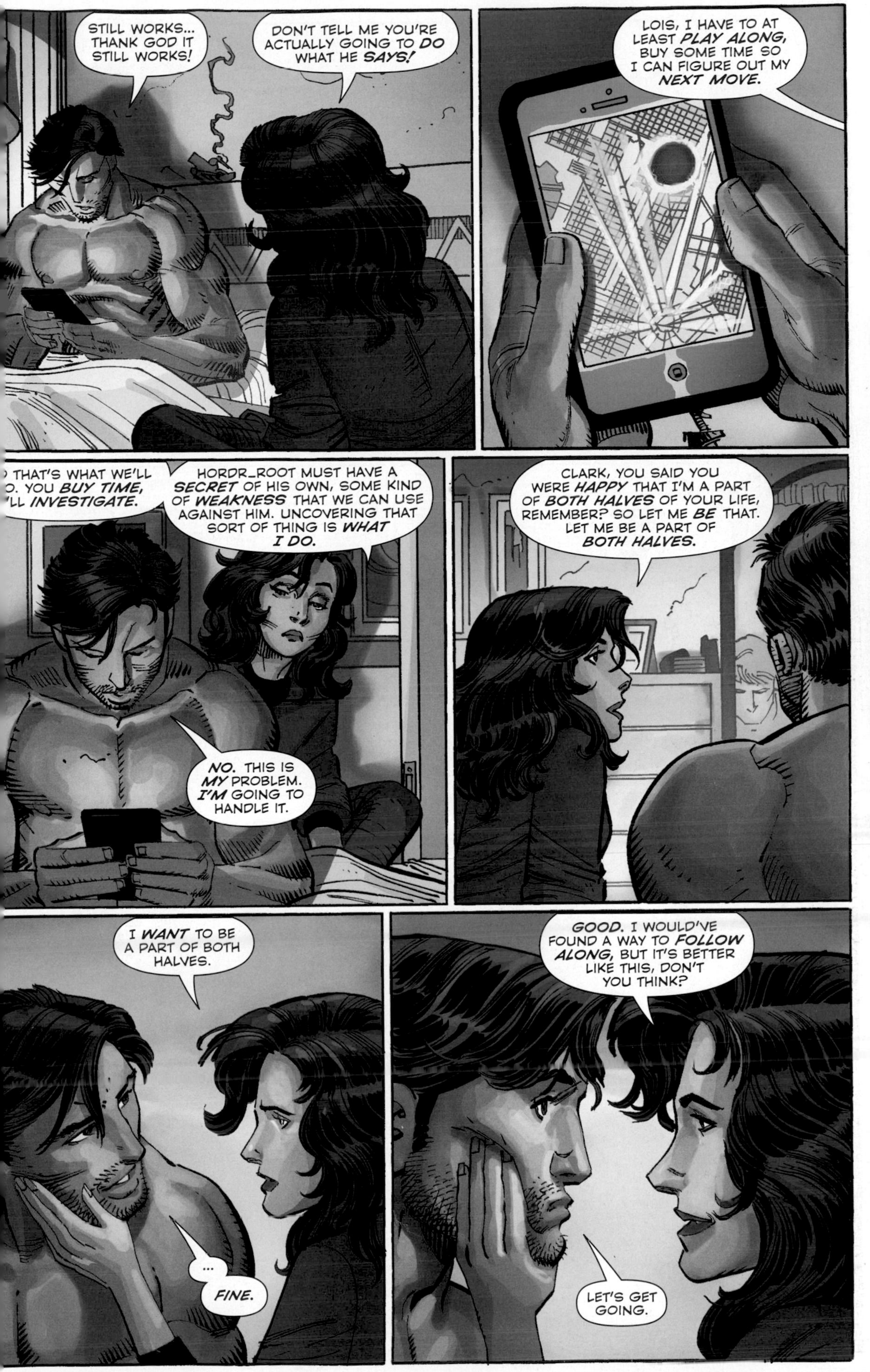
STILL WORKS... THANK GOD IT STILL WORKS!
DON'T TELL ME YOU'RE ACTUALLY GOING TO DO WHAT HE SAYS!
LOIS, I HAVE TO AT LEAST PLAY ALONG, BUY SOME TIME SO I CAN FIGURE OUT MY NEXT MOVE.
THAT'S WHAT WE'LL O. YOU BUY TIME, 'LL INVESTIGATE.
HORDR_ROOT MUST HAVE A SECRET OF HIS OWN, SOME KIND OF WEAKNESS THAT WE CAN USE AGAINST HIM. UNCOVERING THAT SORT OF THING IS WHAT I DO.
NO. THIS IS MY PROBLEM. I'M GOING TO HANDLE IT.
CLARK, YOU SAID YOU WERE HAPPY THAT I'M A PART OF BOTH HALVES OF YOUR LIFE, REMEMBER? SO LET ME BE THAT. LET ME BE A PART OF BOTH HALVES.
I WANT TO BE A PART OF BOTH HALVES.
...
FINE.
GOOD. I WOULD'VE FOUND A WAY TO FOLLOW ALONG, BUT IT'S BETTER LIKE THIS, DON'T YOU THINK?
LET'S GET GOING.

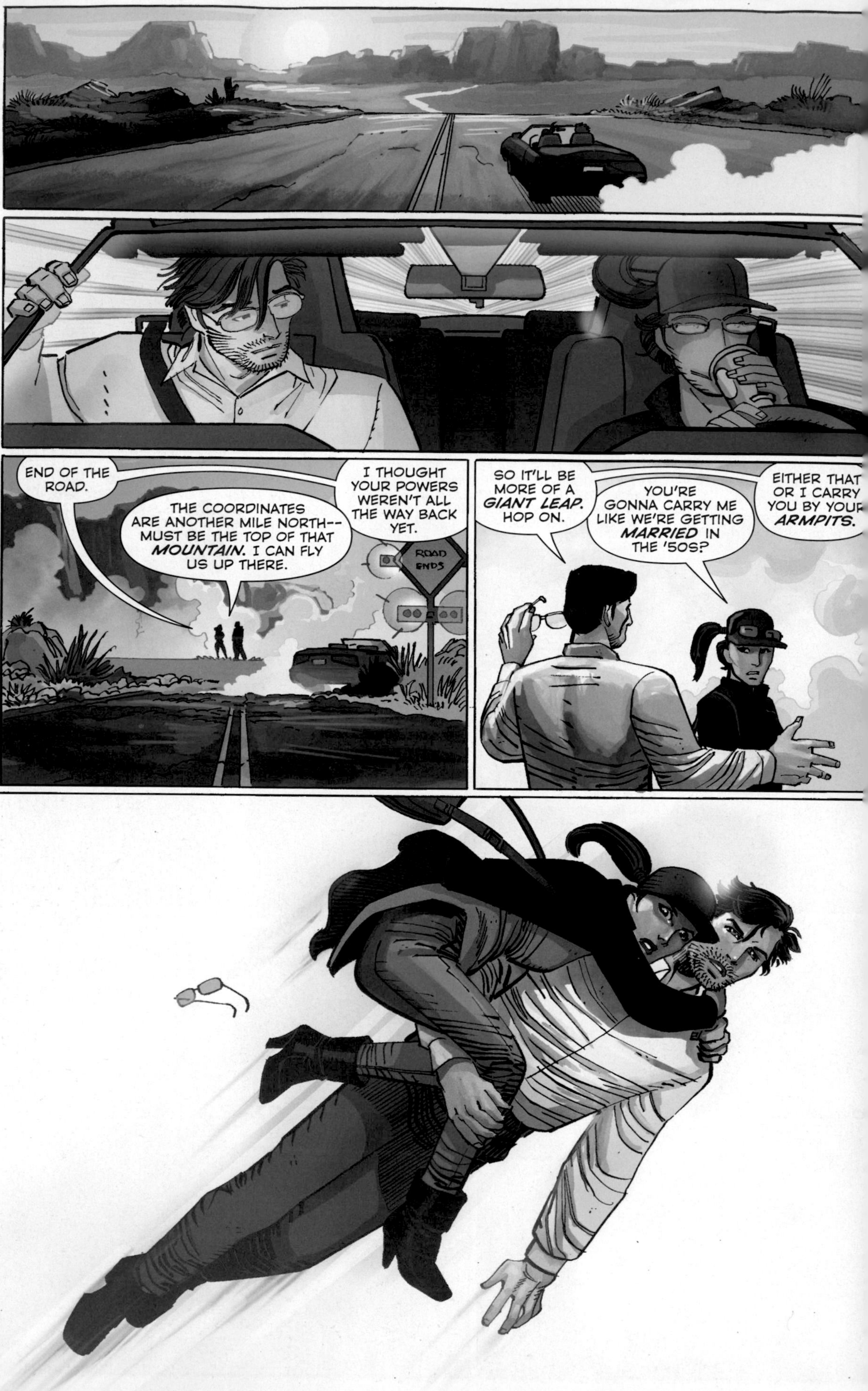
END OF THE ROAD.
THE COORDINATES ARE ANOTHER MILE NORTH-- MUST BE THE TOP OF THAT MOUNTAIN. I CAN FLY US UP THERE.
I THOUGHT YOUR POWERS WEREN'T ALL THE WAY BACK YET.
ROAD ENDS
SO IT'LL BE MORE OF A GIANT LEAP. HOP ON.
YOU'RE GONNA CARRY ME LIKE WE'RE GETTING MARRIED IN THE '50S?
EITHER THAT OR I CARRY YOU BY YOUR ARMPITS.

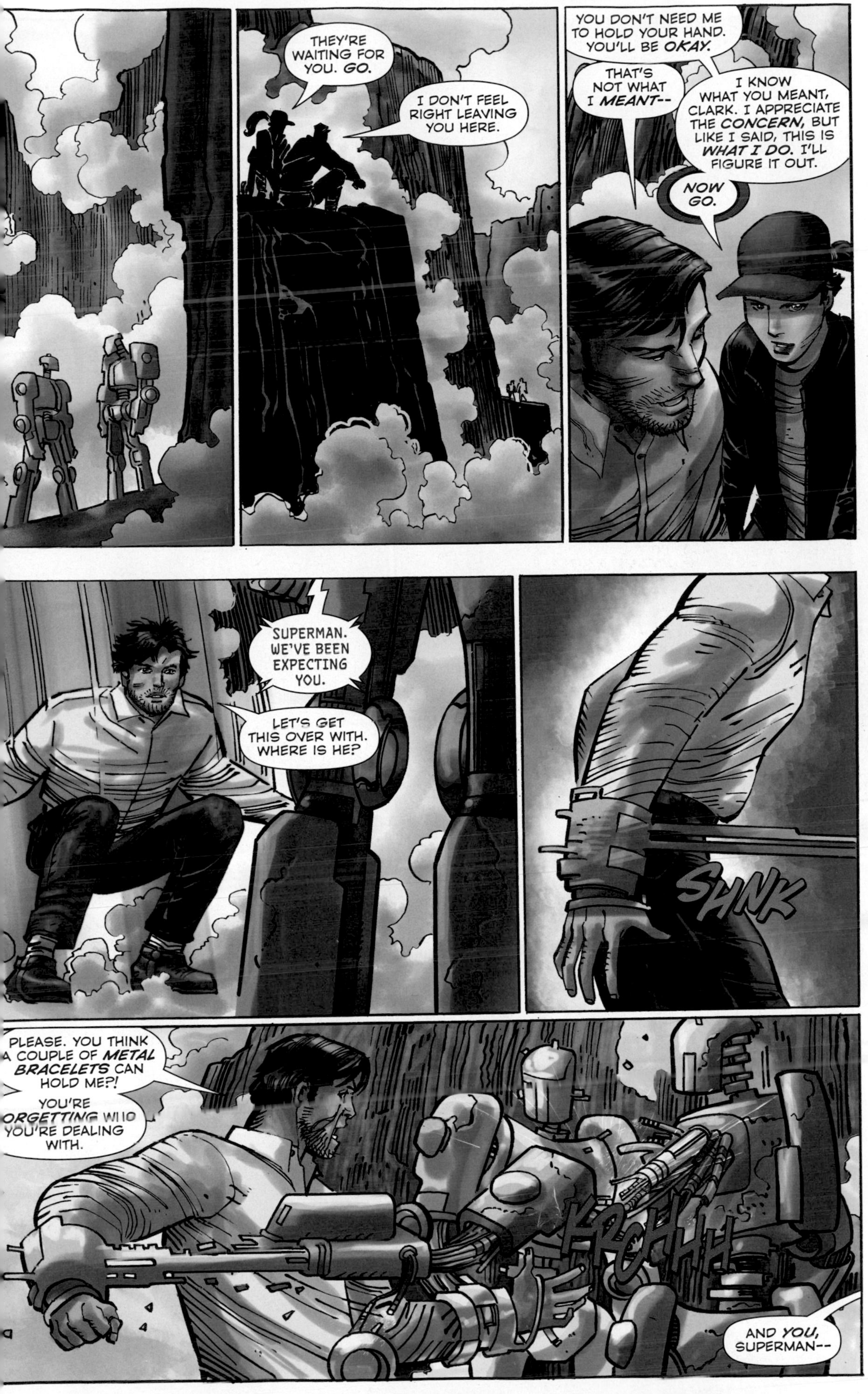
THEY'RE WAITING FOR YOU. GO.
I DON'T FEEL RIGHT LEAVING YOU HERE.
YOU DON'T NEED ME TO HOLD YOUR HAND. YOU'LL BE OKAY.
THAT'S NOT WHAT I MEANT--
I KNOW WHAT YOU MEANT, CLARK. I APPRECIATE THE CONCERN, BUT LIKE I SAID, THIS IS WHAT I DO. I'LL FIGURE IT OUT.
NOW GO.
SUPERMAN. WE'VE BEEN EXPECTING YOU.
LET'S GET THIS OVER WITH. WHERE IS HE?
SHNK
PLEASE. YOU THINK A COUPLE OF METAL BRACELETS CAN HOLD ME?!
YOU'RE ORGETTING WHO YOU'RE DEALING WITH.
KRCHHH
AND YOU, SUPERMAN--

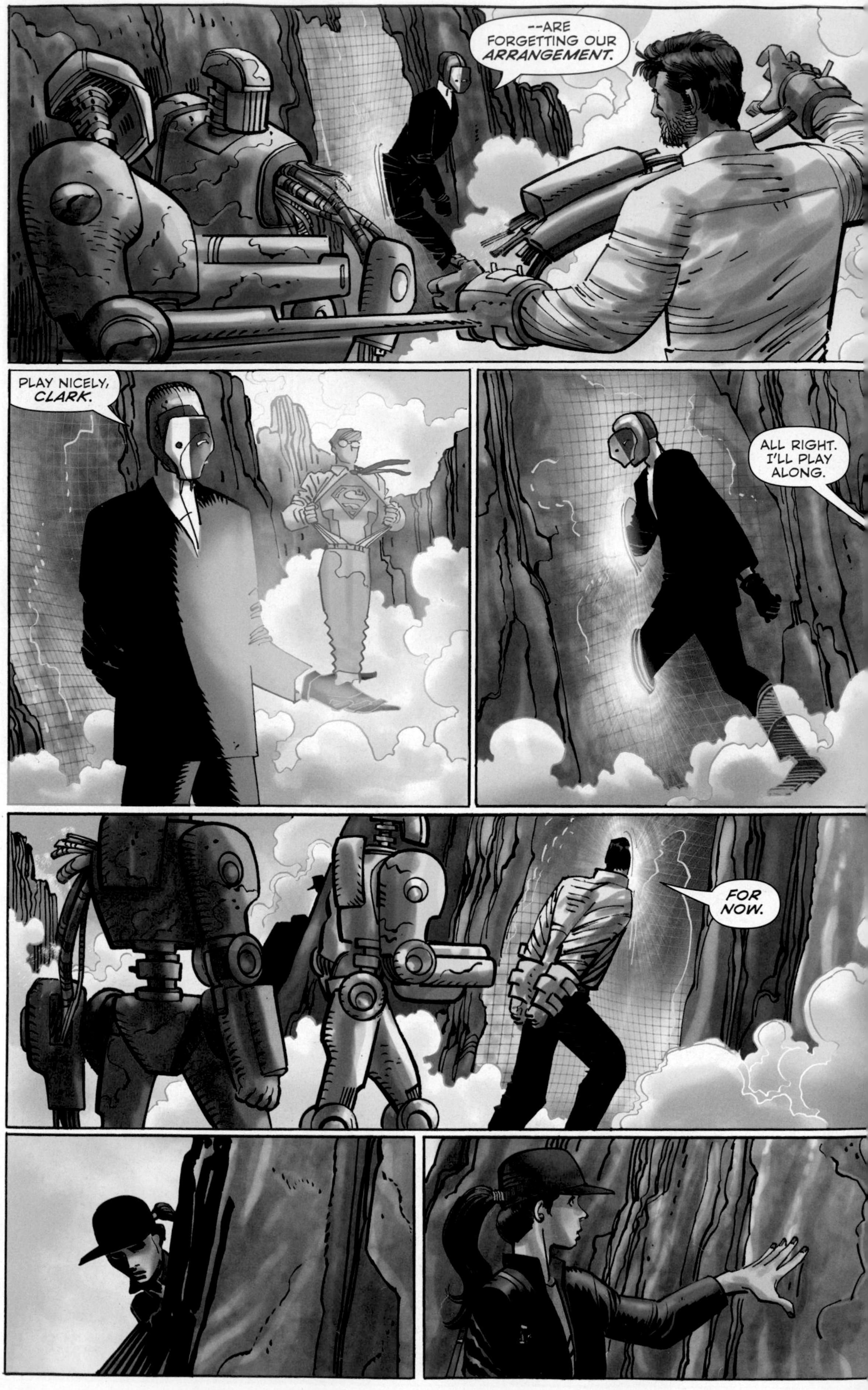
--ARE FORGETTING OUR ARRANGEMENT.
PLAY NICELY, CLARK.
ALL RIGHT. I'LL PLAY ALONG.
FOR NOW.

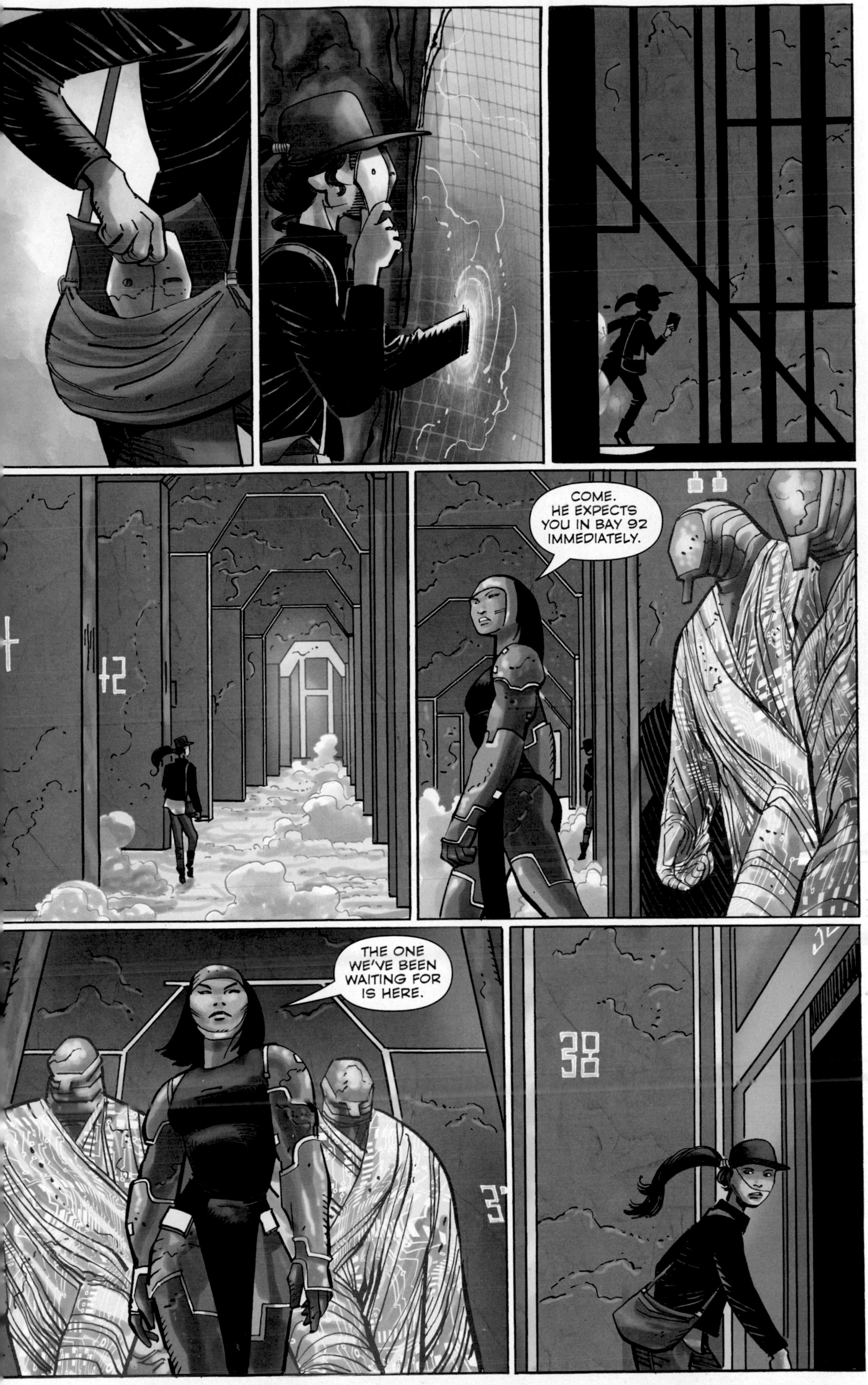
COME. HE EXPECTS YOU IN BAY 92 IMMEDIATELY.
THE ONE WE'VE BEEN WAITING FOR IS HERE.

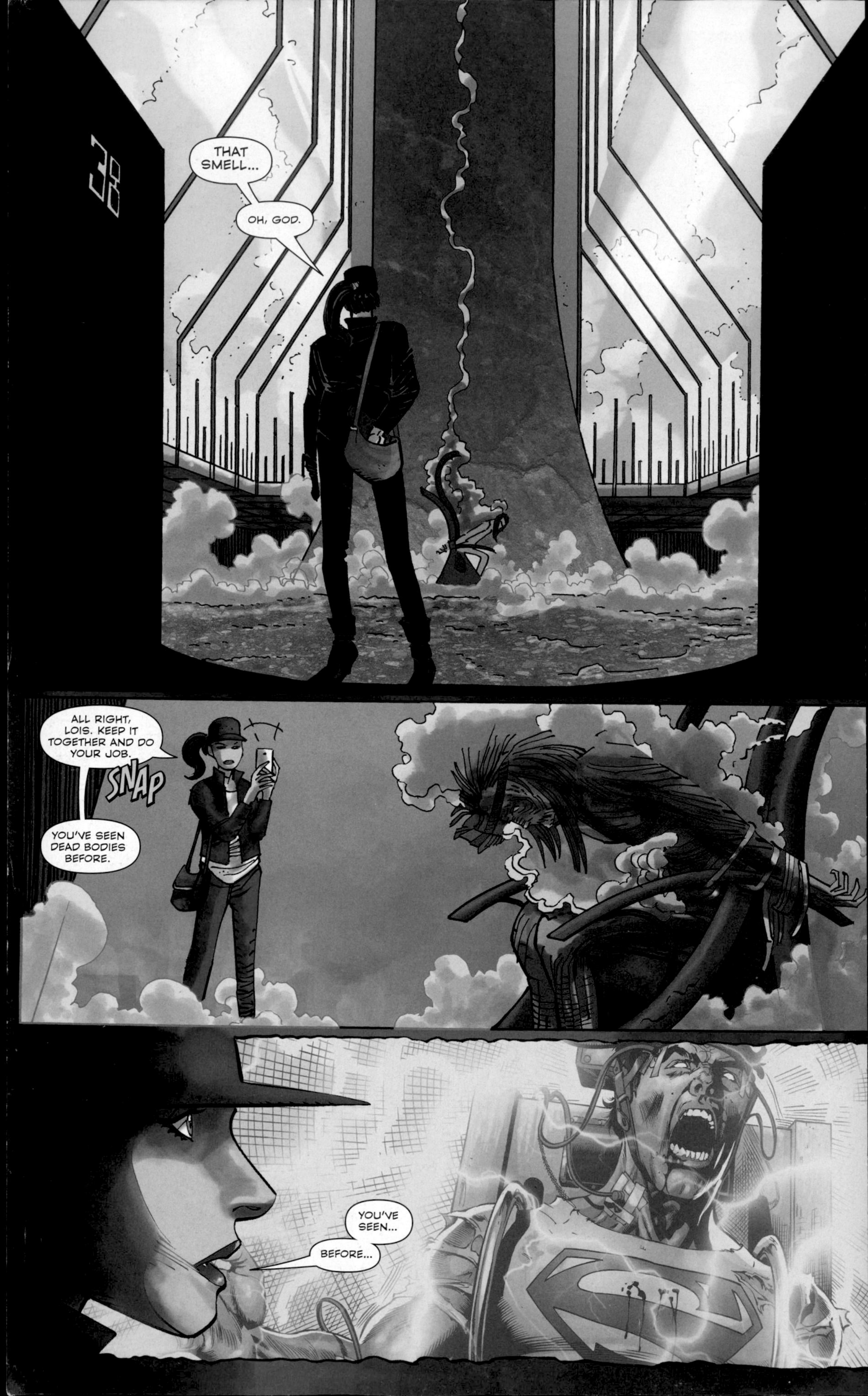

THAT SMELL...
OH, GOD.
ALL RIGHT, LOIS. KEEP IT TOGETHER AND DO YOUR JOB.
SNAP
YOU'VE SEEN DEAD BODIES BEFORE.
YOU'VE SEEN...
BEFORE...

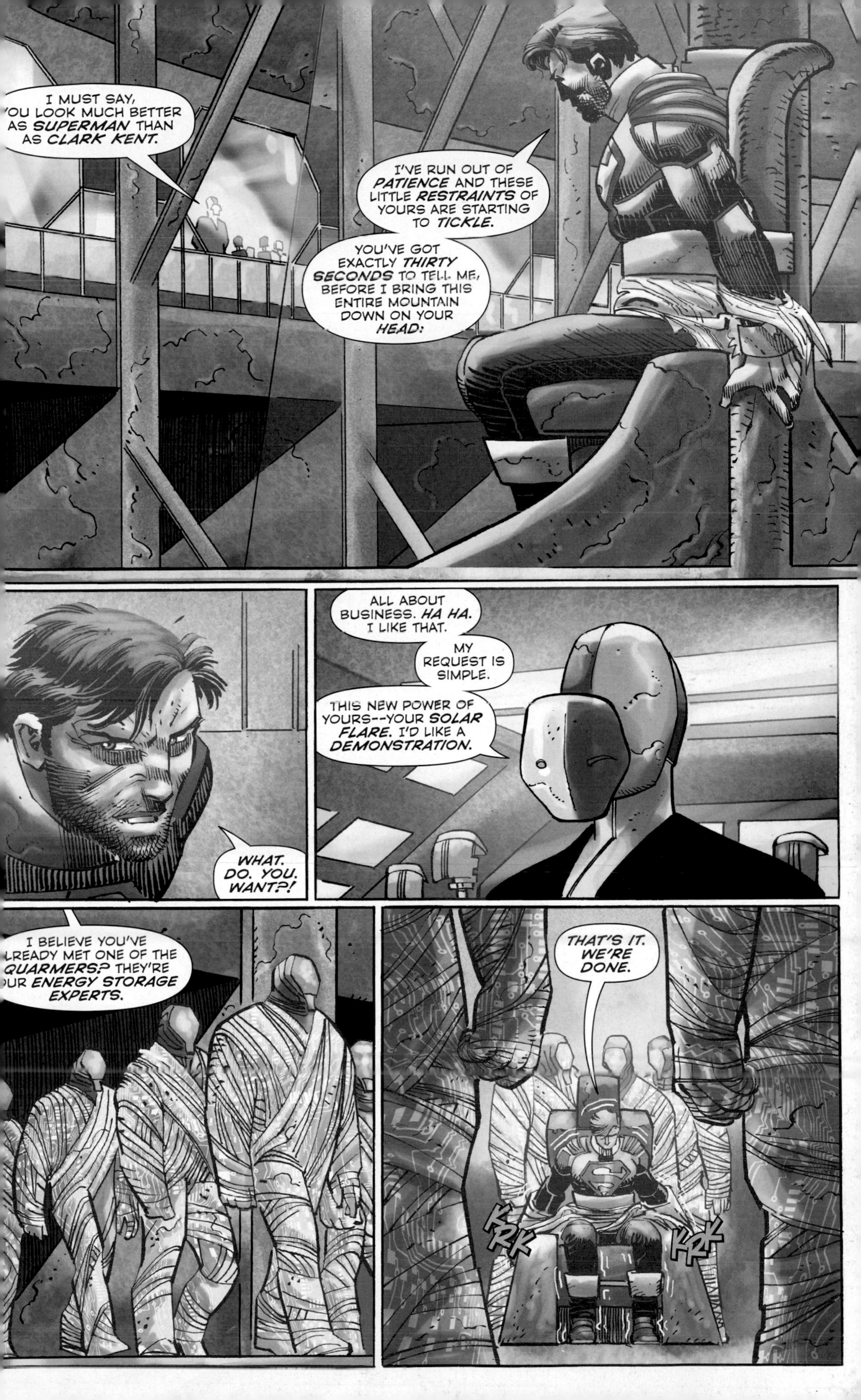

I MUST SAY, YOU LOOK MUCH BETTER AS SUPERMAN THAN AS CLARK KENT.
I'VE RUN OUT OF PATIENCE AND THESE LITTLE RESTRAINTS OF YOURS ARE STARTING TO TICKLE.
YOU'VE GOT EXACTLY THIRTY SECONDS TO TELL ME, BEFORE I BRING THIS ENTIRE MOUNTAIN DOWN ON YOUR HEAD:
WHAT. DO. YOU. WANT?!
ALL ABOUT BUSINESS. HA HA. I LIKE THAT.
MY REQUEST IS SIMPLE.
THIS NEW POWER OF YOURS--YOUR SOLAR FLARE. I'D LIKE A DEMONSTRATION.
I BELIEVE YOU'VE ALREADY MET ONE OF THE QUARMERS? THEY'RE OUR ENERGY STORAGE EXPERTS.
THAT'S IT. WE'RE DONE.
KRK
KRK

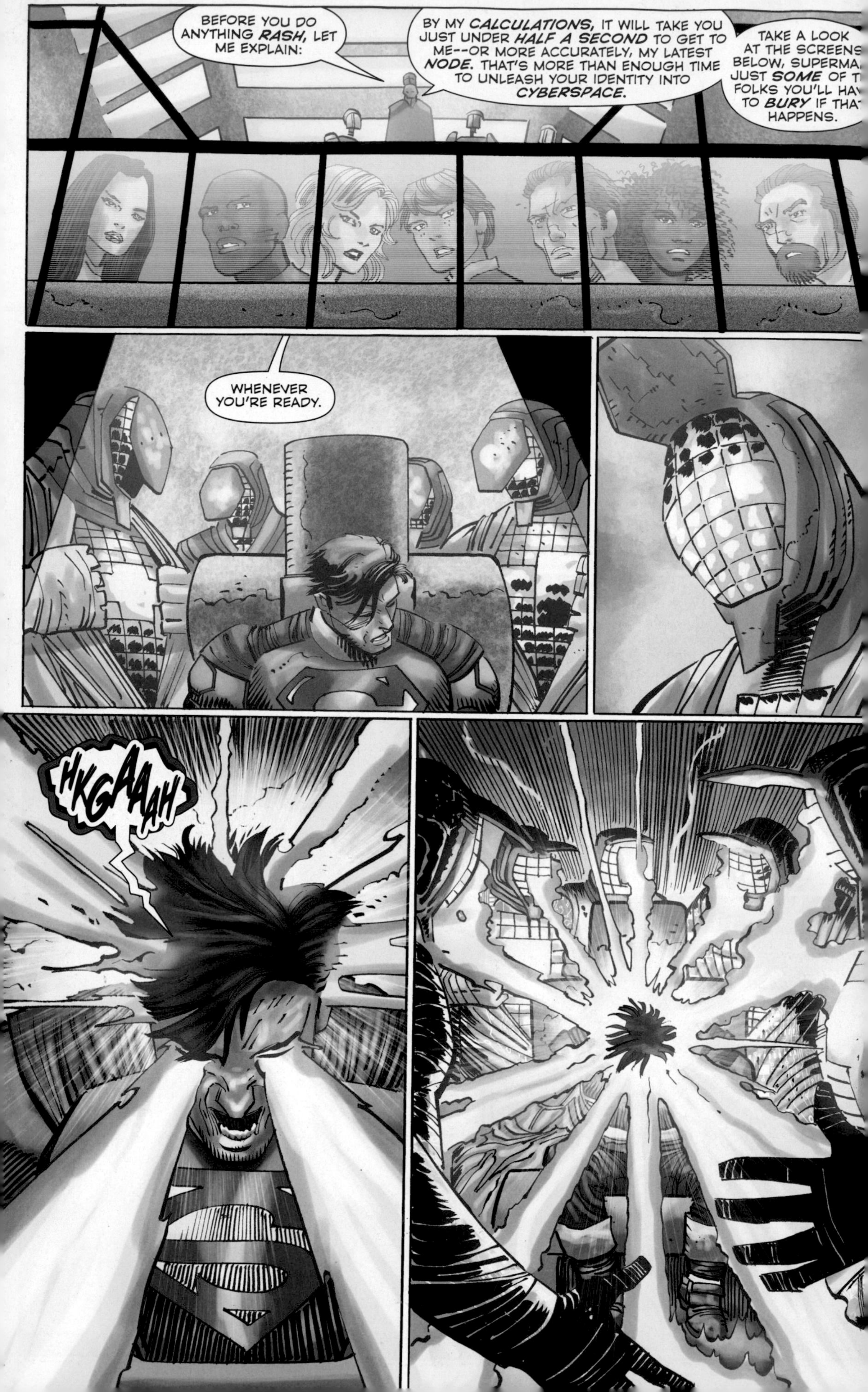
BEFORE YOU DO ANYTHING RASH, LET ME EXPLAIN:
BY MY CALCULATIONS, IT WILL TAKE YOU JUST UNDER HALF A SECOND TO GET TO ME--OR MORE ACCURATELY, MY LATEST NODE. THAT'S MORE THAN ENOUGH TIME TO UNLEASH YOUR IDENTITY INTO CYBERSPACE.
TAKE A LOOK AT THE SCREENS BELOW, SUPERMA JUST SOME OF T FOLKS YOU'LL HAV TO BURY IF THA HAPPENS.
WHENEVER YOU'RE READY.
HKGAAAAH

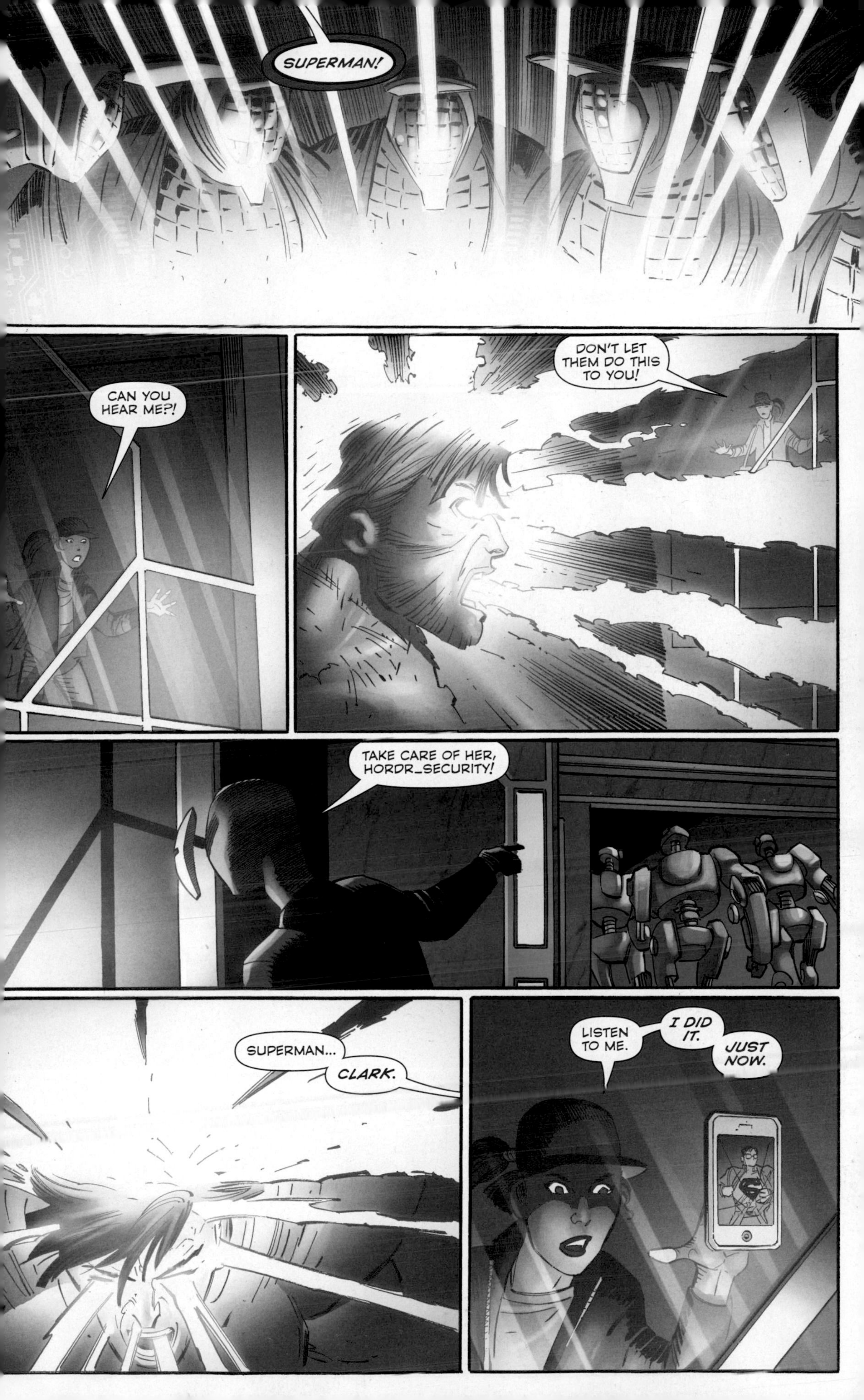
SUPERMAN!
CAN YOU HEAR ME?!
DON'T LET THEM DO THIS TO YOU!
TAKE CARE OF HER, HORDR_SECURITY!
SUPERMAN...
CLARK.
LISTEN TO ME.
I DID IT.
JUST NOW.

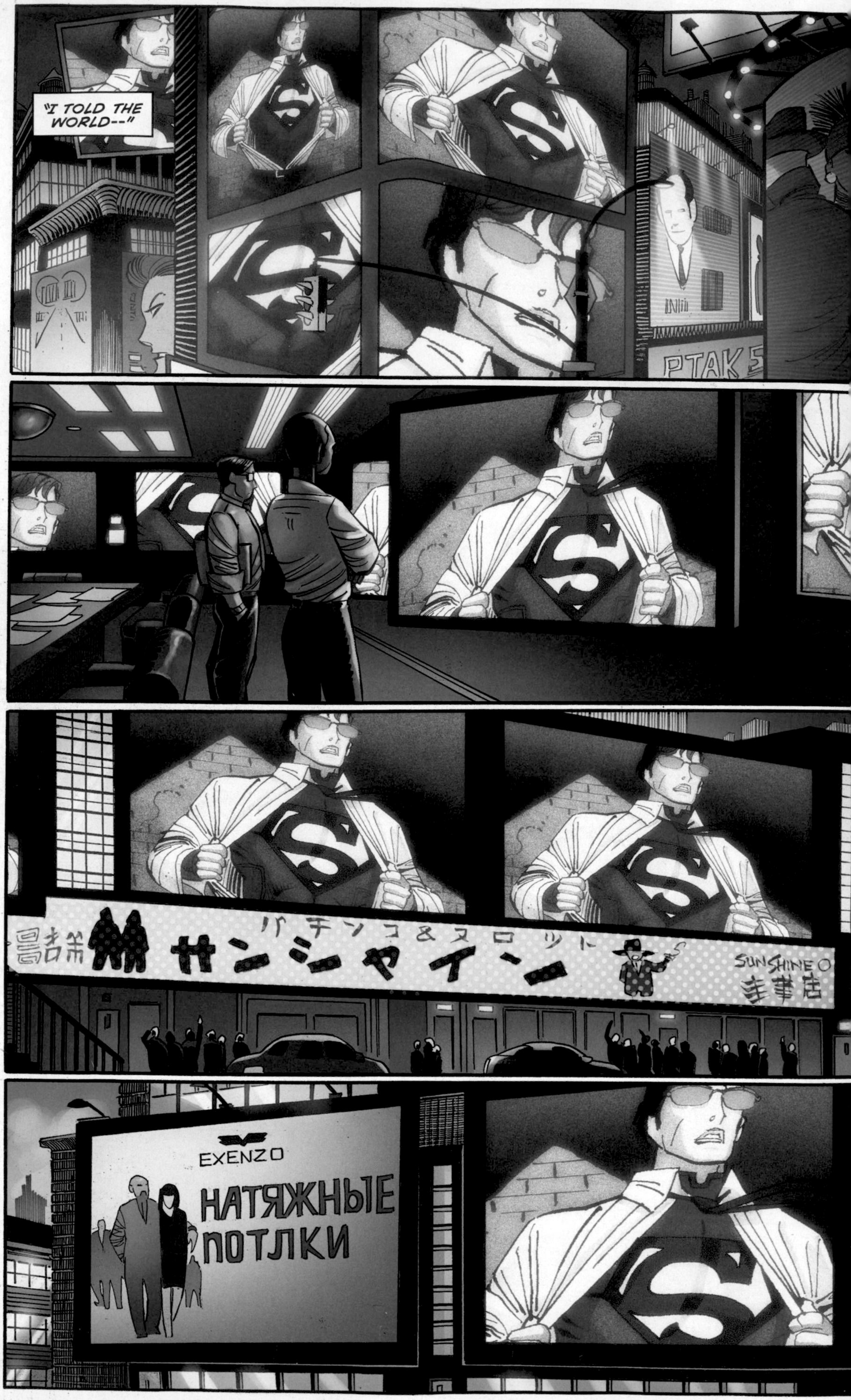
"I TOLD THE WORLD--"
PTAK
SUNSHINE
EXENZO
НАТЯЖНЫЕ
ПОТЛКИ

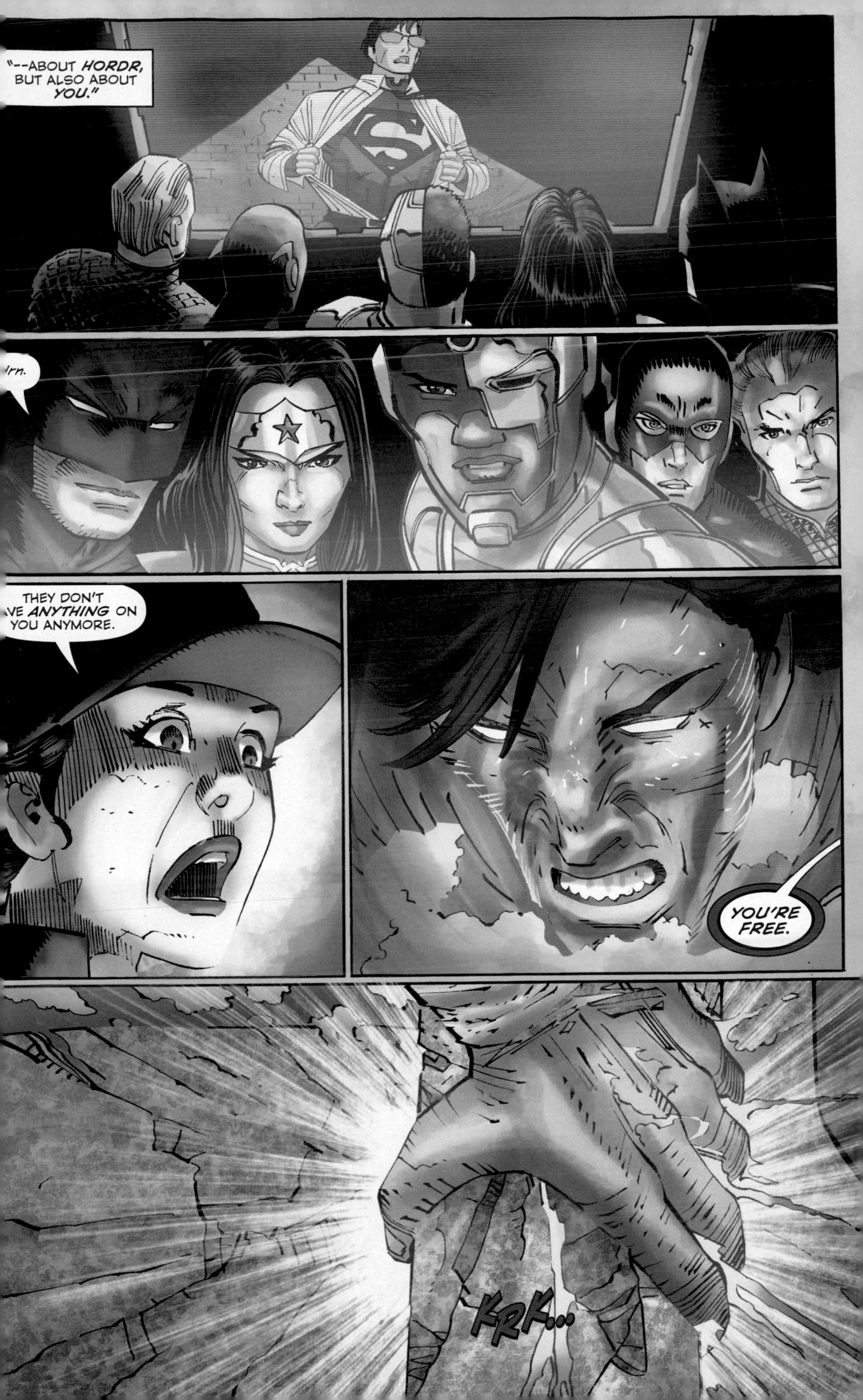
"--ABOUT HORDR, BUT ALSO ABOUT YOU."
THEY DON'T
YOU ANYMORE.
YOU'RE FREE.
KRK...

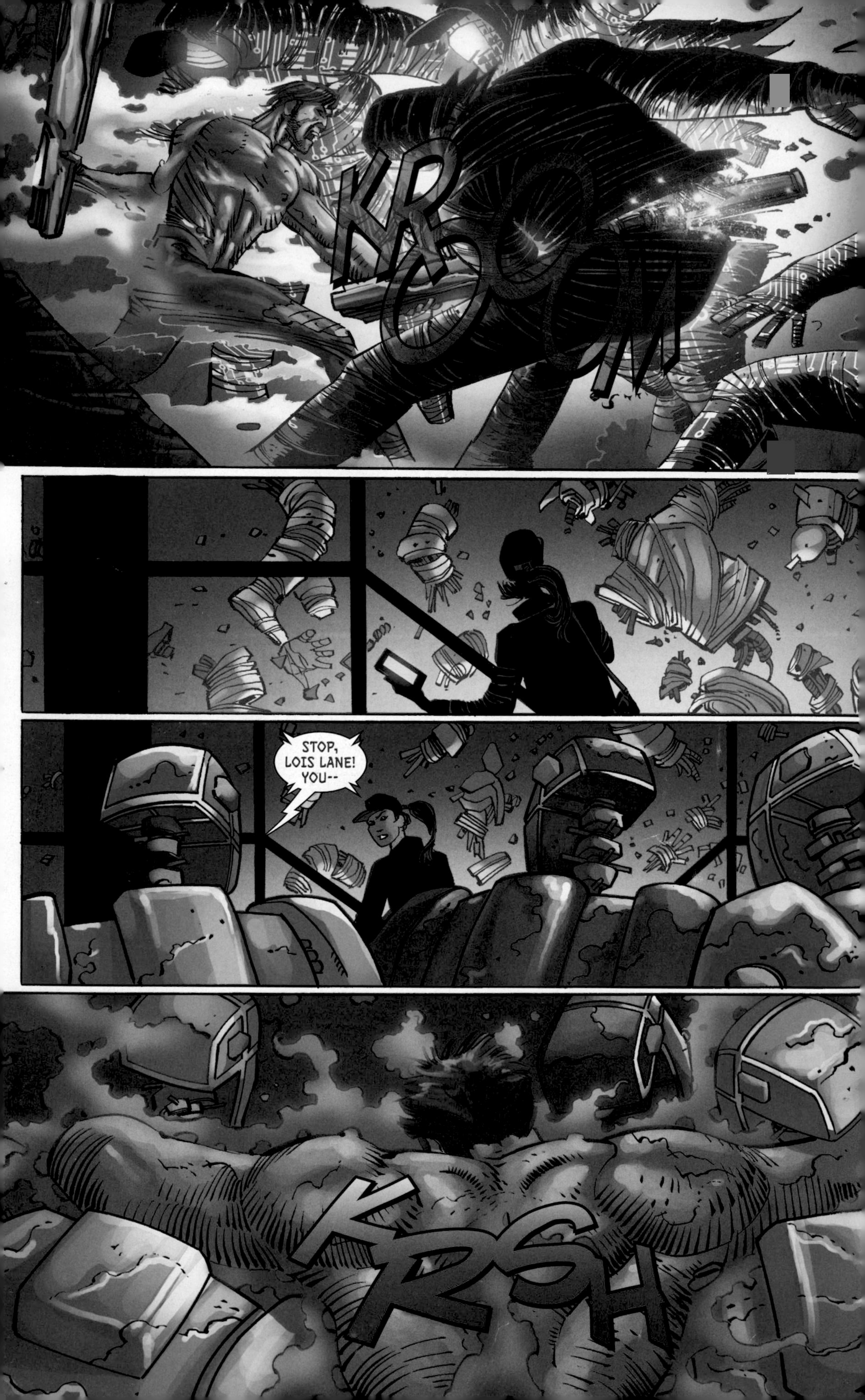
KRAKOOM
STOP, LOIS LANE! YOU--
KRSH

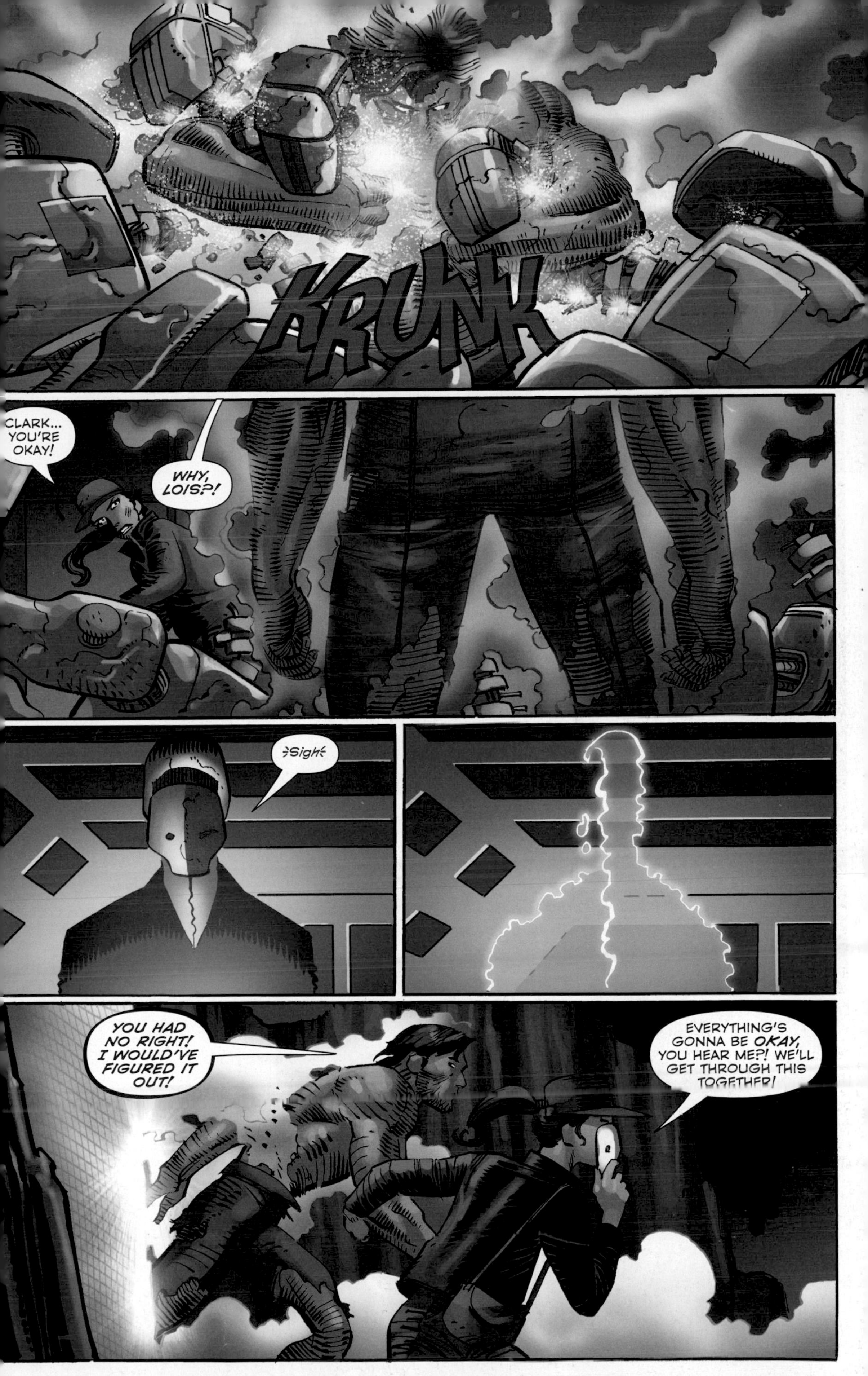
KRUNK
CLARK... YOU'RE OKAY!
WHY, LOIS?!
Sigh
YOU HAD NO RIGHT! I WOULD'VE FIGURED IT OUT!
EVERYTHING'S GONNA BE OKAY, YOU HEAR ME?! WE'LL GET THROUGH THIS TOGETHER!

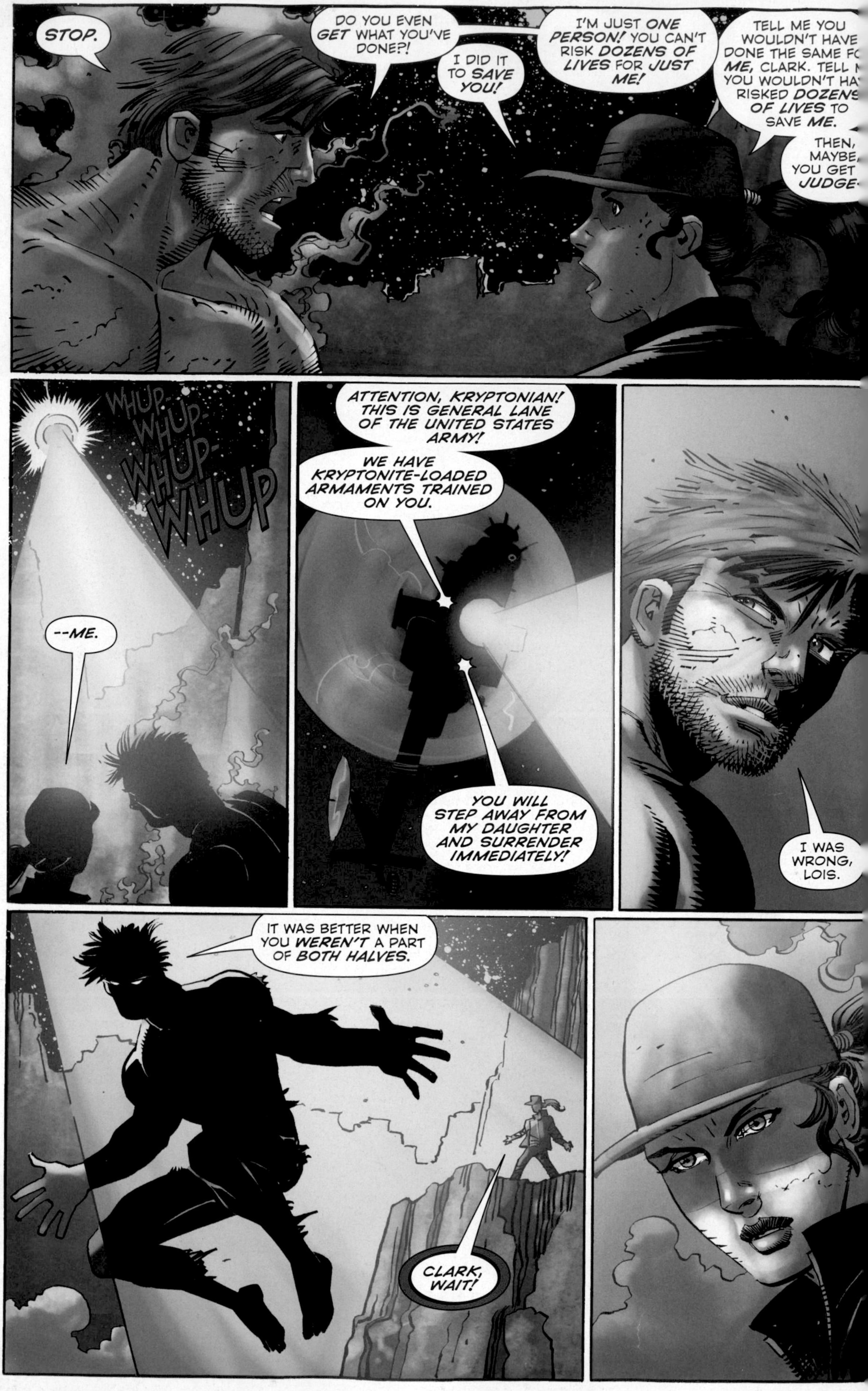
STOP.
DO YOU EVEN GET WHAT YOU'VE DONE?!
I DID IT TO SAVE YOU!
I'M JUST ONE PERSON! YOU CAN'T RISK DOZENS OF LIVES FOR JUST ME!
TELL ME YOU WOULDN'T HAVE DONE THE SAME FO ME, CLARK. TELL M YOU WOULDN'T HA RISKED DOZENS OF LIVES TO SAVE ME.
THEN, MAYBE, YOU GET JUDGE-
WHUP-WHUP-WHUP-WHUP
--ME.
ATTENTION, KRYPTONIAN! THIS IS GENERAL LANE OF THE UNITED STATES ARMY!
WE HAVE KRYPTONITE-LOADED ARMAMENTS TRAINED ON YOU.
YOU WILL STEP AWAY FROM MY DAUGHTER AND SURRENDER IMMEDIATELY!
I WAS WRONG, LOIS.
IT WAS BETTER WHEN YOU WEREN'T A PART OF BOTH HALVES.
CLARK, WAIT!

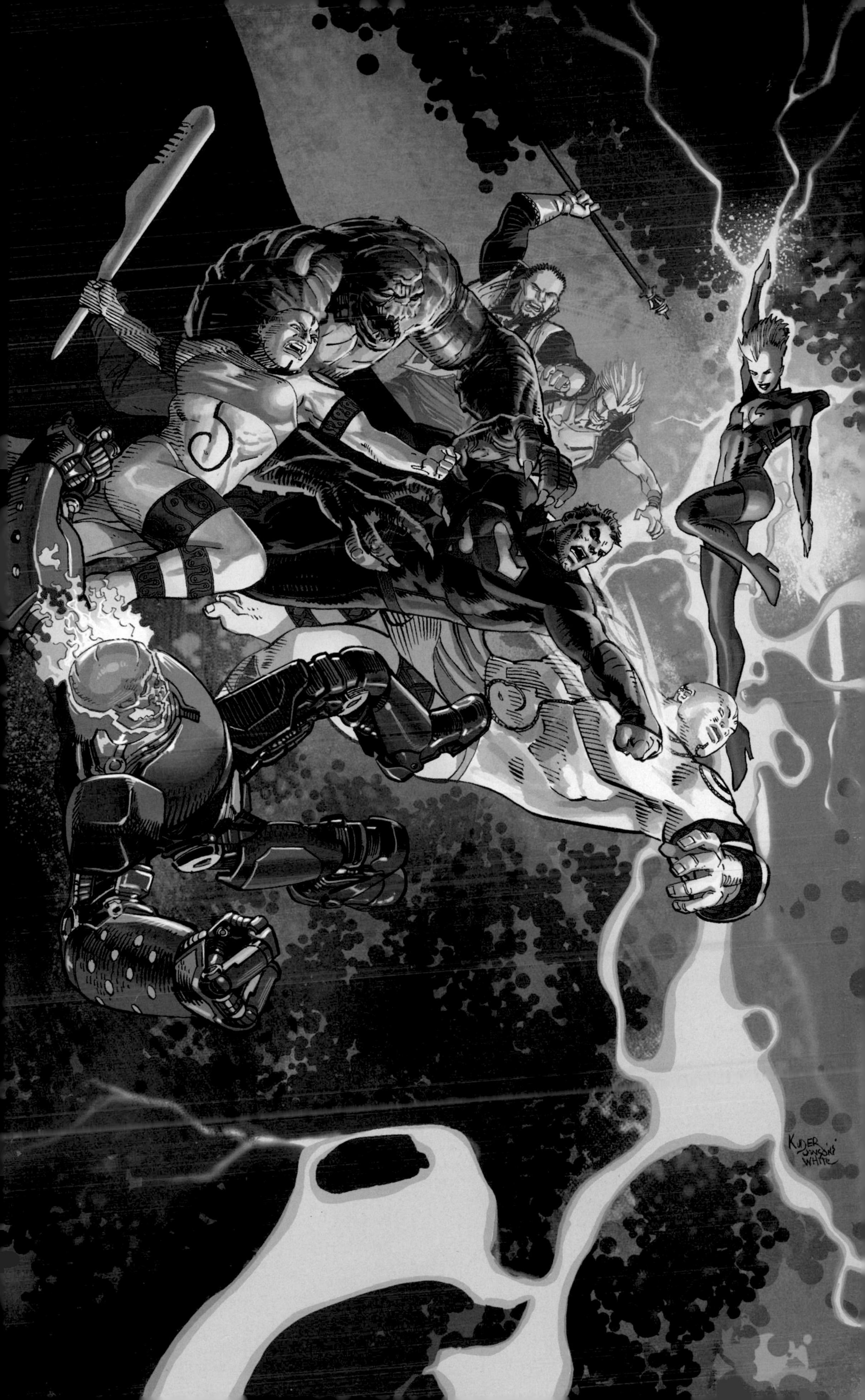
KUDER
JANSON
WHITE

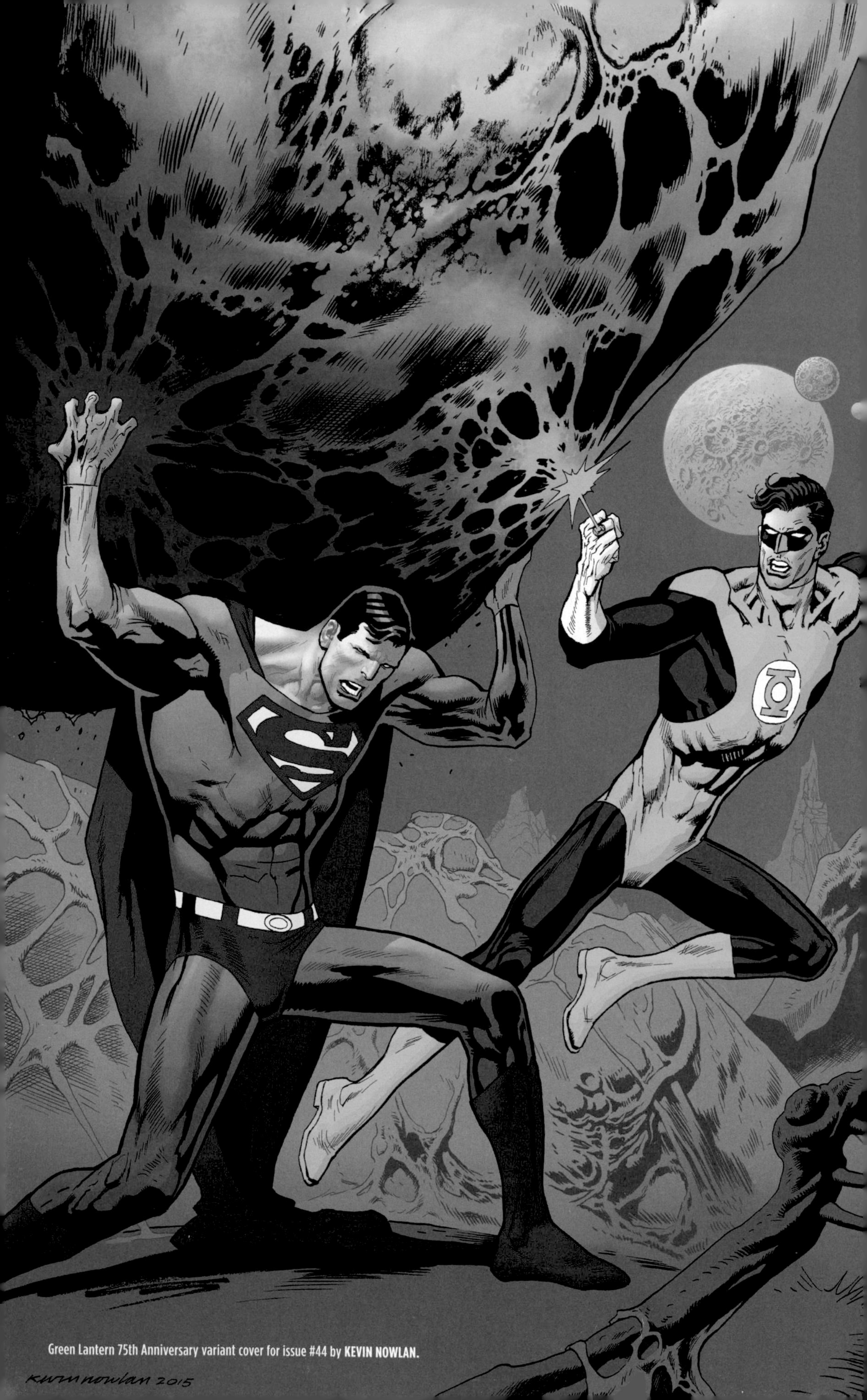
kevin nowlan 2015

Green Lantern 75th Anniversary variant cover for issue #44 by **KEVIN NOWLAN.**

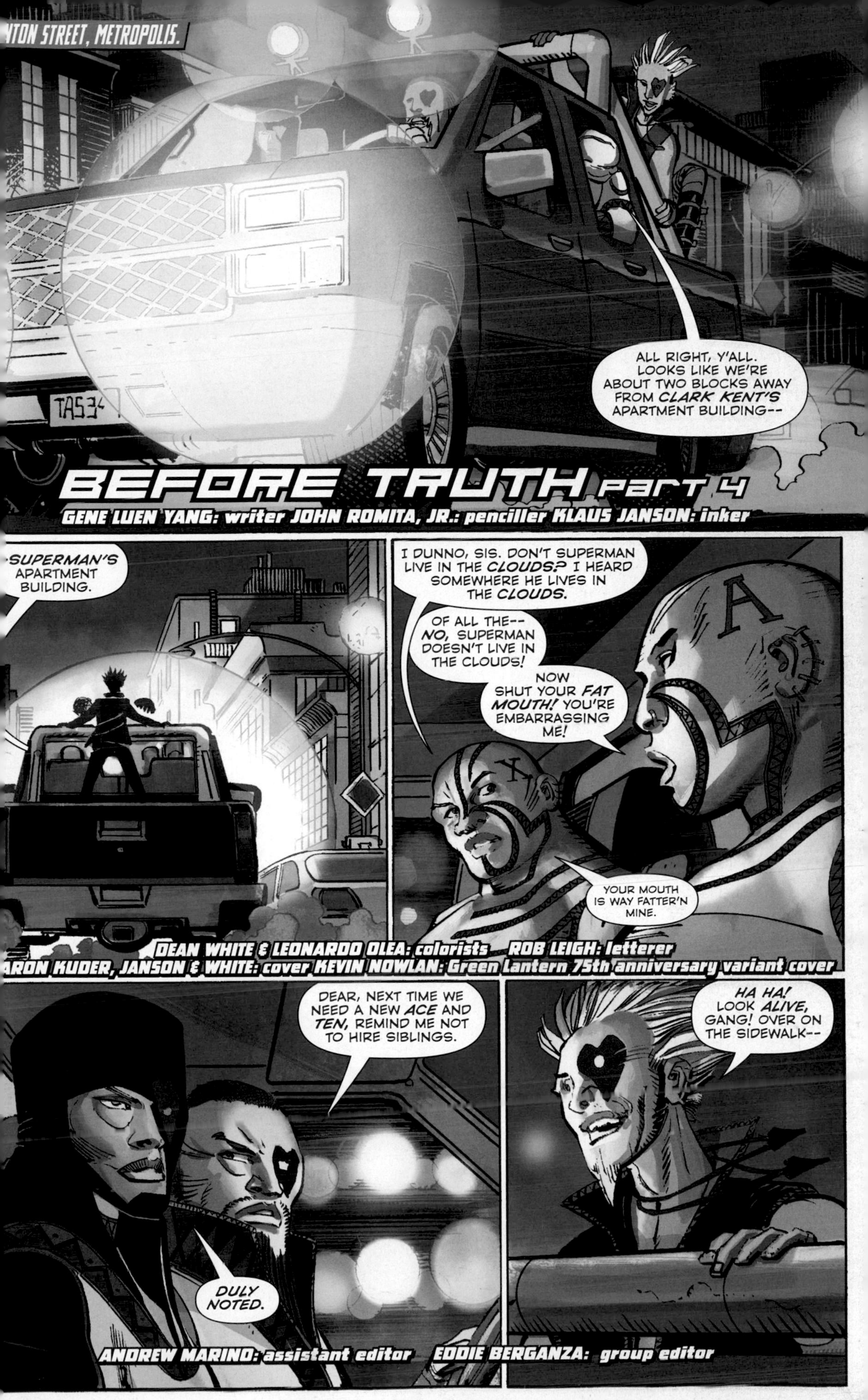

NTON STREET, METROPOLIS.
ALL RIGHT, Y'ALL. LOOKS LIKE WE'RE ABOUT TWO BLOCKS AWAY FROM CLARK KENT'S APARTMENT BUILDING--
BEFORE TRUTH PART 4
GENE LUEN YANG: writer JOHN ROMITA, JR.: penciller KLAUS JANSON: inker
-SUPERMAN'S APARTMENT BUILDING.
I DUNNO, SIS. DON'T SUPERMAN LIVE IN THE CLOUDS? I HEARD SOMEWHERE HE LIVES IN THE CLOUDS.
OF ALL THE-- NO, SUPERMAN DOESN'T LIVE IN THE CLOUDS!
NOW SHUT YOUR FAT MOUTH! YOU'RE EMBARRASSING ME!
YOUR MOUTH IS WAY FATTER'N MINE.
DEAN WHITE & LEONARDO OLEA: colorists ROB LEIGH: letterer
ARON KUDER, JANSON & WHITE: cover KEVIN NOWLAN: Green Lantern 75th anniversary variant cover
DEAR, NEXT TIME WE NEED A NEW ACE AND TEN, REMIND ME NOT TO HIRE SIBLINGS.
DULY NOTED.
HA HA! LOOK ALIVE, GANG! OVER ON THE SIDEWALK--
ANDREW MARINO: assistant editor EDDIE BERGANZA: group editor

JACKPOT!

KZARRT

NGH

WHO--?!

GOOD EVENING, MR. KENT.

I'VE HEARD IT SAID THAT ONCE UPON A TIME, YOU HAD THE ABILITY TO CRUSH *COAL* INTO *DIAMONDS.*

YOU LIVE NOT TOO FAR FROM HERE, NO? THE *ROYAL FLUSH GANG* WOULD LOVE TO COME OVER FOR A *VISIT.*

SORRY, BUDDY. MY BUILDING'S GOT A *NO SOLICITORS* POLICY.

KZARRT

KZARRT

KZARRT

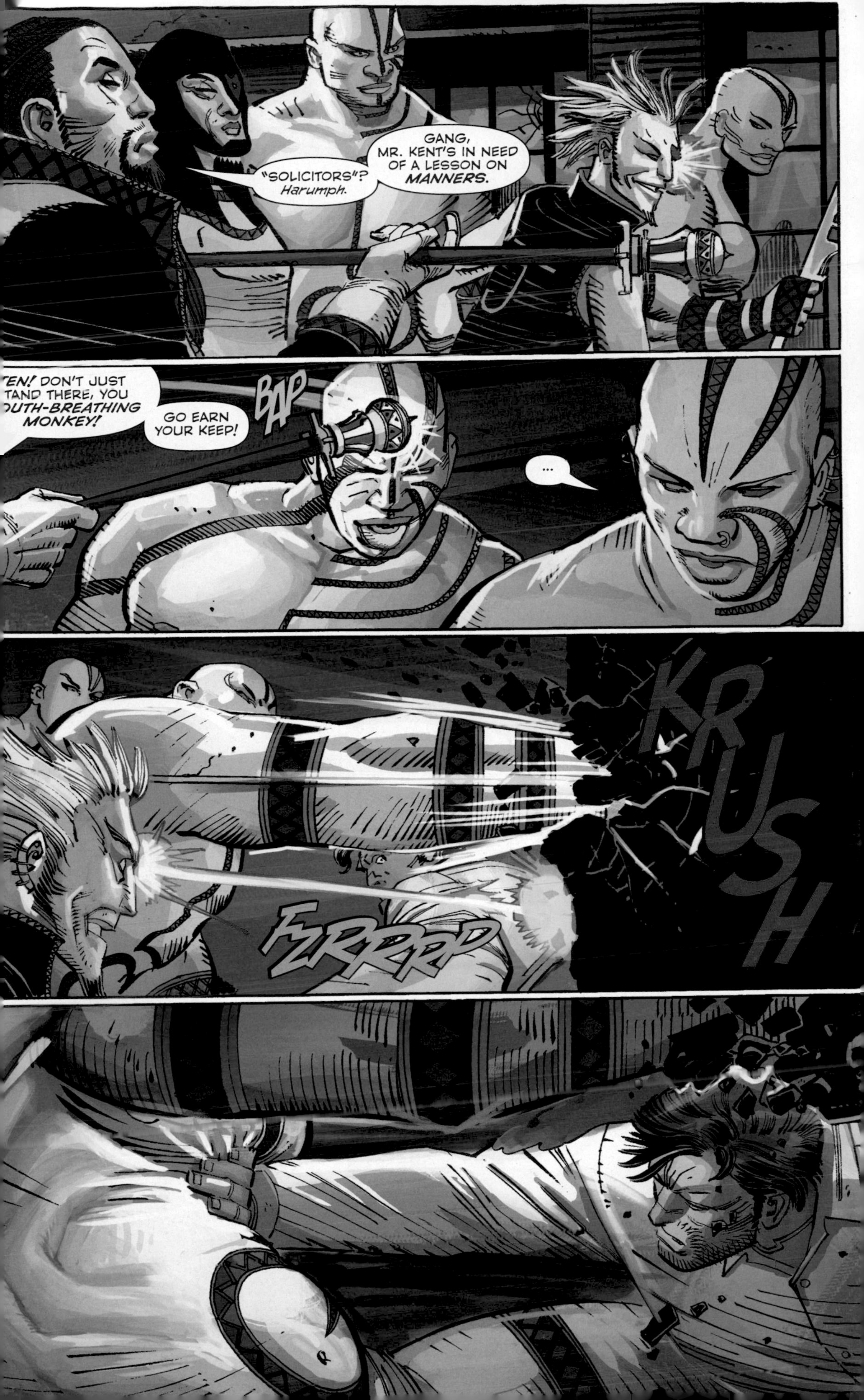

"SOLICITORS"? Harumph.
GANG, MR. KENT'S IN NEED OF A LESSON ON MANNERS.
TEN! DON'T JUST TAND THERE, YOU OUTH-BREATHING MONKEY!
GO EARN YOUR KEEP!
BAP
...
KRUSH
FZRRRD

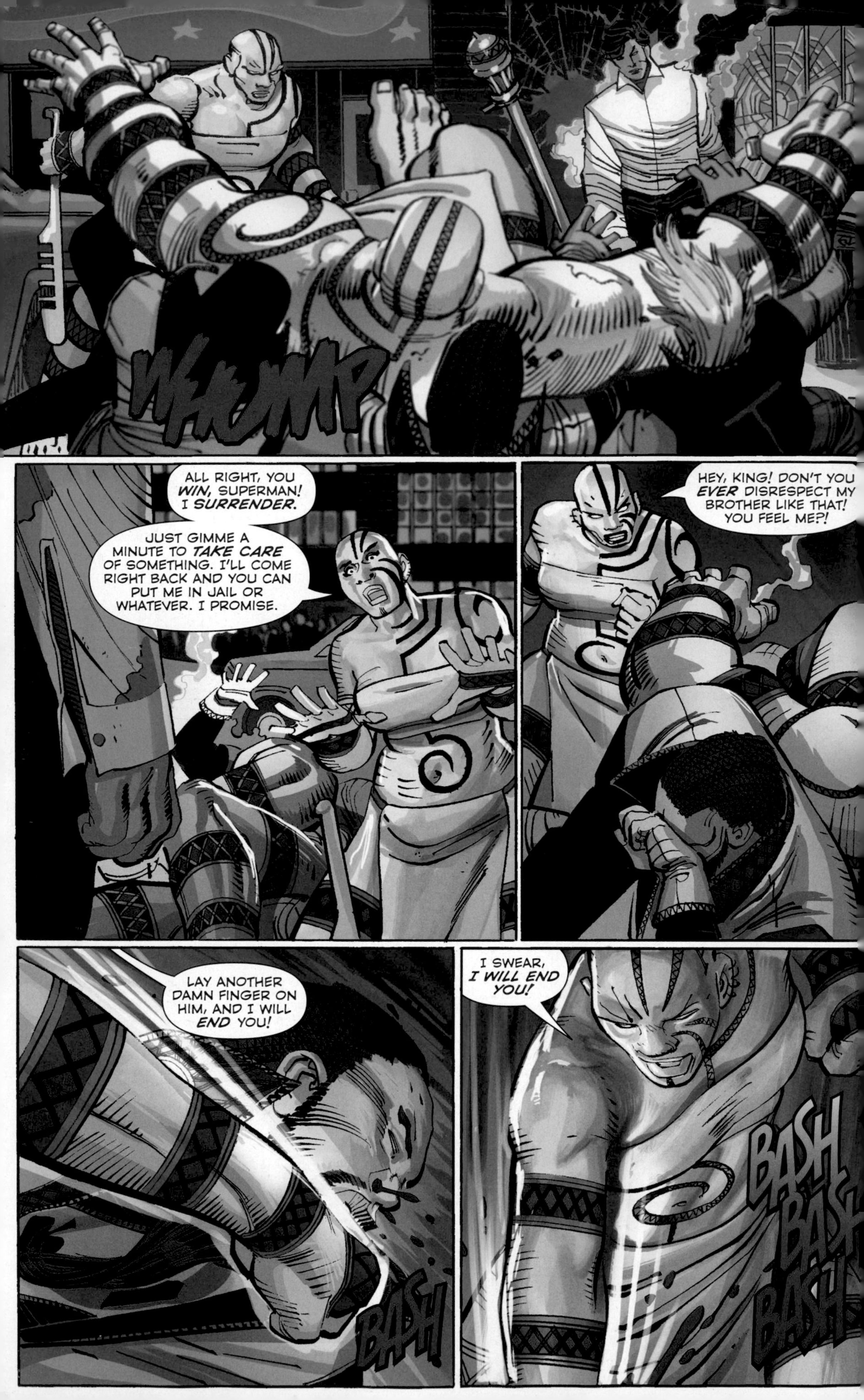
WHUMP
ALL RIGHT, YOU WIN, SUPERMAN! I SURRENDER.
JUST GIMME A MINUTE TO TAKE CARE OF SOMETHING. I'LL COME RIGHT BACK AND YOU CAN PUT ME IN JAIL OR WHATEVER. I PROMISE.
HEY, KING! DON'T YOU EVER DISRESPECT MY BROTHER LIKE THAT! YOU FEEL ME?!
LAY ANOTHER DAMN FINGER ON HIM, AND I WILL END YOU!
BASH
I SWEAR, I WILL END YOU!
BASH
BASH
BASH

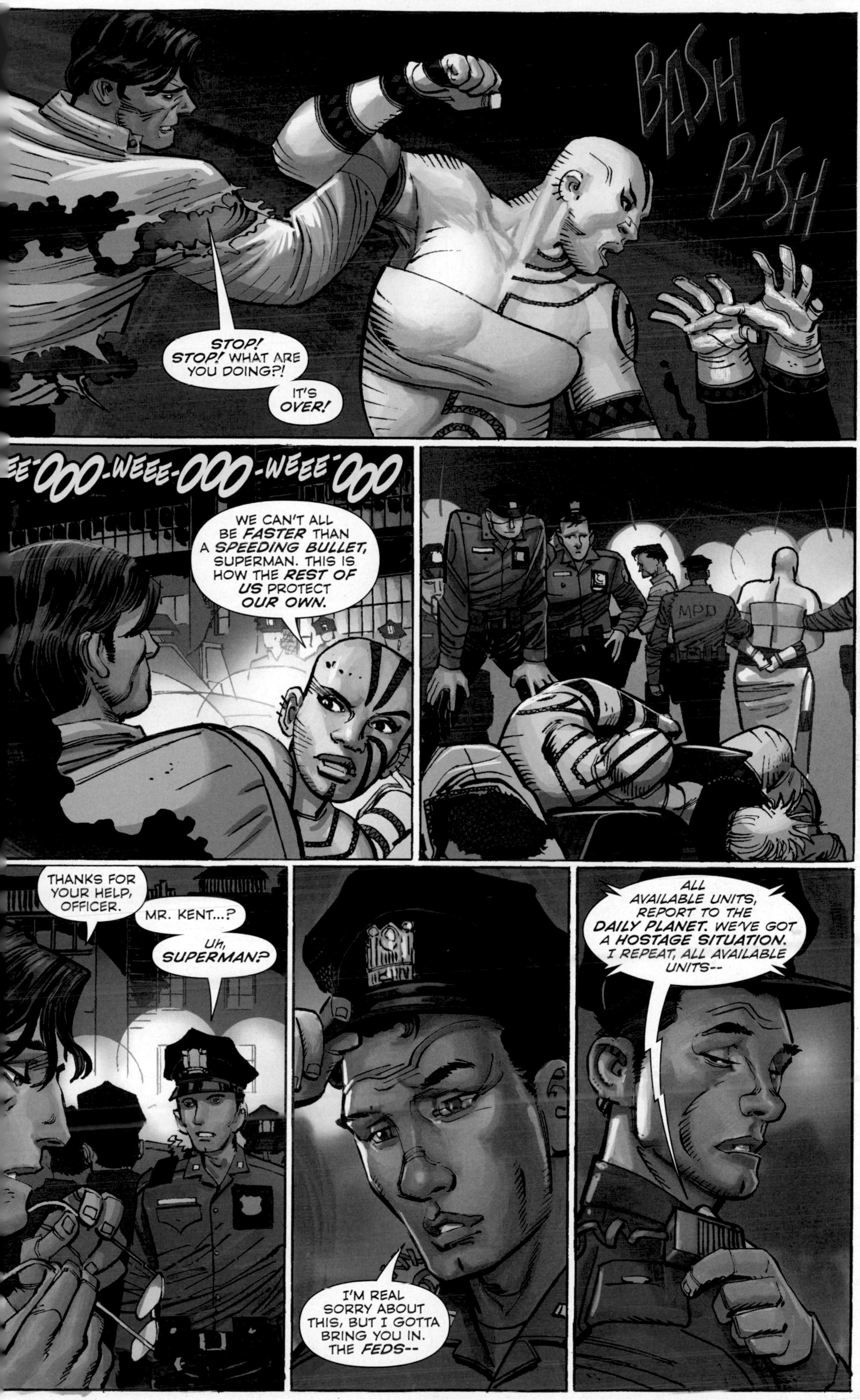
BASH
BASH
STOP! STOP! WHAT ARE YOU DOING?!
IT'S OVER!
EE-OOO-WEEE-OOO-WEEE-OOO
WE CAN'T ALL BE FASTER THAN A SPEEDING BULLET, SUPERMAN. THIS IS HOW THE REST OF US PROTECT OUR OWN.
MPD
THANKS FOR YOUR HELP, OFFICER.
MR. KENT...?
Uh, SUPERMAN?
I'M REAL SORRY ABOUT THIS, BUT I GOTTA BRING YOU IN. THE FEDS--
ALL AVAILABLE UNITS, REPORT TO THE DAILY PLANET. WE'VE GOT A HOSTAGE SITUATION. I REPEAT, ALL AVAILABLE UNITS--

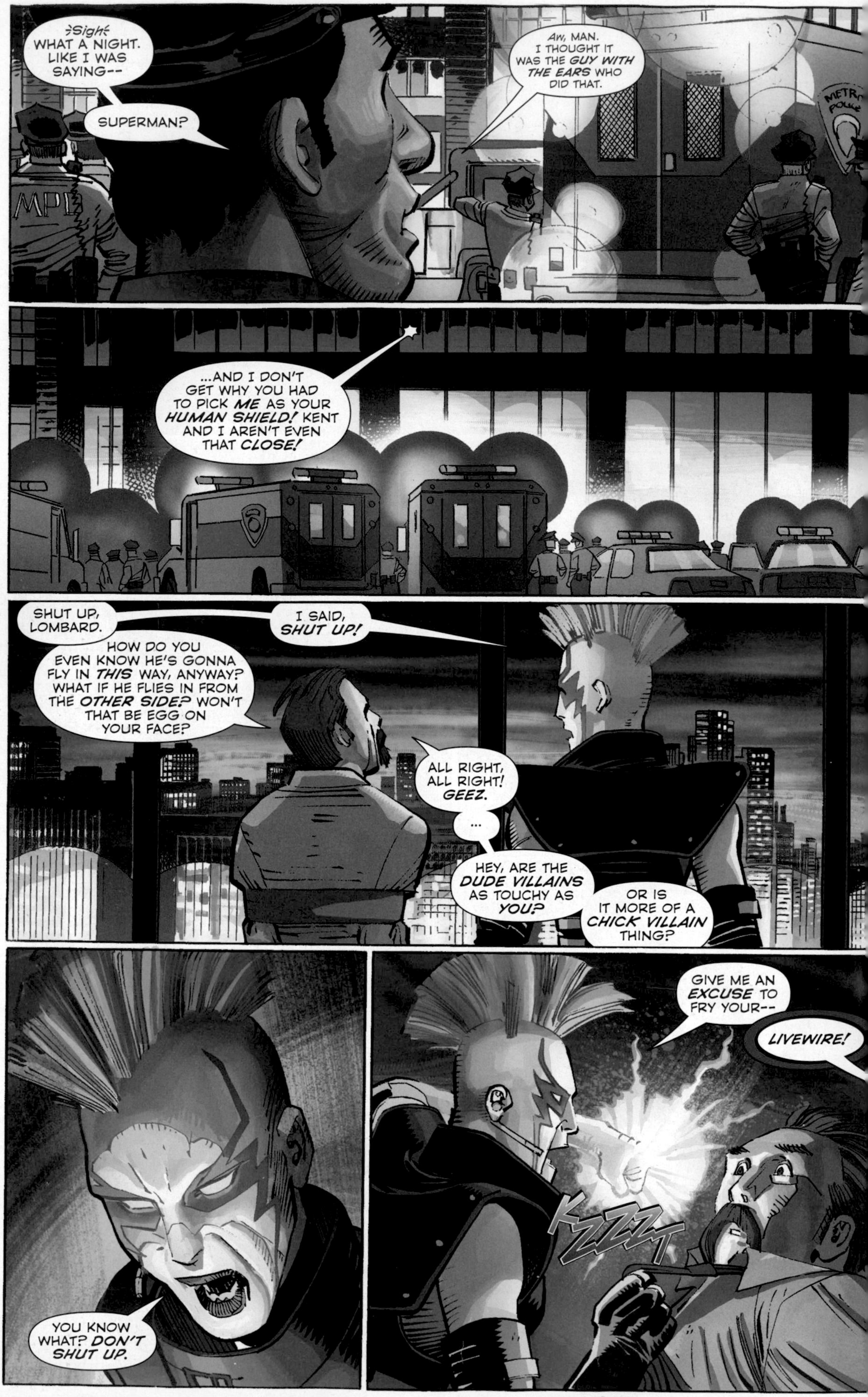

Sigh
WHAT A NIGHT. LIKE I WAS SAYING--
SUPERMAN?
Aw, MAN. I THOUGHT IT WAS THE GUY WITH THE EARS WHO DID THAT.
MPD
METRO POLICE
...AND I DON'T GET WHY YOU HAD TO PICK ME AS YOUR HUMAN SHIELD! KENT AND I AREN'T EVEN THAT CLOSE!
SHUT UP, LOMBARD.
HOW DO YOU EVEN KNOW HE'S GONNA FLY IN THIS WAY, ANYWAY? WHAT IF HE FLIES IN FROM THE OTHER SIDE? WON'T THAT BE EGG ON YOUR FACE?
I SAID, SHUT UP!
ALL RIGHT, ALL RIGHT! GEEZ.
...
HEY, ARE THE DUDE VILLAINS AS TOUCHY AS YOU?
OR IS IT MORE OF A CHICK VILLAIN THING?
YOU KNOW WHAT? DON'T SHUT UP.
GIVE ME AN EXCUSE TO FRY YOUR--
LIVEWIRE!
KZZZZT

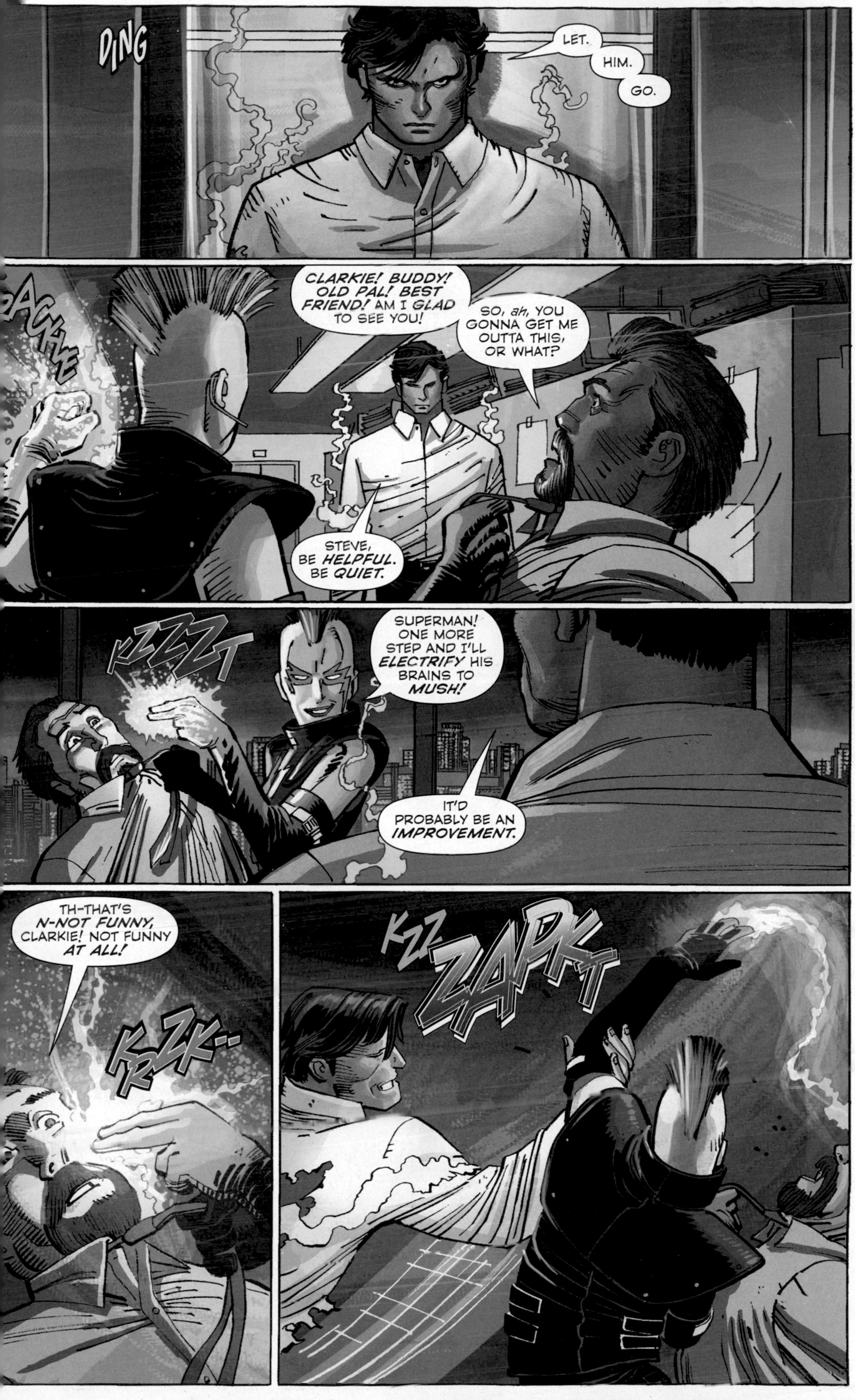
DING
LET.
HIM.
GO.
CLARKIE! BUDDY! OLD PAL! BEST FRIEND! AM I GLAD TO SEE YOU!
SO, ah, YOU GONNA GET ME OUTTA THIS, OR WHAT?
STEVE, BE HELPFUL. BE QUIET.
KZZZZT
SUPERMAN! ONE MORE STEP AND I'LL ELECTRIFY HIS BRAINS TO MUSH!
IT'D PROBABLY BE AN IMPROVEMENT.
TH-THAT'S N-NOT FUNNY, CLARKIE! NOT FUNNY AT ALL!
KRZK...
KZZ
ZAPKT

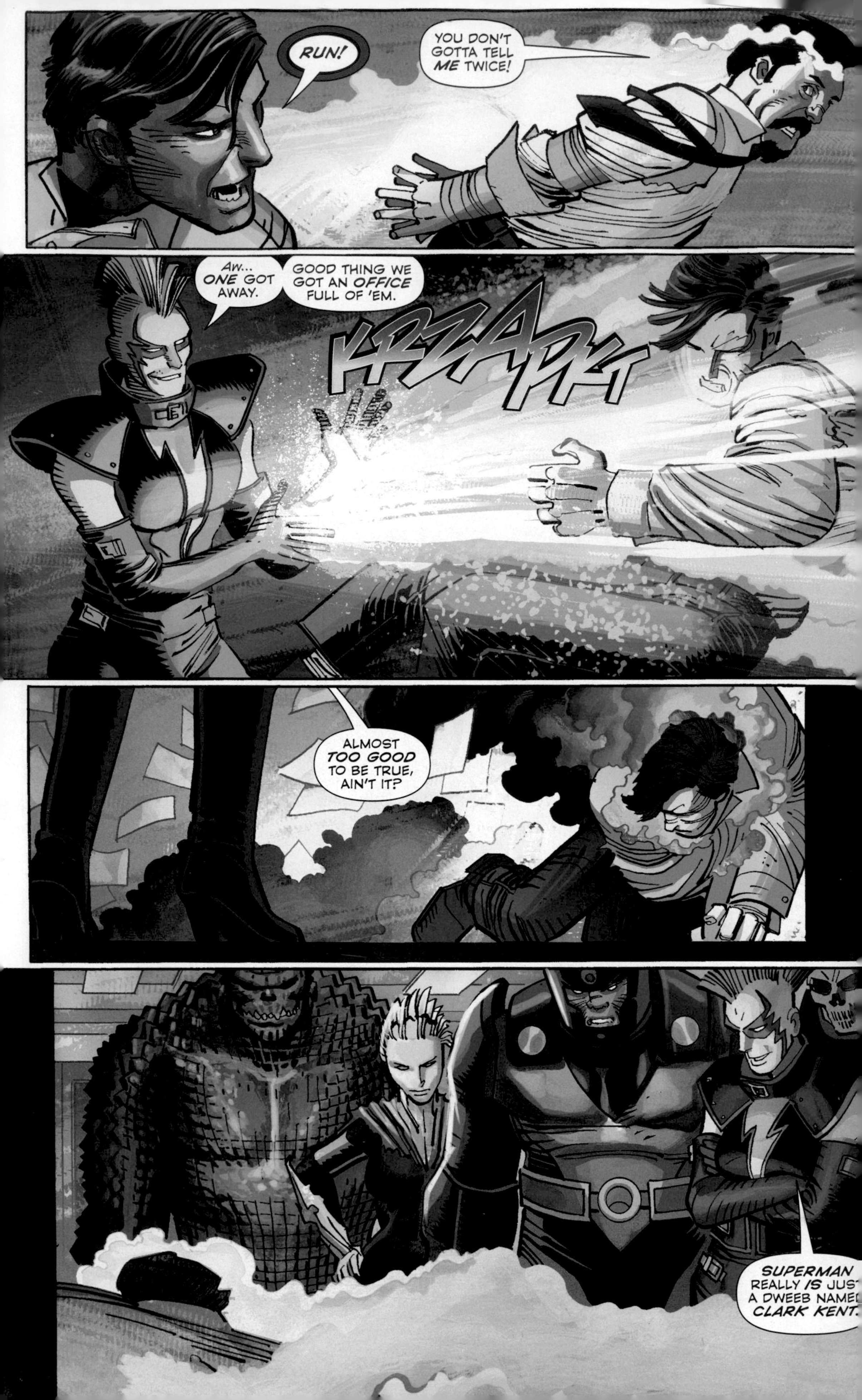
RUN!
YOU DON'T GOTTA TELL ME TWICE!
AW... ONE GOT AWAY.
GOOD THING WE GOT AN OFFICE FULL OF 'EM.
KRZAAKT
ALMOST TOO GOOD TO BE TRUE, AIN'T IT?
SUPERMAN REALLY IS JUST A DWEEB NAMED CLARK KENT.

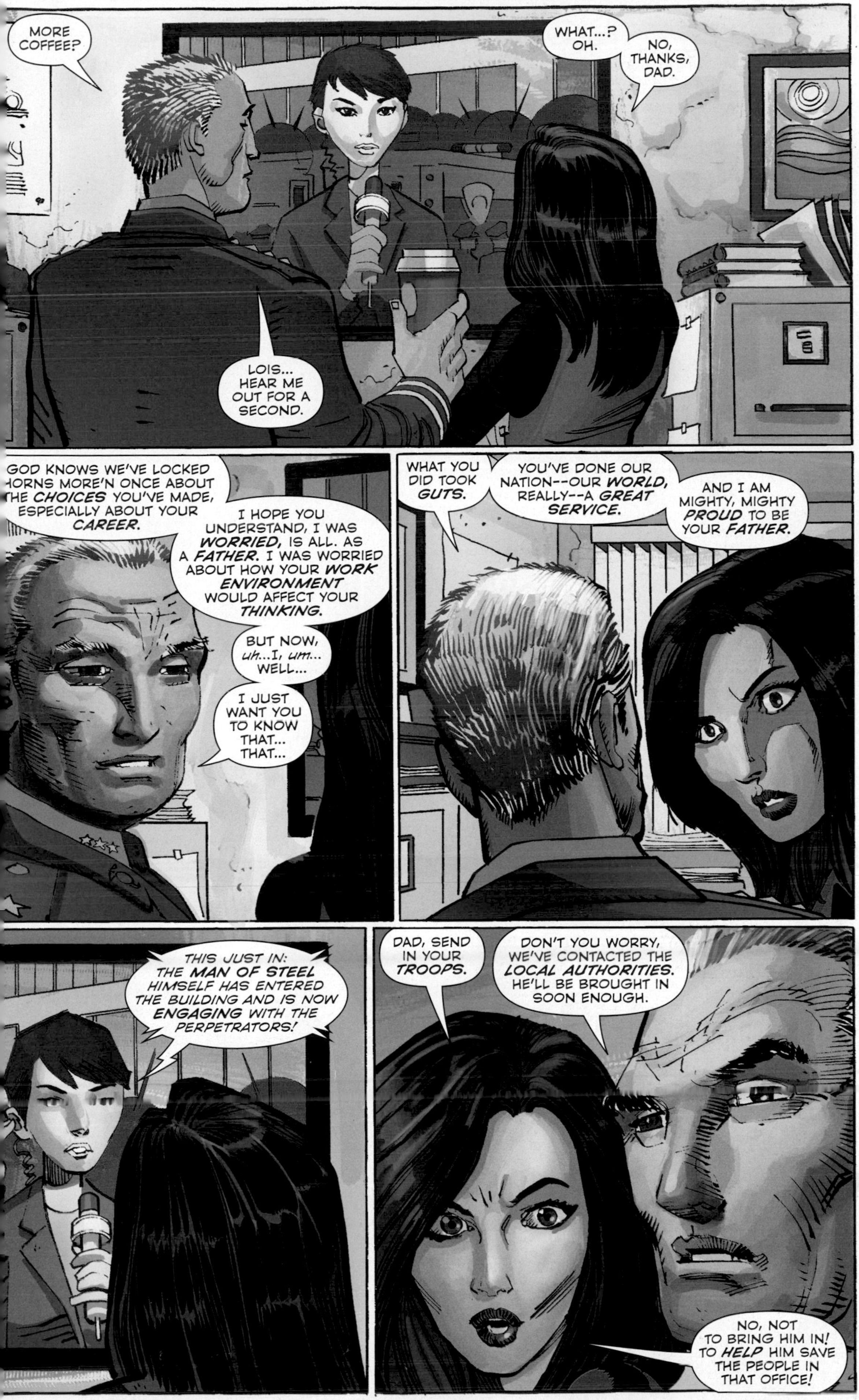
MORE COFFEE?
WHAT...? OH.
NO, THANKS, DAD.
LOIS... HEAR ME OUT FOR A SECOND.
GOD KNOWS WE'VE LOCKED HORNS MORE'N ONCE ABOUT THE *CHOICES* YOU'VE MADE, ESPECIALLY ABOUT YOUR *CAREER.*
I HOPE YOU UNDERSTAND, I WAS *WORRIED,* IS ALL. AS A *FATHER.* I WAS WORRIED ABOUT HOW YOUR *WORK ENVIRONMENT* WOULD AFFECT YOUR *THINKING.*
BUT NOW, *uh*...I, *um*... WELL...
I JUST WANT YOU TO KNOW THAT... THAT...
WHAT YOU DID TOOK *GUTS.*
YOU'VE DONE OUR NATION--OUR *WORLD,* REALLY--A *GREAT SERVICE.*
AND I AM MIGHTY, MIGHTY *PROUD* TO BE YOUR *FATHER.*
THIS JUST IN: THE *MAN OF STEEL* HIMSELF HAS ENTERED THE BUILDING AND IS NOW *ENGAGING* WITH THE PERPETRATORS!
DAD, SEND IN YOUR *TROOPS.*
DON'T YOU WORRY, WE'VE CONTACTED THE *LOCAL AUTHORITIES.* HE'LL BE BROUGHT IN SOON ENOUGH.
NO, NOT TO BRING HIM IN! TO *HELP* HIM SAVE THE PEOPLE IN THAT OFFICE!

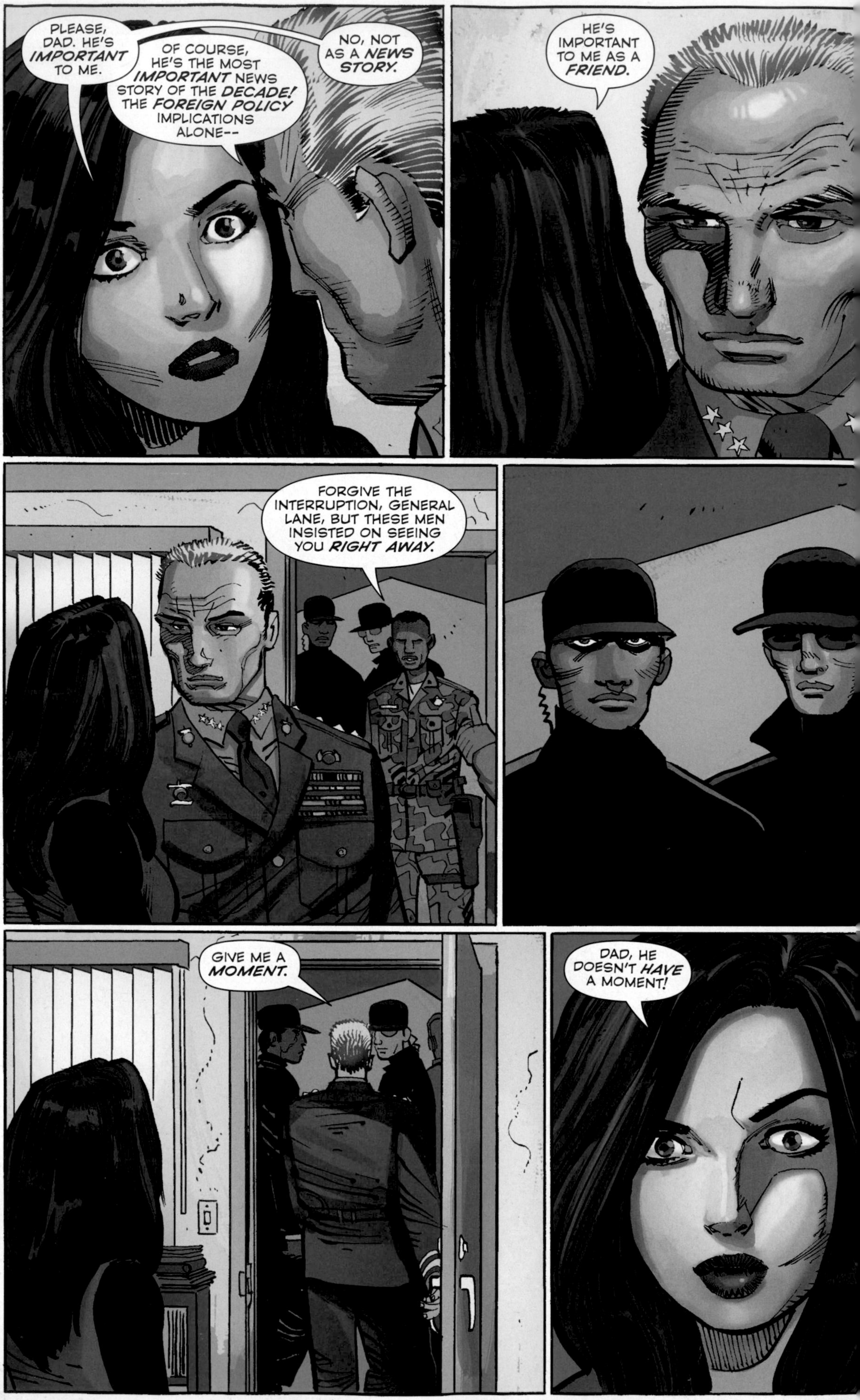
PLEASE, DAD. HE'S IMPORTANT TO ME.
OF COURSE, HE'S THE MOST IMPORTANT NEWS STORY OF THE DECADE! THE FOREIGN POLICY IMPLICATIONS ALONE--
NO, NOT AS A NEWS STORY.
HE'S IMPORTANT TO ME AS A FRIEND.
FORGIVE THE INTERRUPTION, GENERAL LANE, BUT THESE MEN INSISTED ON SEEING YOU RIGHT AWAY.
GIVE ME A MOMENT.
DAD, HE DOESN'T HAVE A MOMENT!

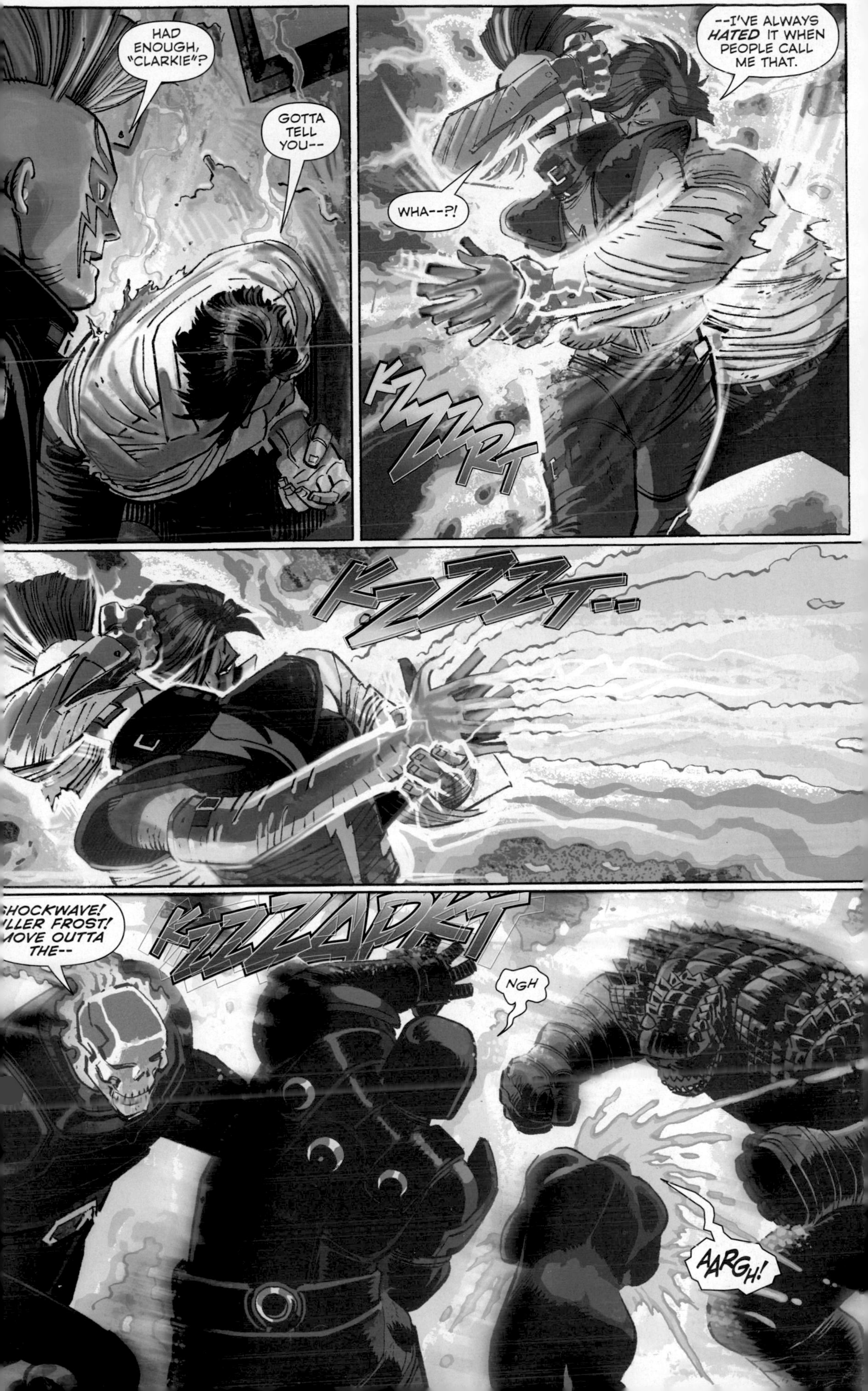
HAD ENOUGH, "CLARKIE"?
GOTTA TELL YOU--
--I'VE ALWAYS *HATED* IT WHEN PEOPLE CALL ME THAT.
WHA--?!
KZZZZRT
KZZZT--
SHOCKWAVE! LLER FROST! MOVE OUTTA THE--
KZZZAPKT
NGH
AARGH!

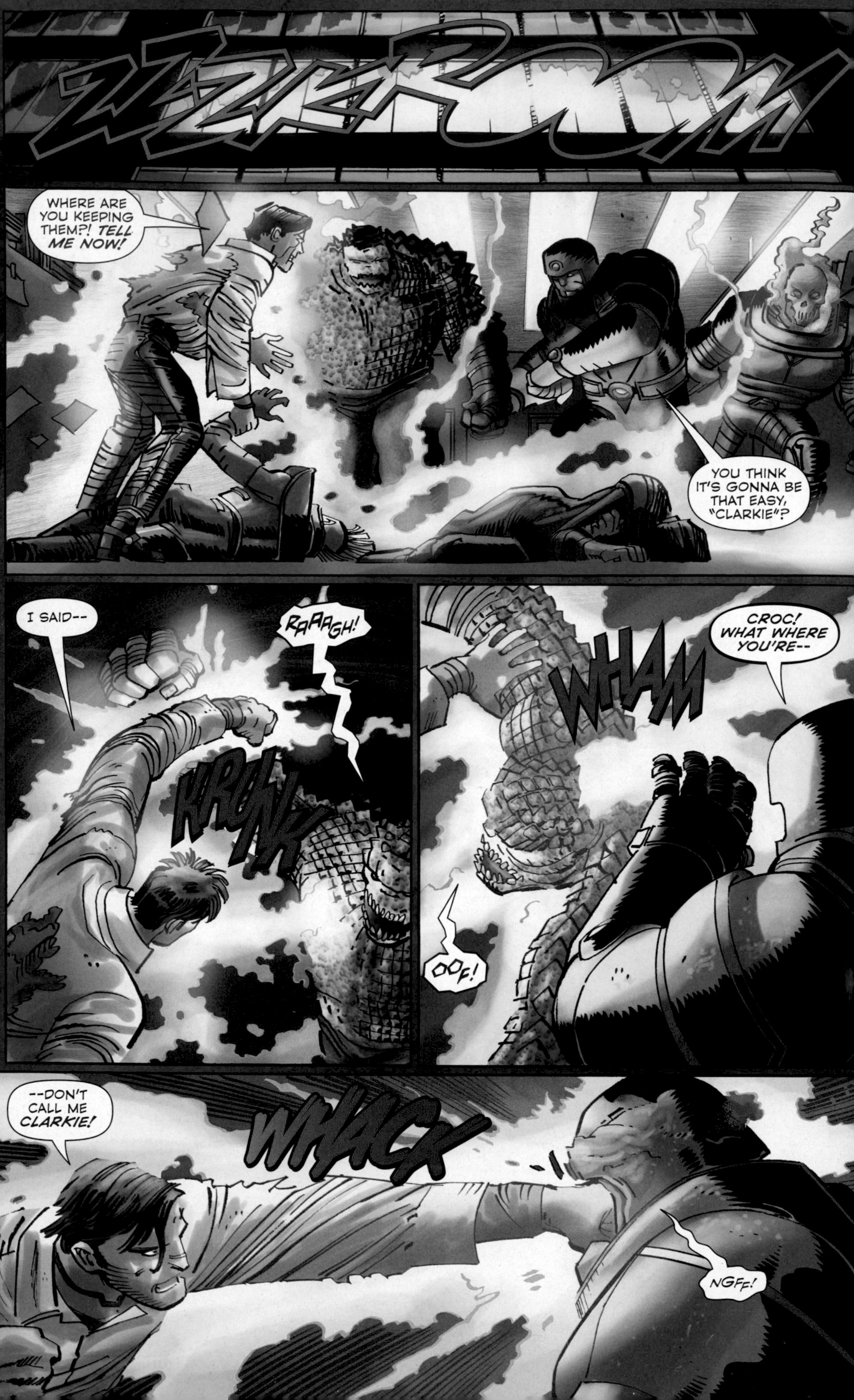
ZZZKROOM
WHERE ARE YOU KEEPING THEM?! TELL ME NOW!
YOU THINK IT'S GONNA BE THAT EASY, "CLARKIE"?
I SAID--
RAAAGH!
KRUNK
WHAM
CROC! WHAT WHERE YOU'RE--
OOF!
--DON'T CALL ME CLARKIE!
WHACK
NGFF!

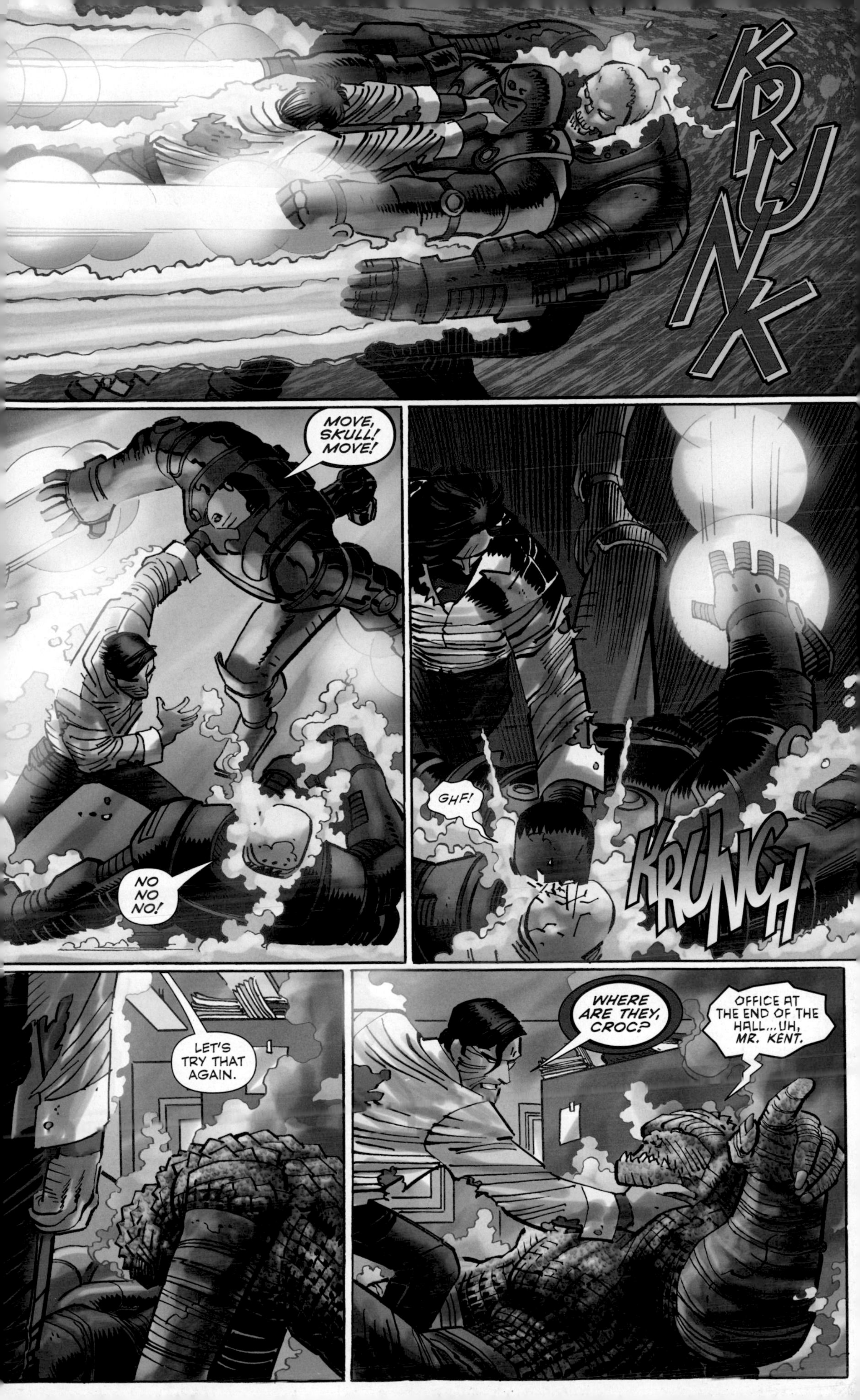
KRUNK
MOVE, SKULL! MOVE!
NO NO NO!
GHF!
KRUNCH
LET'S TRY THAT AGAIN.
WHERE ARE THEY, CROC?
OFFICE AT THE END OF THE HALL...UH, MR. KENT.

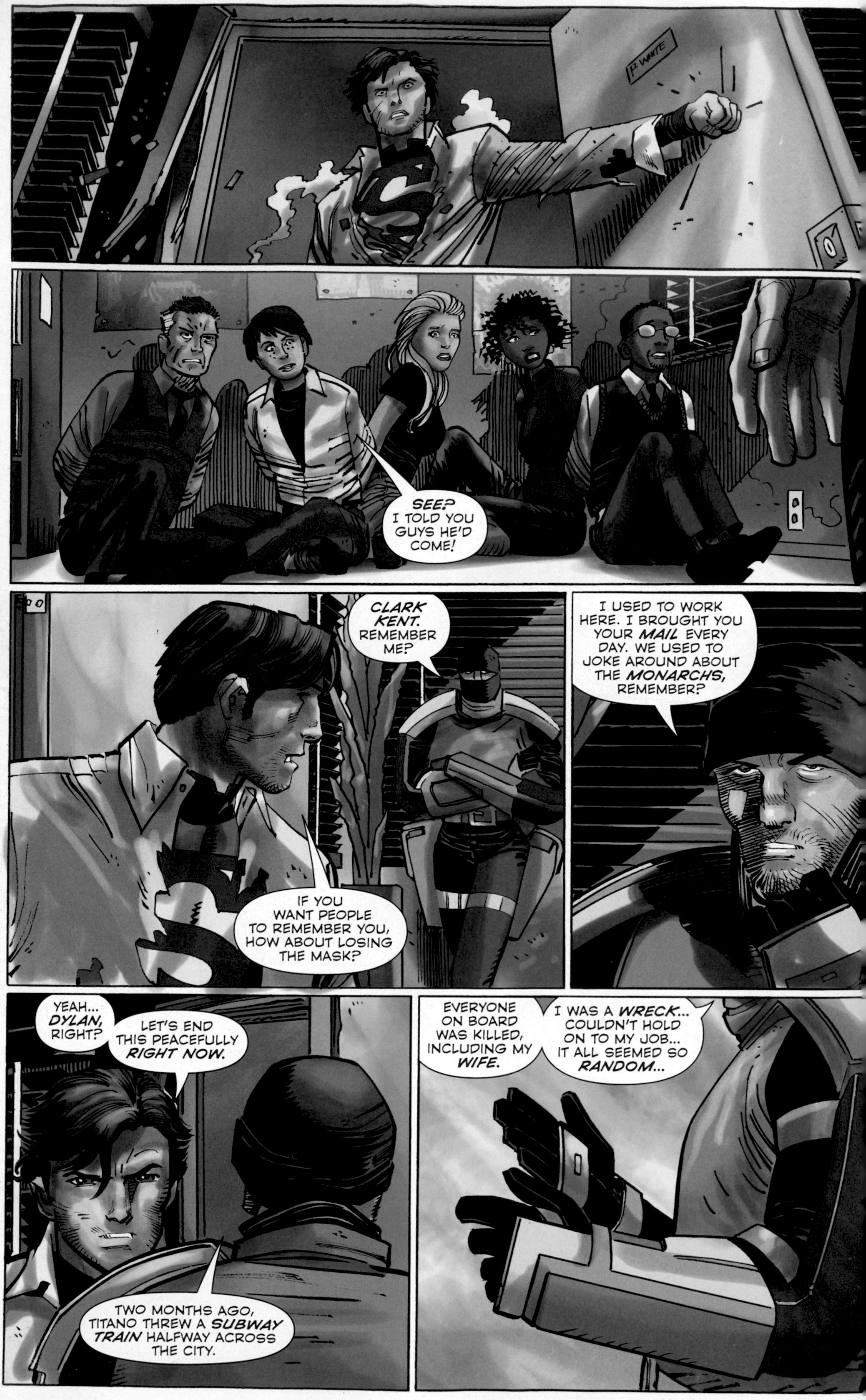
P. WHITE
SEE? I TOLD YOU GUYS HE'D COME!
CLARK KENT. REMEMBER ME?
IF YOU WANT PEOPLE TO REMEMBER YOU, HOW ABOUT LOSING THE MASK?
I USED TO WORK HERE. I BROUGHT YOU YOUR MAIL EVERY DAY. WE USED TO JOKE AROUND ABOUT THE MONARCHS, REMEMBER?
YEAH... DYLAN, RIGHT?
LET'S END THIS PEACEFULLY RIGHT NOW.
TWO MONTHS AGO, TITANO THREW A SUBWAY TRAIN HALFWAY ACROSS THE CITY.
EVERYONE ON BOARD WAS KILLED, INCLUDING MY WIFE.
I WAS A WRECK... COULDN'T HOLD ON TO MY JOB... IT ALL SEEMED SO RANDOM...

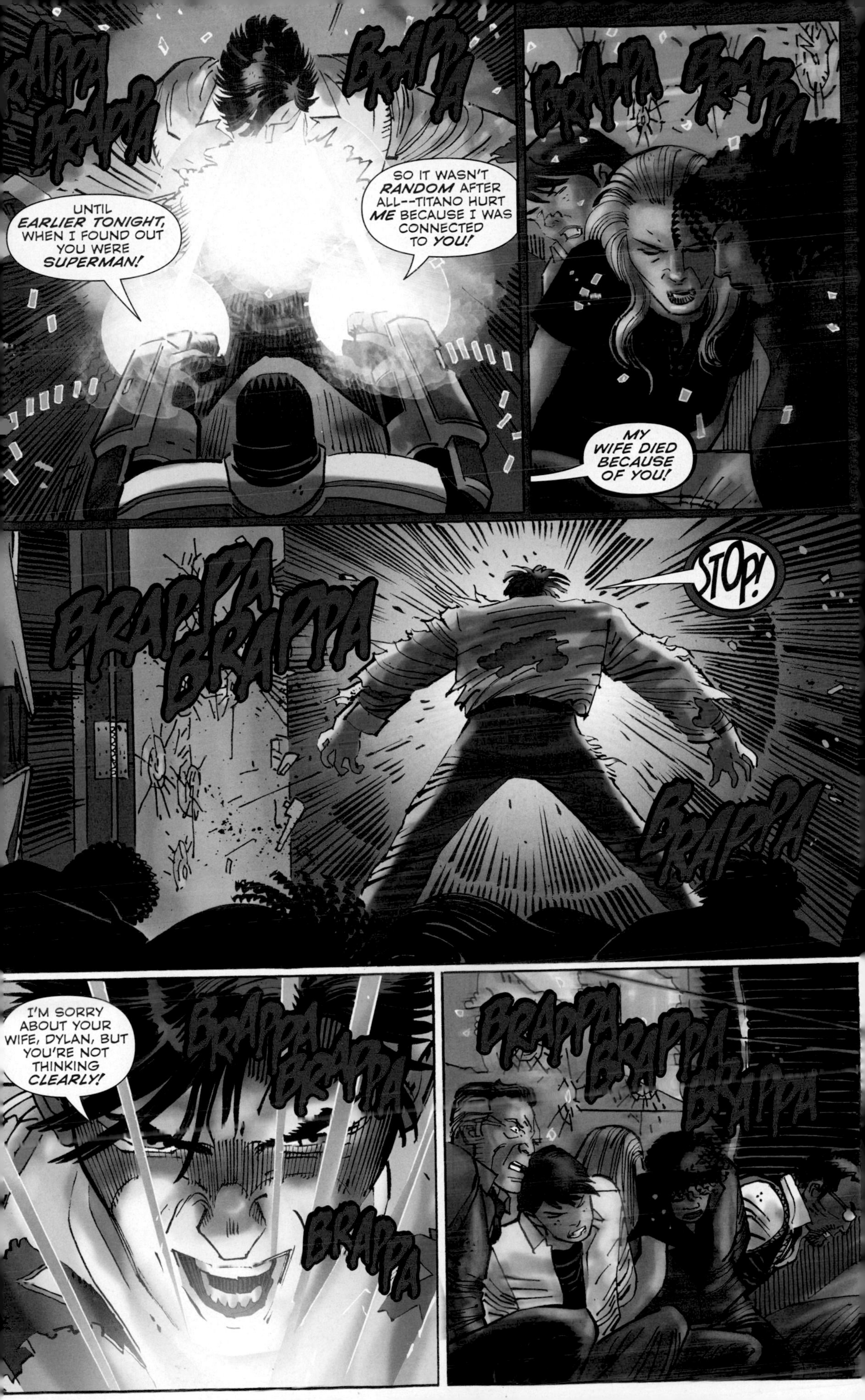
BRAPPA BRAPPA
BRAPPA
UNTIL EARLIER TONIGHT, WHEN I FOUND OUT YOU WERE SUPERMAN!
SO IT WASN'T RANDOM AFTER ALL--TITANO HURT ME BECAUSE I WAS CONNECTED TO YOU!
BRAPPA BRAPPA
MY WIFE DIED BECAUSE OF YOU!
BRAPPA BRAPPA
STOP!
BRAPPA
I'M SORRY ABOUT YOUR WIFE, DYLAN, BUT YOU'RE NOT THINKING CLEARLY!
BRAPPA BRAPPA
BRAPPA
BRAPPA BRAPPA BRAPPA

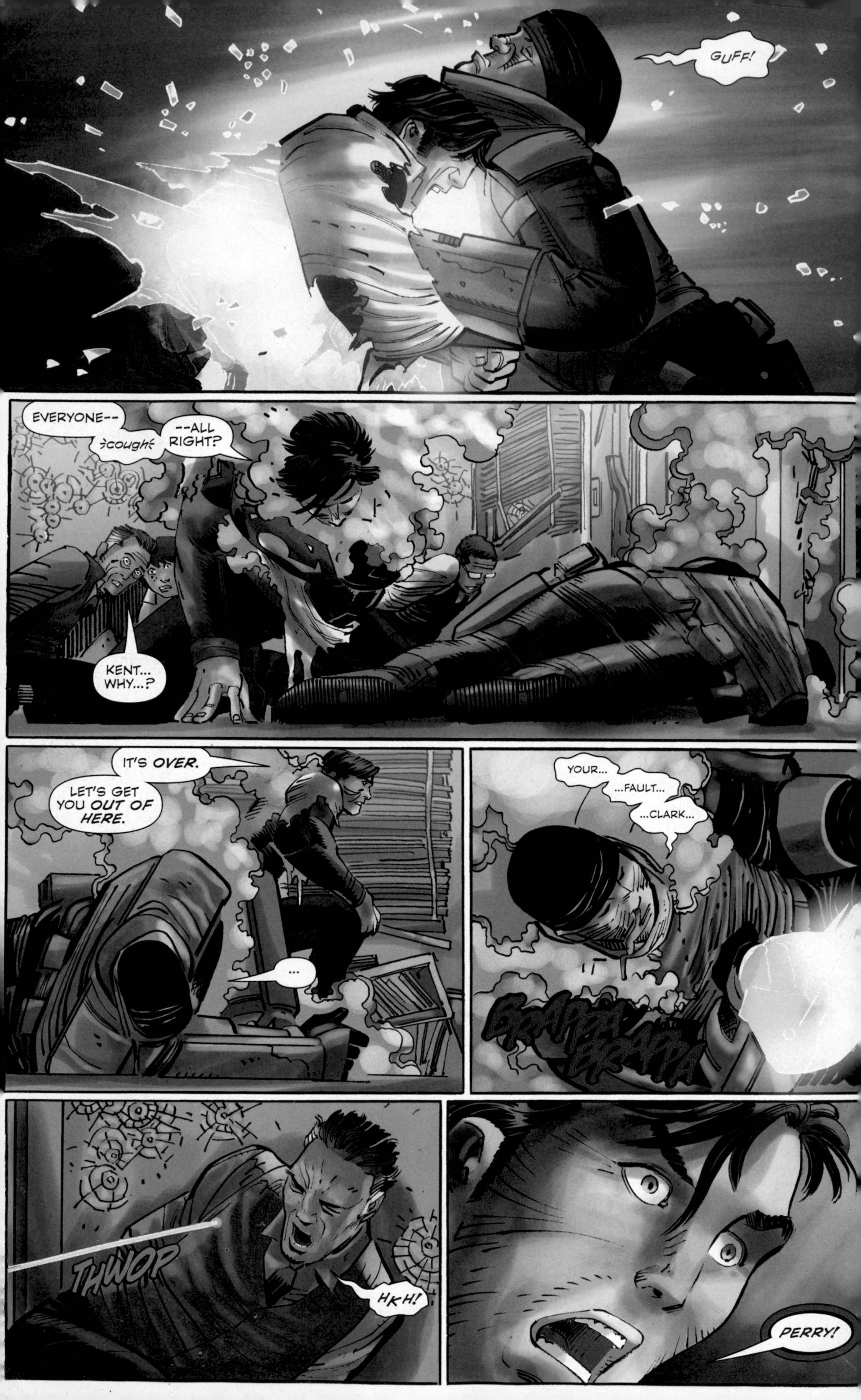
GUFF!
EVERYONE--
>cough<
--ALL RIGHT?
KENT... WHY...?
IT'S OVER.
LET'S GET YOU OUT OF HERE.
...
YOUR...
...FAULT...
...CLARK...
BRAPPA BRAPPA
THWOP
HKH!
PERRY!

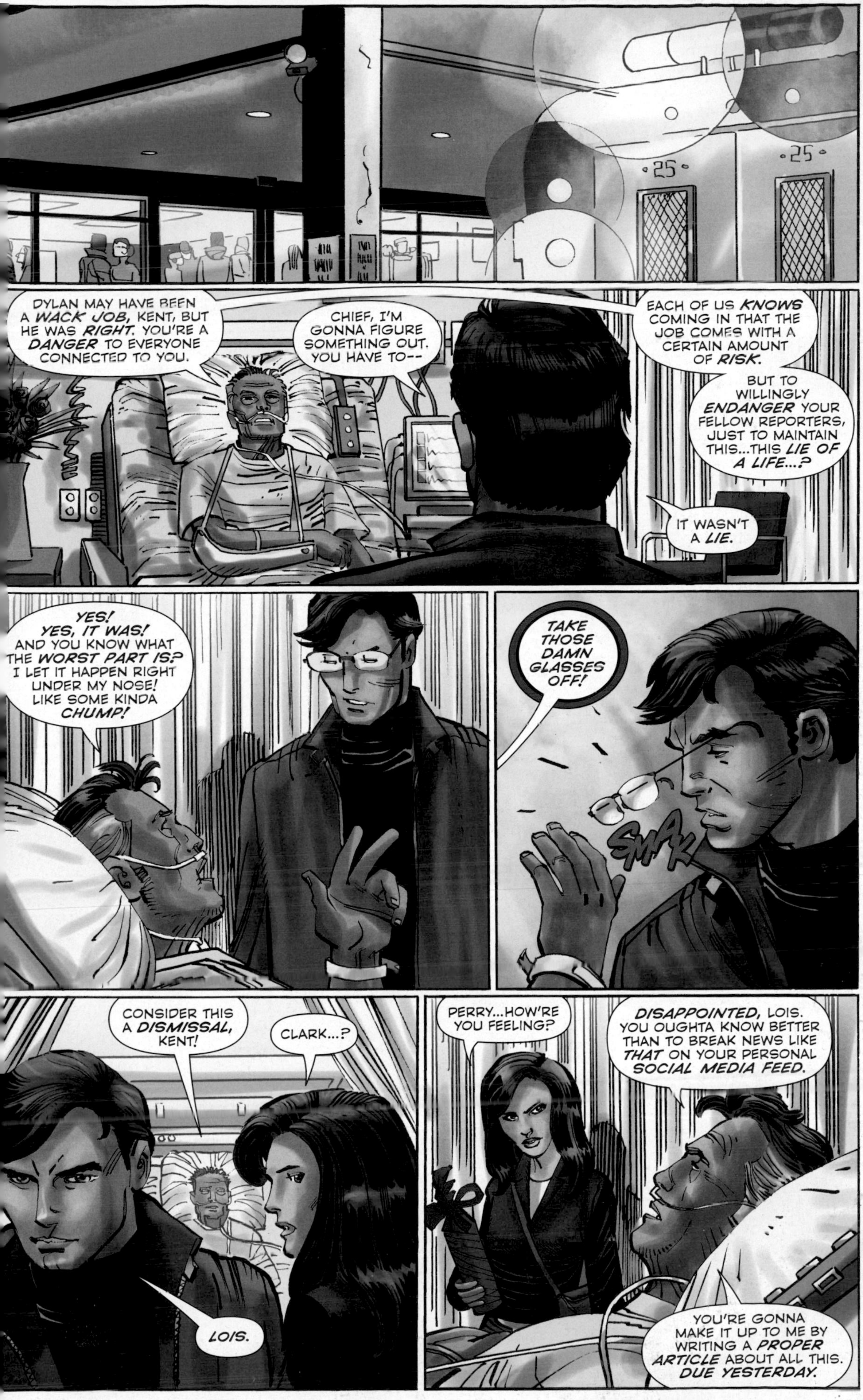
DYLAN MAY HAVE BEEN A WACK JOB, KENT, BUT HE WAS RIGHT. YOU'RE A DANGER TO EVERYONE CONNECTED TO YOU.
CHIEF, I'M GONNA FIGURE SOMETHING OUT. YOU HAVE TO--
EACH OF US KNOWS COMING IN THAT THE JOB COMES WITH A CERTAIN AMOUNT OF RISK.
BUT TO WILLINGLY ENDANGER YOUR FELLOW REPORTERS, JUST TO MAINTAIN THIS...THIS LIE OF A LIFE...?
IT WASN'T A LIE.
YES! YES, IT WAS! AND YOU KNOW WHAT THE WORST PART IS? I LET IT HAPPEN RIGHT UNDER MY NOSE! LIKE SOME KINDA CHUMP!
TAKE THOSE DAMN GLASSES OFF!
SMAK
CONSIDER THIS A DISMISSAL, KENT!
CLARK...?
LOIS.
PERRY...HOW'RE YOU FEELING?
DISAPPOINTED, LOIS. YOU OUGHTA KNOW BETTER THAN TO BREAK NEWS LIKE THAT ON YOUR PERSONAL SOCIAL MEDIA FEED.
YOU'RE GONNA MAKE IT UP TO ME BY WRITING A PROPER ARTICLE ABOUT ALL THIS. DUE YESTERDAY.

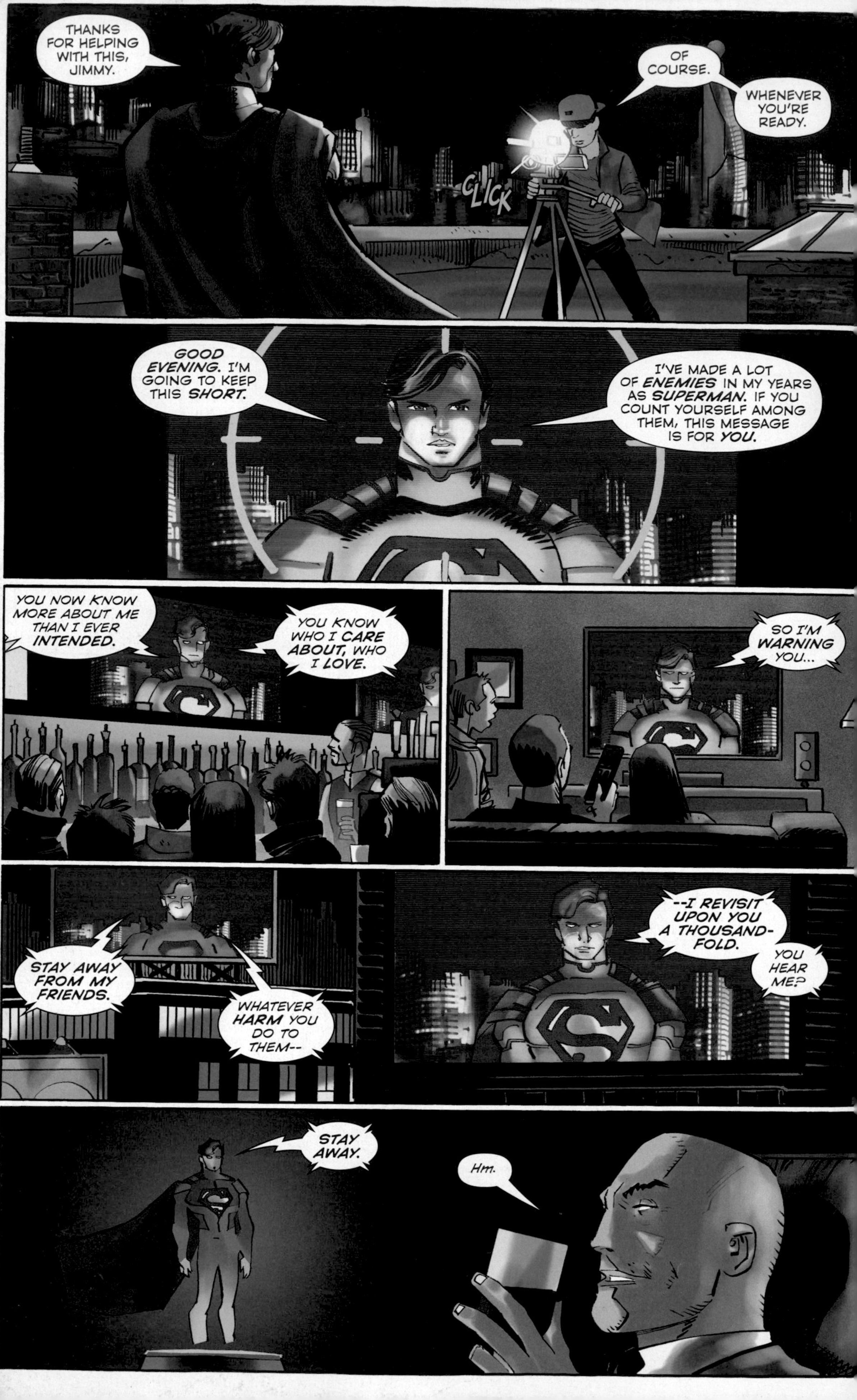
THANKS FOR HELPING WITH THIS, JIMMY.
OF COURSE.
WHENEVER YOU'RE READY.
CLICK
GOOD EVENING. I'M GOING TO KEEP THIS SHORT.
I'VE MADE A LOT OF ENEMIES IN MY YEARS AS SUPERMAN. IF YOU COUNT YOURSELF AMONG THEM, THIS MESSAGE IS FOR YOU.
YOU NOW KNOW MORE ABOUT ME THAN I EVER INTENDED.
YOU KNOW WHO I CARE ABOUT, WHO I LOVE.
SO I'M WARNING YOU...
STAY AWAY FROM MY FRIENDS.
WHATEVER HARM YOU DO TO THEM--
--I REVISIT UPON YOU A THOUSAND-FOLD.
YOU HEAR ME?
STAY AWAY.
Hm.

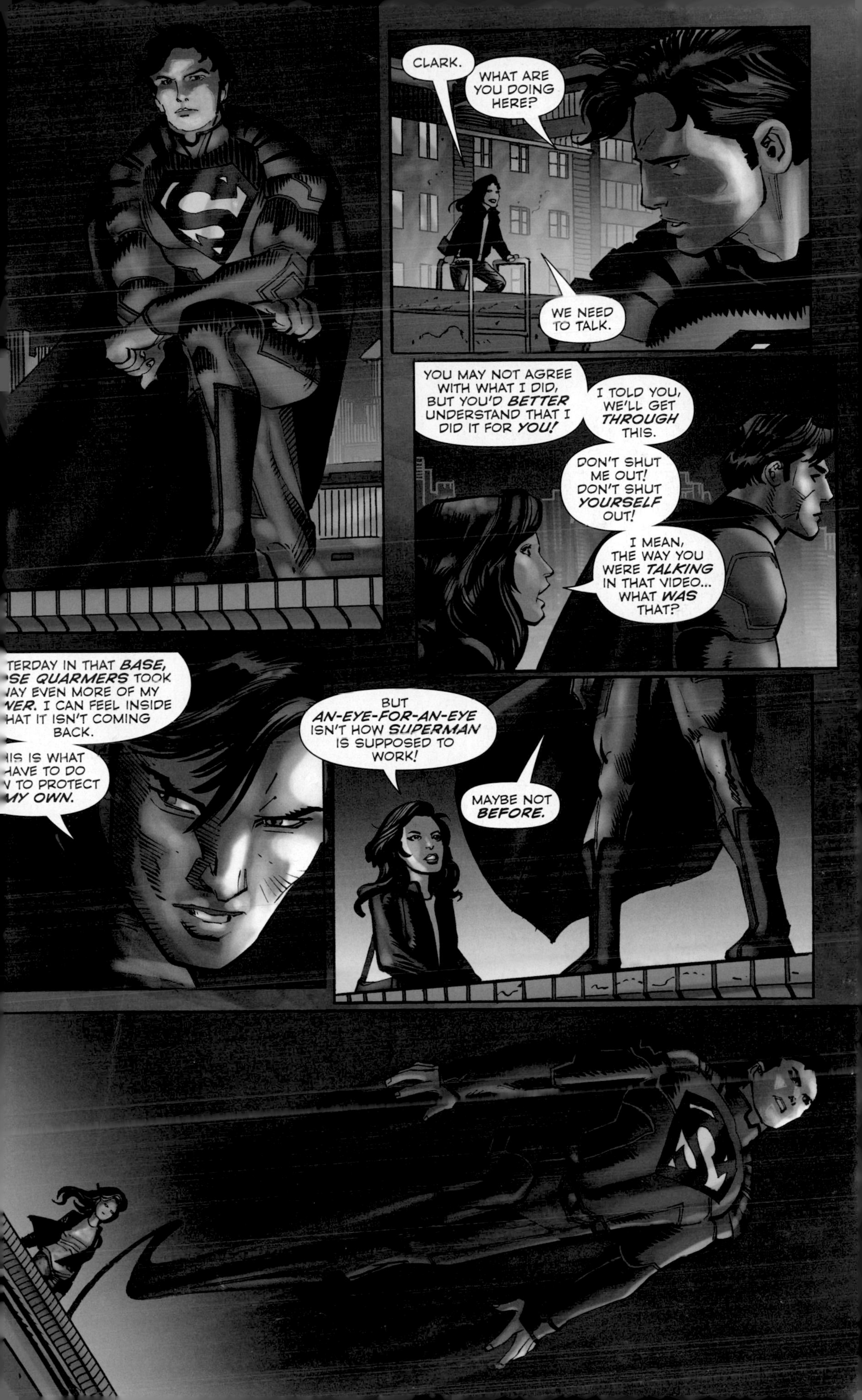
CLARK.
WHAT ARE YOU DOING HERE?
WE NEED TO TALK.
YOU MAY NOT AGREE WITH WHAT I DID, BUT YOU'D BETTER UNDERSTAND THAT I DID IT FOR YOU!
I TOLD YOU, WE'LL GET THROUGH THIS.
DON'T SHUT ME OUT! DON'T SHUT YOURSELF OUT!
I MEAN, THE WAY YOU WERE TALKING IN THAT VIDEO... WHAT WAS THAT?
TERDAY IN THAT BASE, OSE QUARMERS TOOK VAY EVEN MORE OF MY VER. I CAN FEEL INSIDE HAT IT ISN'T COMING BACK.
HIS IS WHAT HAVE TO DO V TO PROTECT MY OWN.
BUT AN-EYE-FOR-AN-EYE ISN'T HOW SUPERMAN IS SUPPOSED TO WORK!
MAYBE NOT BEFORE.

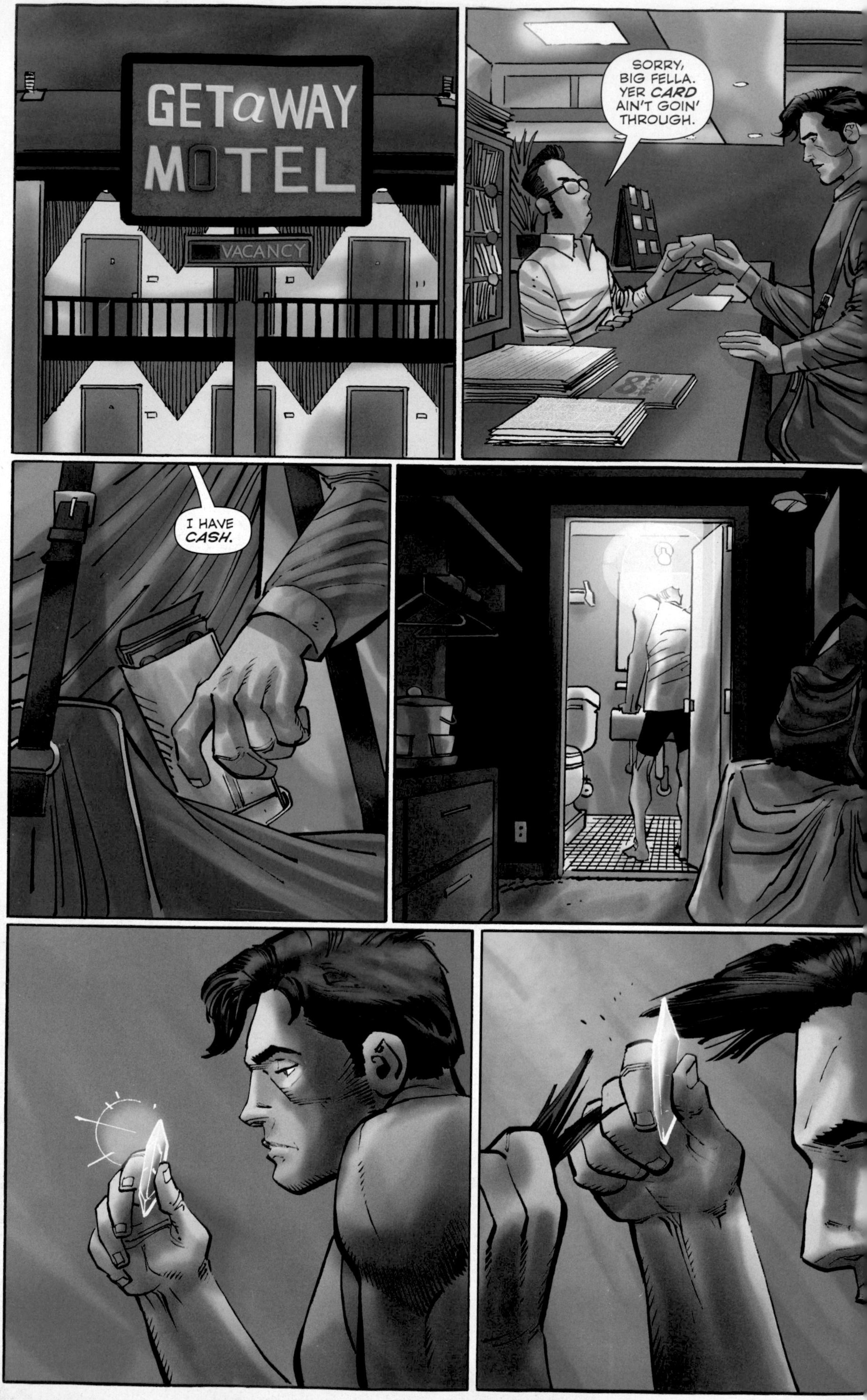
GETaWAY
MOTEL
VACANCY
SORRY, BIG FELLA. YER CARD AIN'T GOIN' THROUGH.
I HAVE CASH.

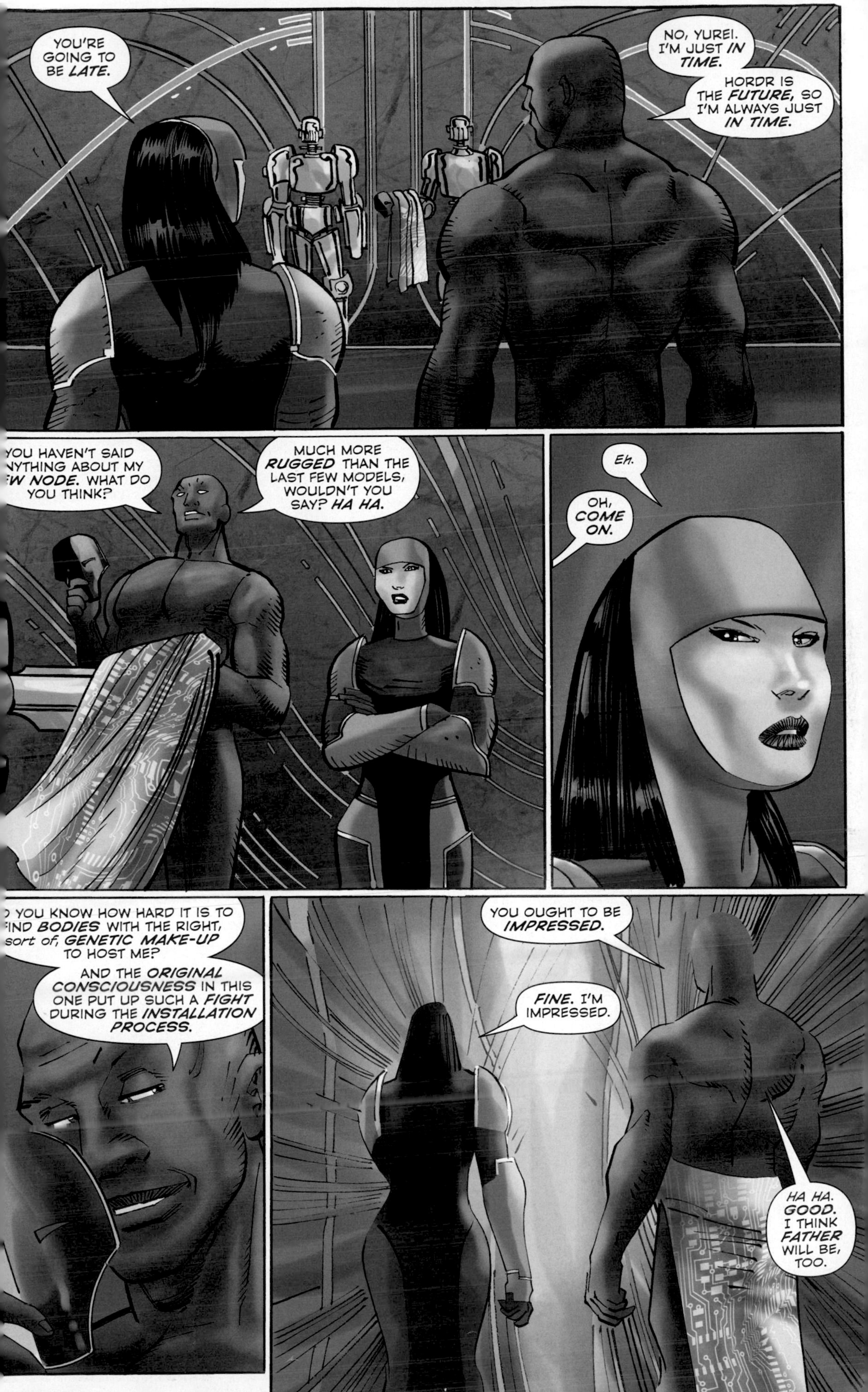
YOU'RE GOING TO BE LATE.
NO, YUREI. I'M JUST IN TIME.
HORDR IS THE FUTURE, SO I'M ALWAYS JUST IN TIME.
YOU HAVEN'T SAID NYTHING ABOUT MY EW NODE. WHAT DO YOU THINK?
MUCH MORE RUGGED THAN THE LAST FEW MODELS, WOULDN'T YOU SAY? HA HA.
Eh.
OH, COME ON.
O YOU KNOW HOW HARD IT IS TO FIND BODIES WITH THE RIGHT, sort of, GENETIC MAKE-UP TO HOST ME?
AND THE ORIGINAL CONSCIOUSNESS IN THIS ONE PUT UP SUCH A FIGHT DURING THE INSTALLATION PROCESS.
YOU OUGHT TO BE IMPRESSED.
FINE. I'M IMPRESSED.
HA HA. GOOD. I THINK FATHER WILL BE, TOO.

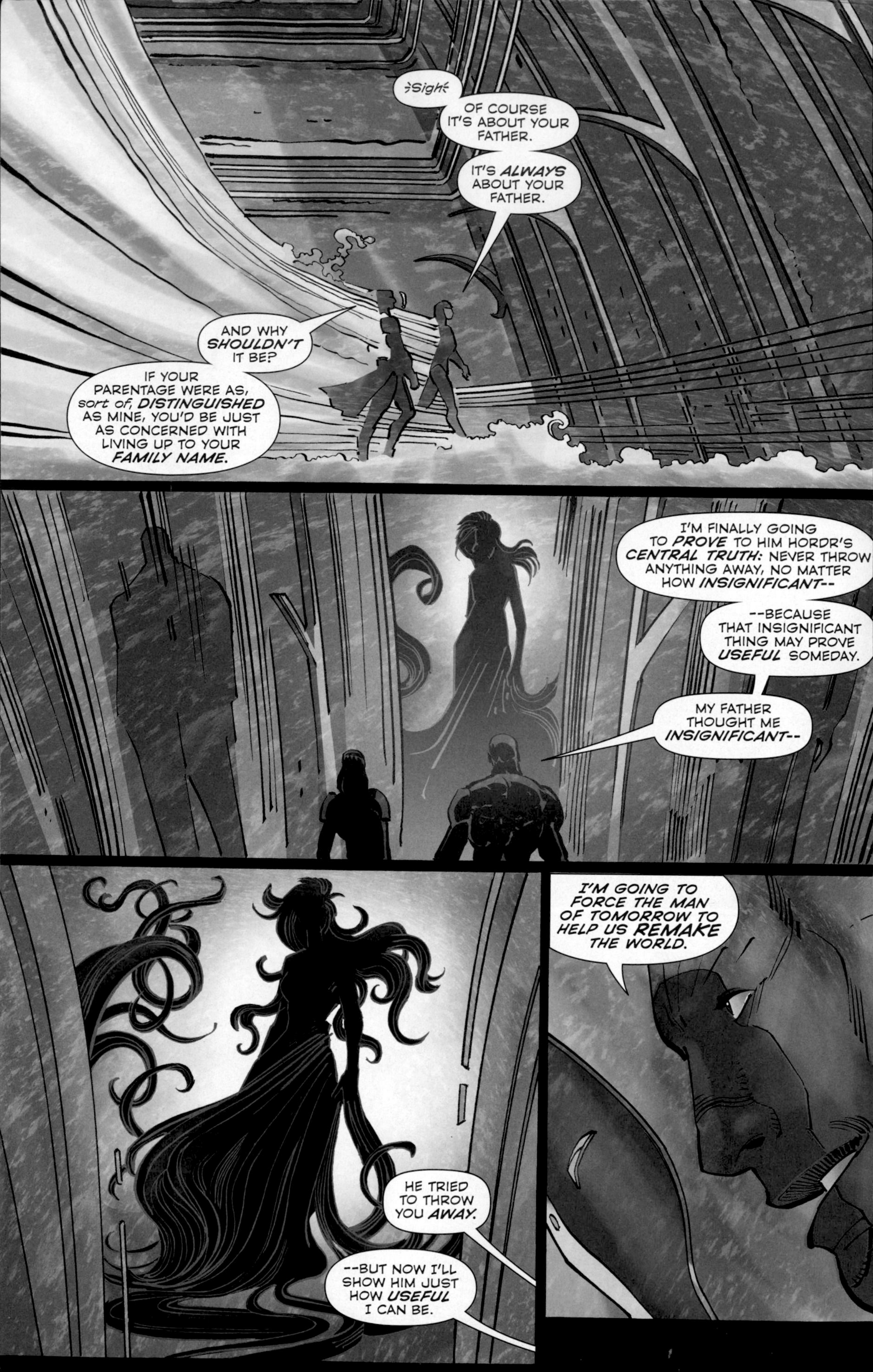

Sigh
OF COURSE IT'S ABOUT YOUR FATHER.
IT'S ALWAYS ABOUT YOUR FATHER.
AND WHY SHOULDN'T IT BE?
IF YOUR PARENTAGE WERE AS, sort of, DISTINGUISHED AS MINE, YOU'D BE JUST AS CONCERNED WITH LIVING UP TO YOUR FAMILY NAME.
I'M FINALLY GOING TO PROVE TO HIM HORDR'S CENTRAL TRUTH: NEVER THROW ANYTHING AWAY, NO MATTER HOW INSIGNIFICANT--
--BECAUSE THAT INSIGNIFICANT THING MAY PROVE USEFUL SOMEDAY.
MY FATHER THOUGHT ME INSIGNIFICANT--
HE TRIED TO THROW YOU AWAY.
--BUT NOW I'LL SHOW HIM JUST HOW USEFUL I CAN BE.
I'M GOING TO FORCE THE MAN OF TOMORROW TO HELP US REMAKE THE WORLD.

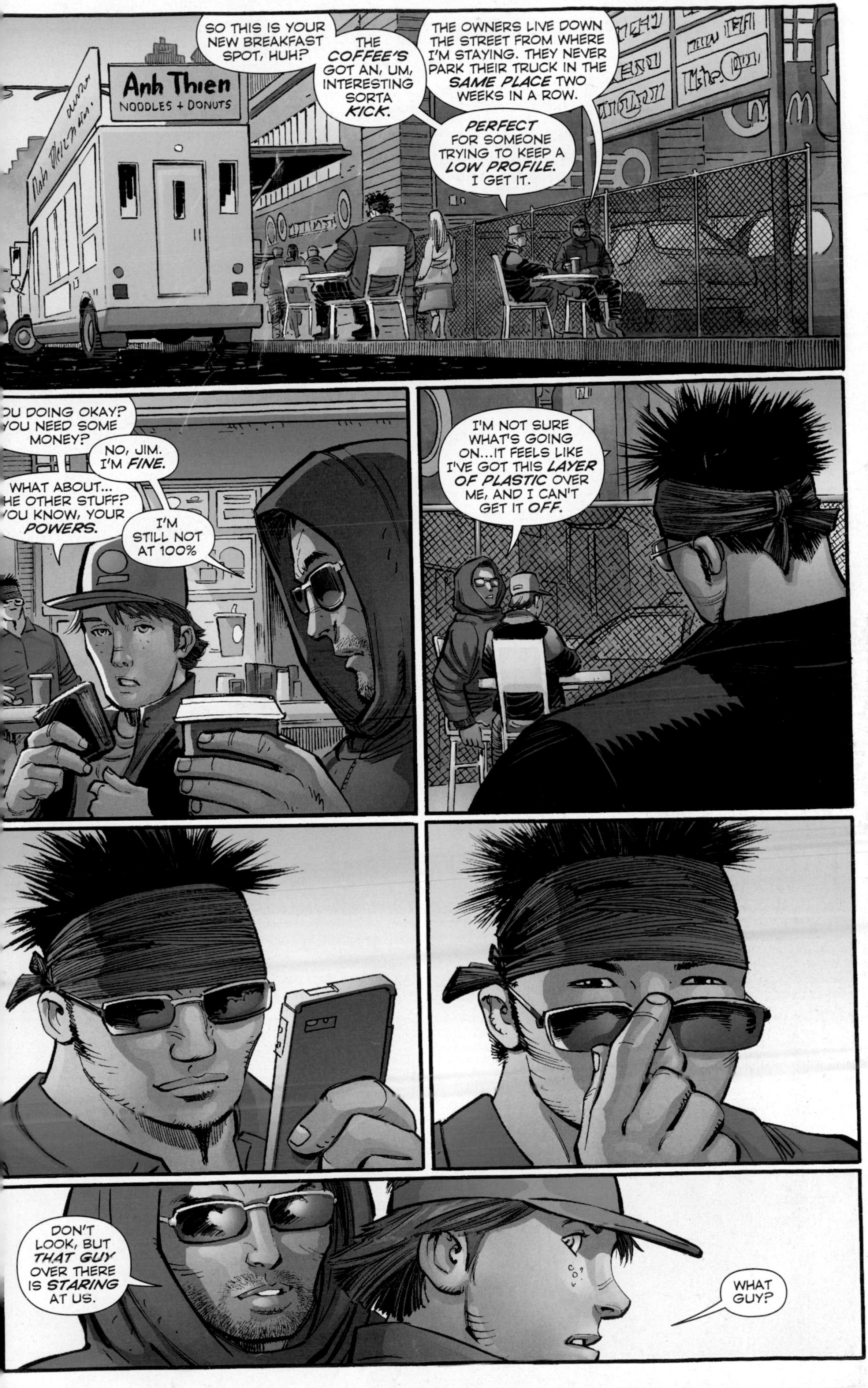

Anh Thien
NOODLES + DONUTS
SO THIS IS YOUR NEW BREAKFAST SPOT, HUH?
THE COFFEE'S GOT AN, UM, INTERESTING SORTA KICK.
THE OWNERS LIVE DOWN THE STREET FROM WHERE I'M STAYING. THEY NEVER PARK THEIR TRUCK IN THE SAME PLACE TWO WEEKS IN A ROW.
PERFECT FOR SOMEONE TRYING TO KEEP A LOW PROFILE. I GET IT.
OU DOING OKAY? YOU NEED SOME MONEY?
NO, JIM. I'M FINE.
WHAT ABOUT... HE OTHER STUFF? OU KNOW, YOUR POWERS.
I'M STILL NOT AT 100%
I'M NOT SURE WHAT'S GOING ON...IT FEELS LIKE I'VE GOT THIS LAYER OF PLASTIC OVER ME, AND I CAN'T GET IT OFF.
DON'T LOOK, BUT THAT GUY OVER THERE IS STARING AT US.
WHAT GUY?

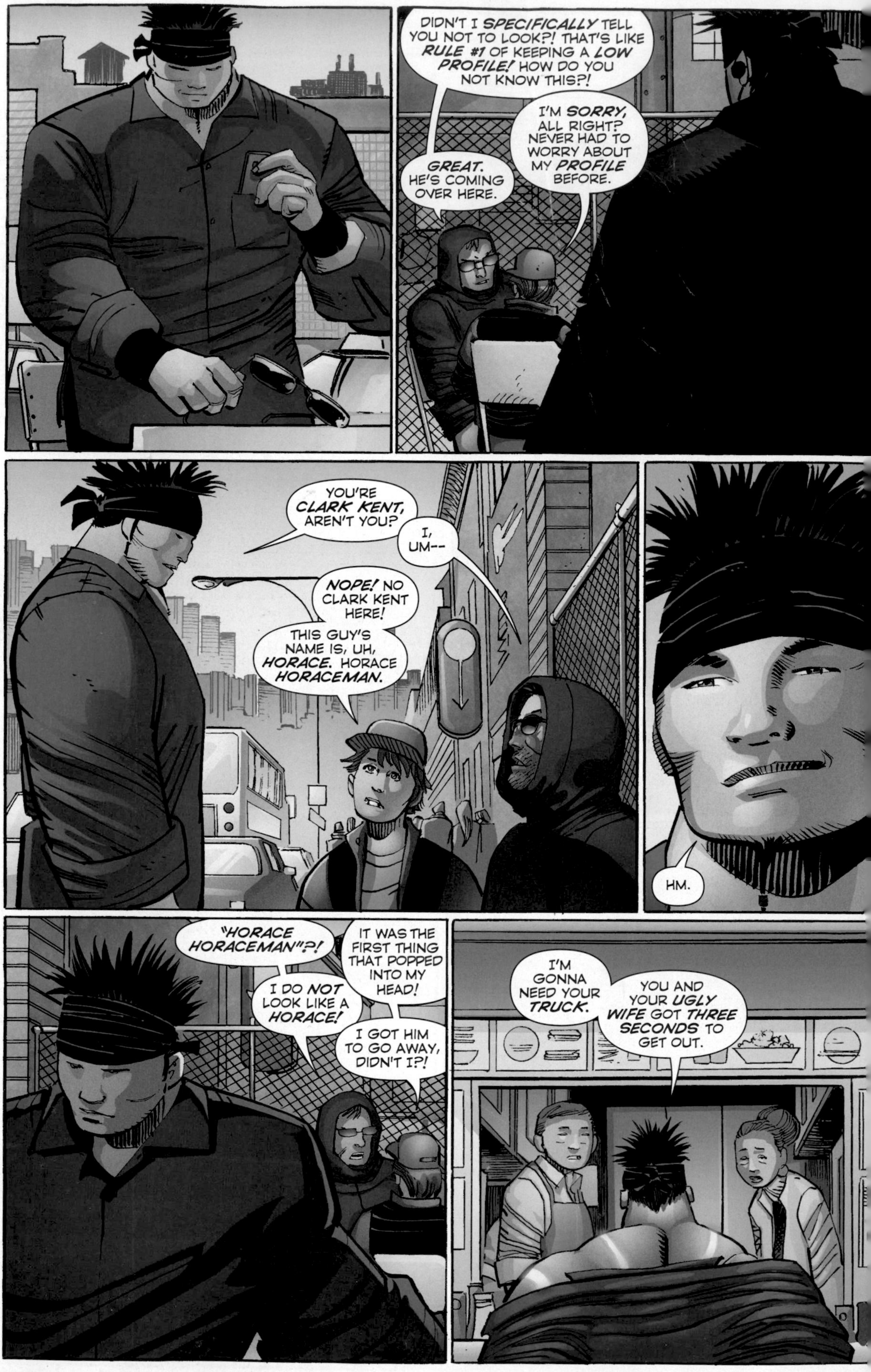

DIDN'T I SPECIFICALLY TELL YOU NOT TO LOOK?! THAT'S LIKE RULE #1 OF KEEPING A LOW PROFILE! HOW DO YOU NOT KNOW THIS?!
I'M SORRY, ALL RIGHT? NEVER HAD TO WORRY ABOUT MY PROFILE BEFORE.
GREAT. HE'S COMING OVER HERE.
YOU'RE CLARK KENT, AREN'T YOU?
I, UM--
NOPE! NO CLARK KENT HERE!
THIS GUY'S NAME IS, UH, HORACE. HORACE HORACEMAN.
HM.
"HORACE HORACEMAN"?!
I DO NOT LOOK LIKE A HORACE!
IT WAS THE FIRST THING THAT POPPED INTO MY HEAD!
I GOT HIM TO GO AWAY, DIDN'T I?!
I'M GONNA NEED YOUR TRUCK.
YOU AND YOUR UGLY WIFE GOT THREE SECONDS TO GET OUT.

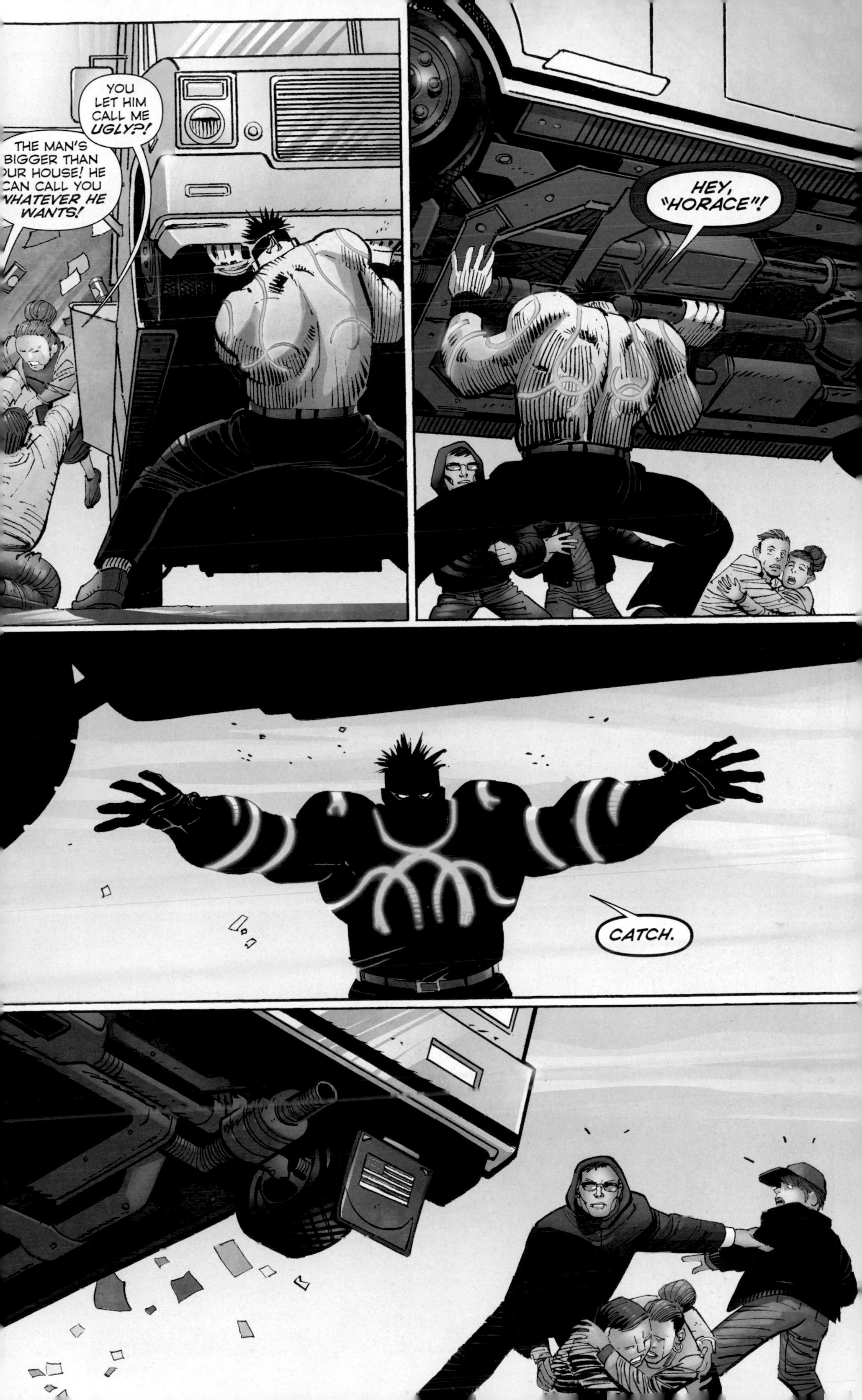
YOU LET HIM CALL ME UGLY?!
THE MAN'S BIGGER THAN OUR HOUSE! HE CAN CALL YOU WHATEVER HE WANTS!
HEY, "HORACE"!
CATCH.

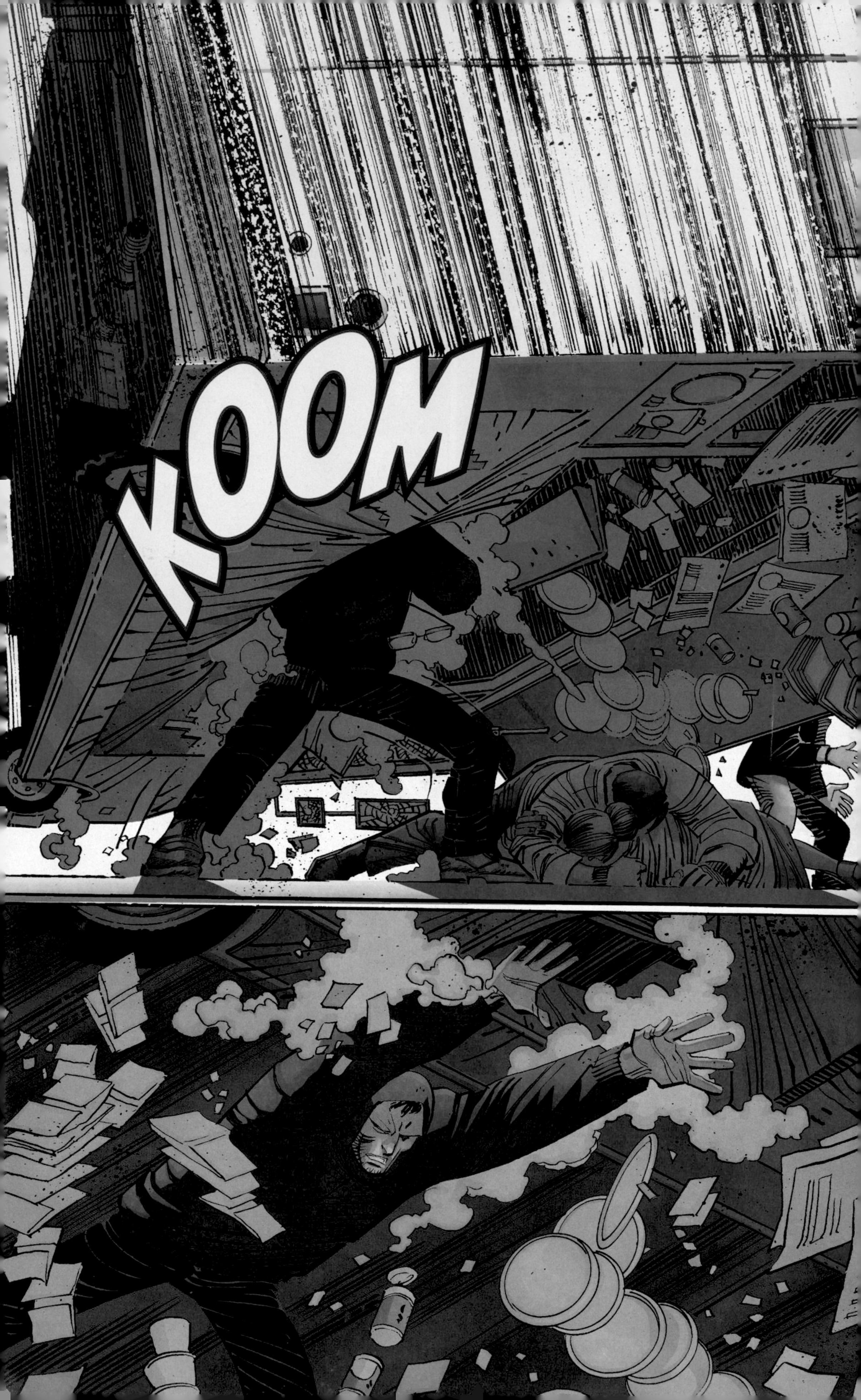
KOOM

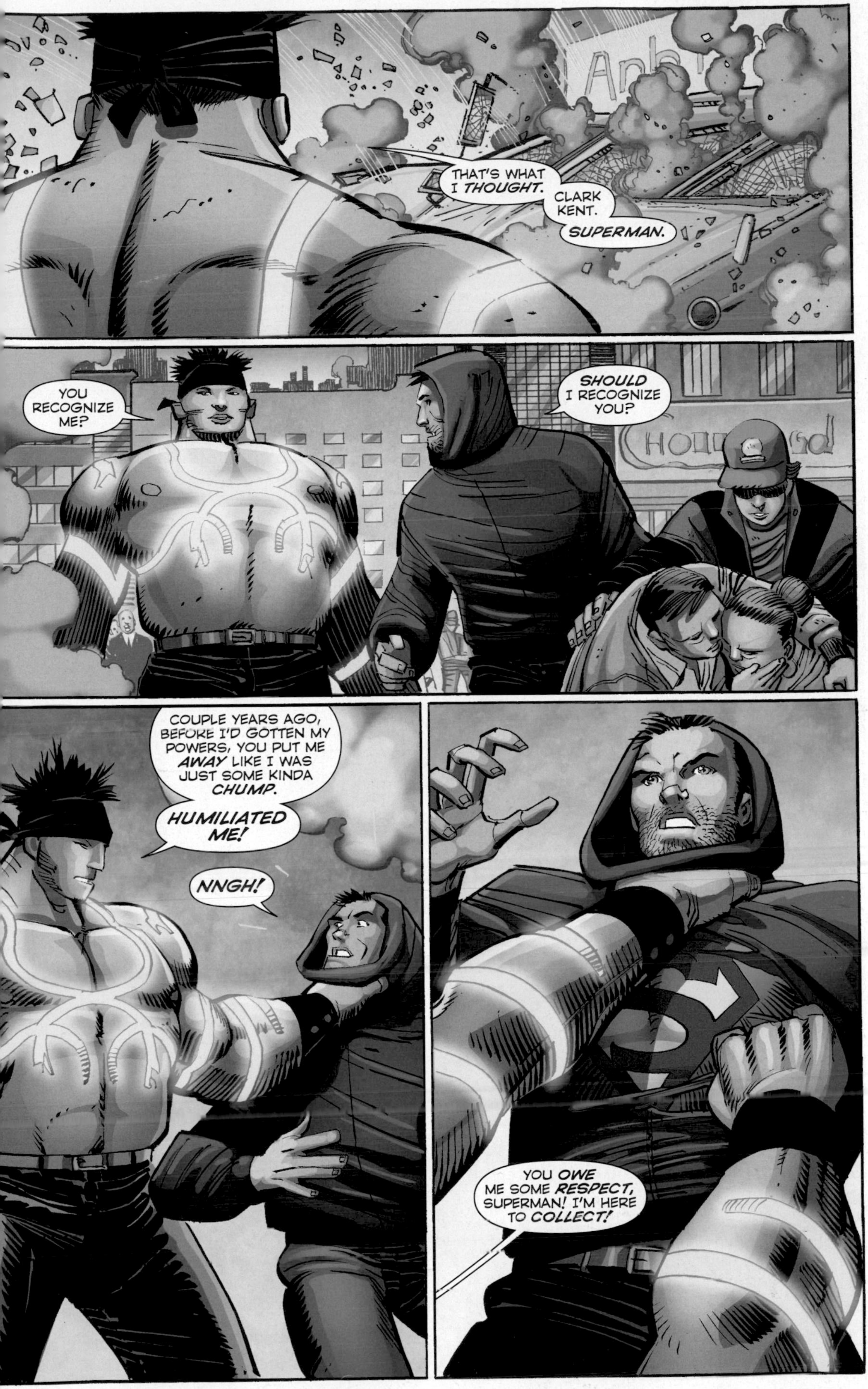
THAT'S WHAT I *THOUGHT*.
CLARK KENT.
SUPERMAN.
YOU RECOGNIZE ME?
SHOULD I RECOGNIZE YOU?
COUPLE YEARS AGO, BEFORE I'D GOTTEN MY POWERS, YOU PUT ME *AWAY* LIKE I WAS JUST SOME KINDA *CHUMP*.
HUMILIATED ME!
NNGH!
YOU *OWE* ME SOME *RESPECT*, SUPERMAN! I'M HERE TO *COLLECT!*

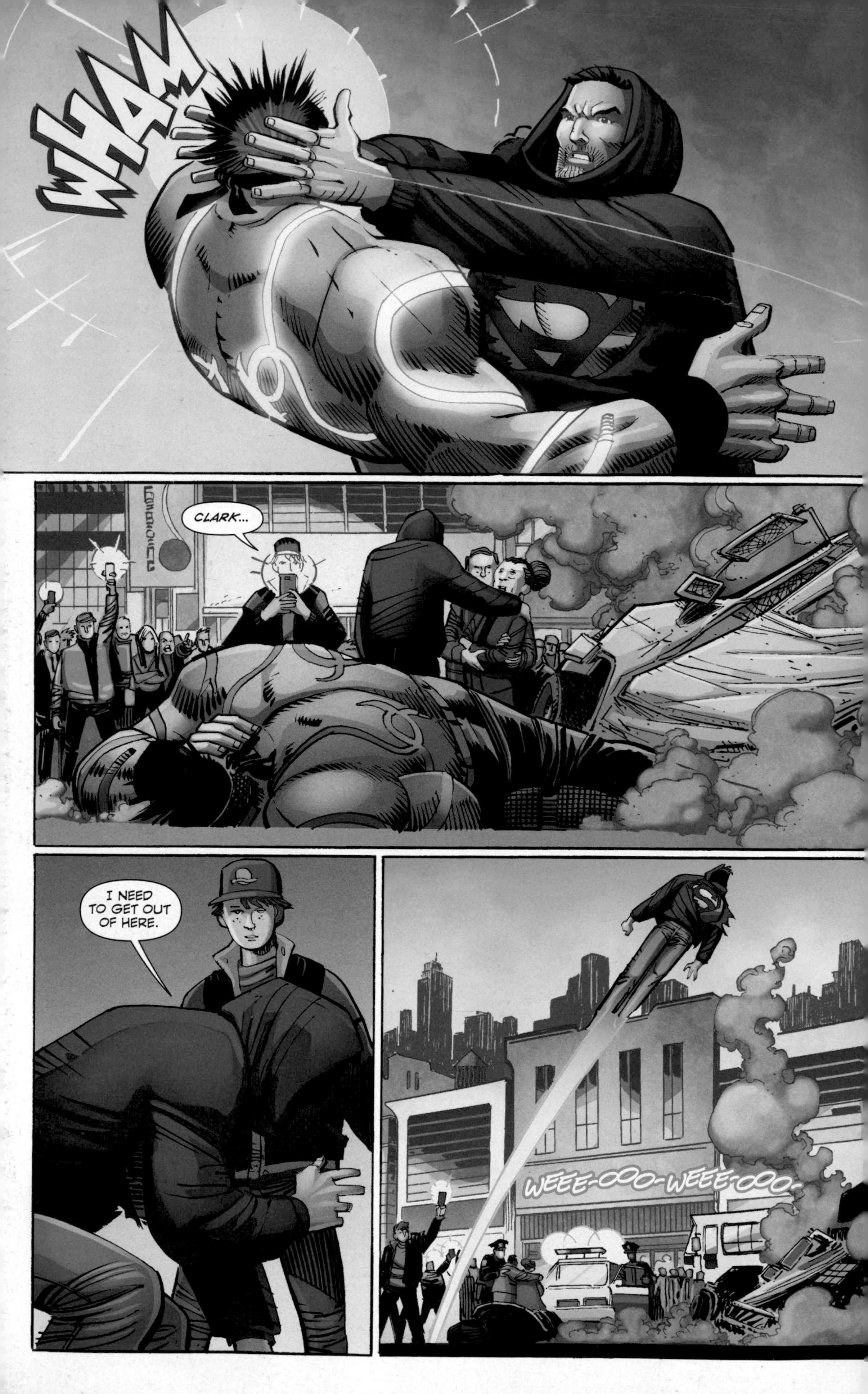
WHAM
CLARK...
I NEED TO GET OUT OF HERE.
WEEE-OOO-WEEE-OOO-

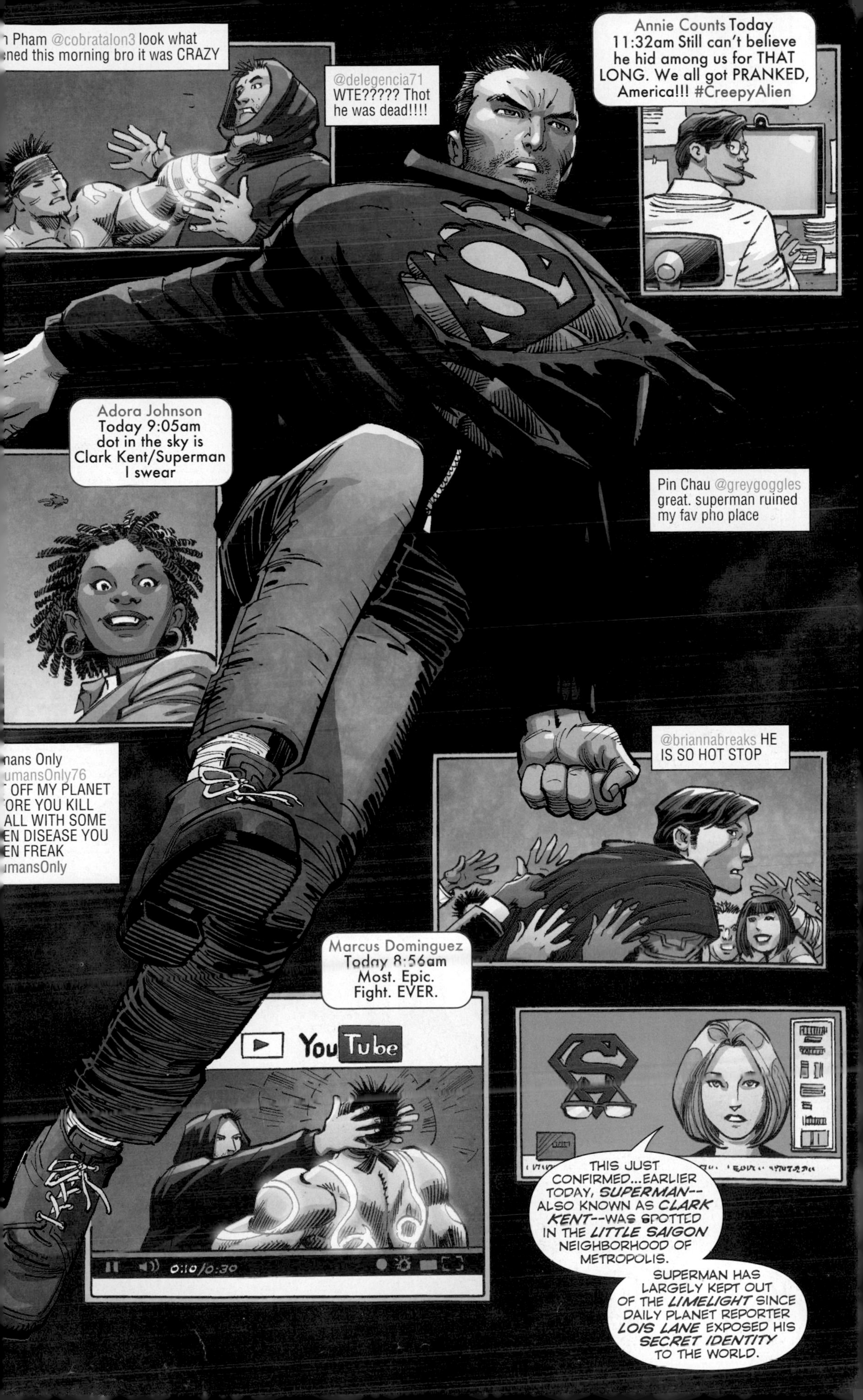

n Pham @cobratalon3 look what
ened this morning bro it was CRAZY
@delegencia71
WTE????? Thot
he was dead!!!!
Annie Counts Today
11:32am Still can't believe
he hid among us for THAT
LONG. We all got PRANKED,
America!!! #CreepyAlien
Adora Johnson
Today 9:05am
dot in the sky is
Clark Kent/Superman
I swear
Pin Chau @greygoggles
great. superman ruined
my fav pho place
nans Only
umansOnly76
T OFF MY PLANET
ORE YOU KILL
ALL WITH SOME
EN DISEASE YOU
EN FREAK
umansOnly
@briannabreaks HE
IS SO HOT STOP
Marcus Dominguez
Today 8:56am
Most. Epic.
Fight. EVER.
YouTube
0:10/0:30
THIS JUST CONFIRMED...EARLIER TODAY, *SUPERMAN*-- ALSO KNOWN AS *CLARK KENT*--WAS SPOTTED IN THE *LITTLE SAIGON* NEIGHBORHOOD OF METROPOLIS.
SUPERMAN HAS LARGELY KEPT OUT OF THE *LIMELIGHT* SINCE DAILY PLANET REPORTER *LOIS LANE* EXPOSED HIS *SECRET IDENTITY* TO THE WORLD.

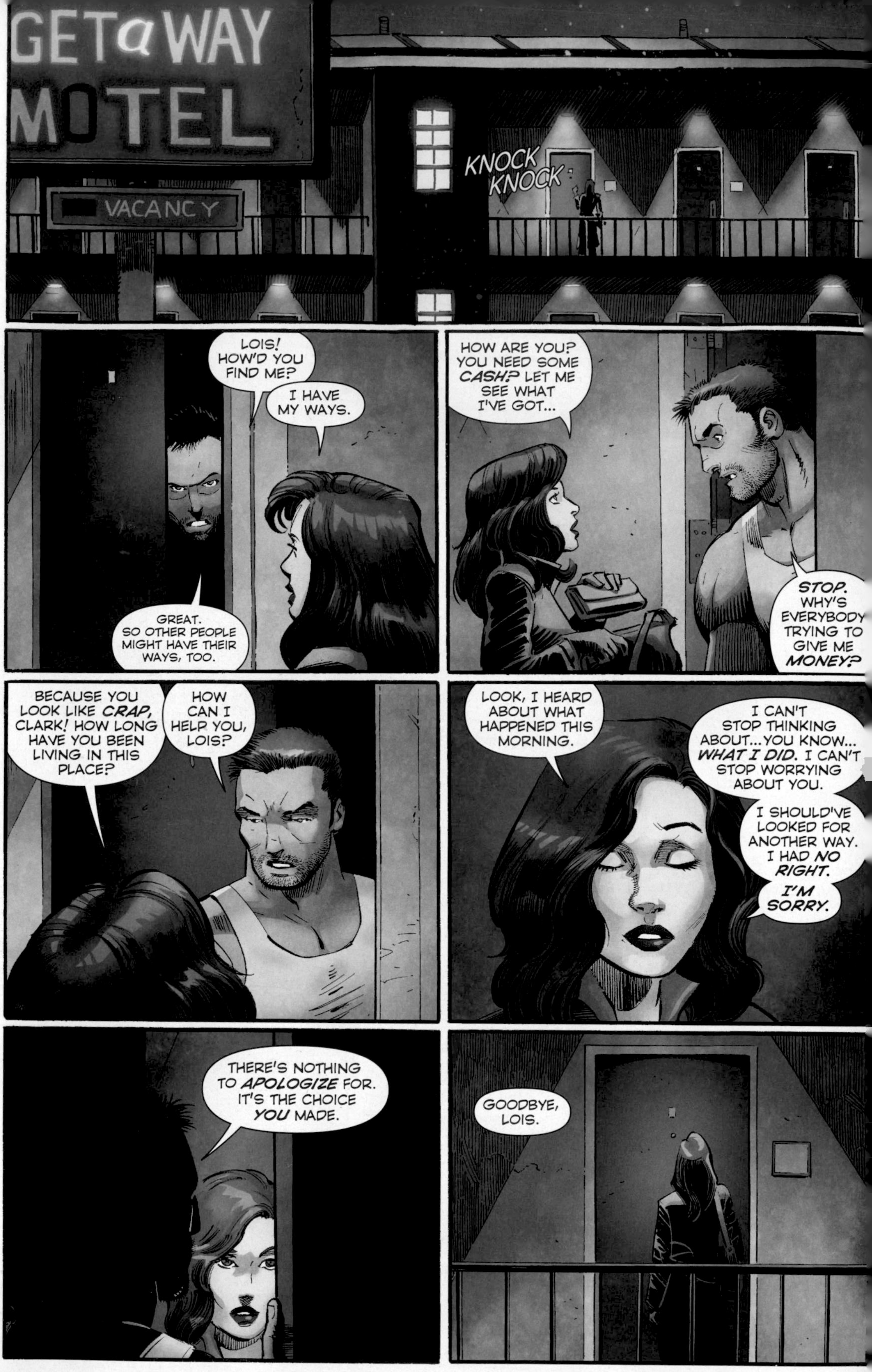
GETaWAY MOTEL
VACANCY
KNOCK KNOCK
LOIS! HOW'D YOU FIND ME?
I HAVE MY WAYS.
GREAT. SO OTHER PEOPLE MIGHT HAVE THEIR WAYS, TOO.
HOW ARE YOU? YOU NEED SOME CASH? LET ME SEE WHAT I'VE GOT...
STOP. WHY'S EVERYBODY TRYING TO GIVE ME MONEY?
BECAUSE YOU LOOK LIKE CRAP, CLARK! HOW LONG HAVE YOU BEEN LIVING IN THIS PLACE?
HOW CAN I HELP YOU, LOIS?
LOOK, I HEARD ABOUT WHAT HAPPENED THIS MORNING.
I CAN'T STOP THINKING ABOUT...YOU KNOW... WHAT I DID. I CAN'T STOP WORRYING ABOUT YOU.
I SHOULD'VE LOOKED FOR ANOTHER WAY. I HAD NO RIGHT.
I'M SORRY.
THERE'S NOTHING TO APOLOGIZE FOR. IT'S THE CHOICE YOU MADE.
GOODBYE, LOIS.

EXPOSED

GENE LUEN YANG script · JOHN ROMITA, JR. pencils · KLAUS JANSON with SCOTT HANNA inks · HI-F color

TRAVIS LANHAM: letterer RICKEY PURDIN: associate editor EDDIE BERGANZA: group editor

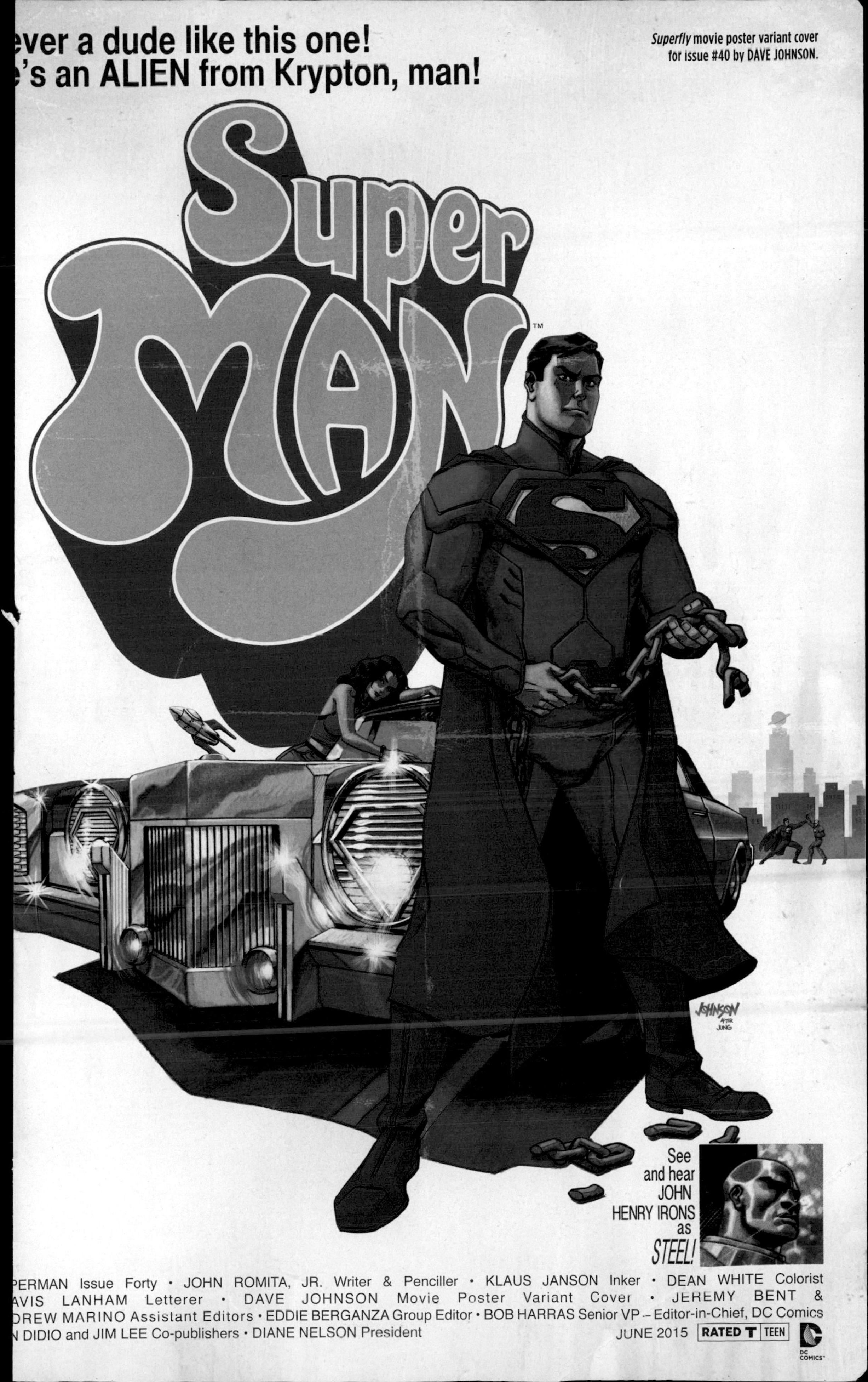
ever a dude like this one!
'e's an ALIEN from Krypton, man!
Superfly movie poster variant cover for issue #40 by DAVE JOHNSON.
SuperMAN™
JOHNSON AFTER JUNG
See and hear JOHN HENRY IRONS as STEEL!
PERMAN Issue Forty • JOHN ROMITA, JR. Writer & Penciller • KLAUS JANSON Inker • DEAN WHITE Colorist
AVIS LANHAM Letterer • DAVE JOHNSON Movie Poster Variant Cover • JEREMY BENT &
DREW MARINO Assistant Editors • EDDIE BERGANZA Group Editor • BOB HARRAS Senior VP – Editor-in-Chief, DC Comics
N DIDIO and JIM LEE Co-publishers • DIANE NELSON President
JUNE 2015
RATED T TEEN
DC COMICS

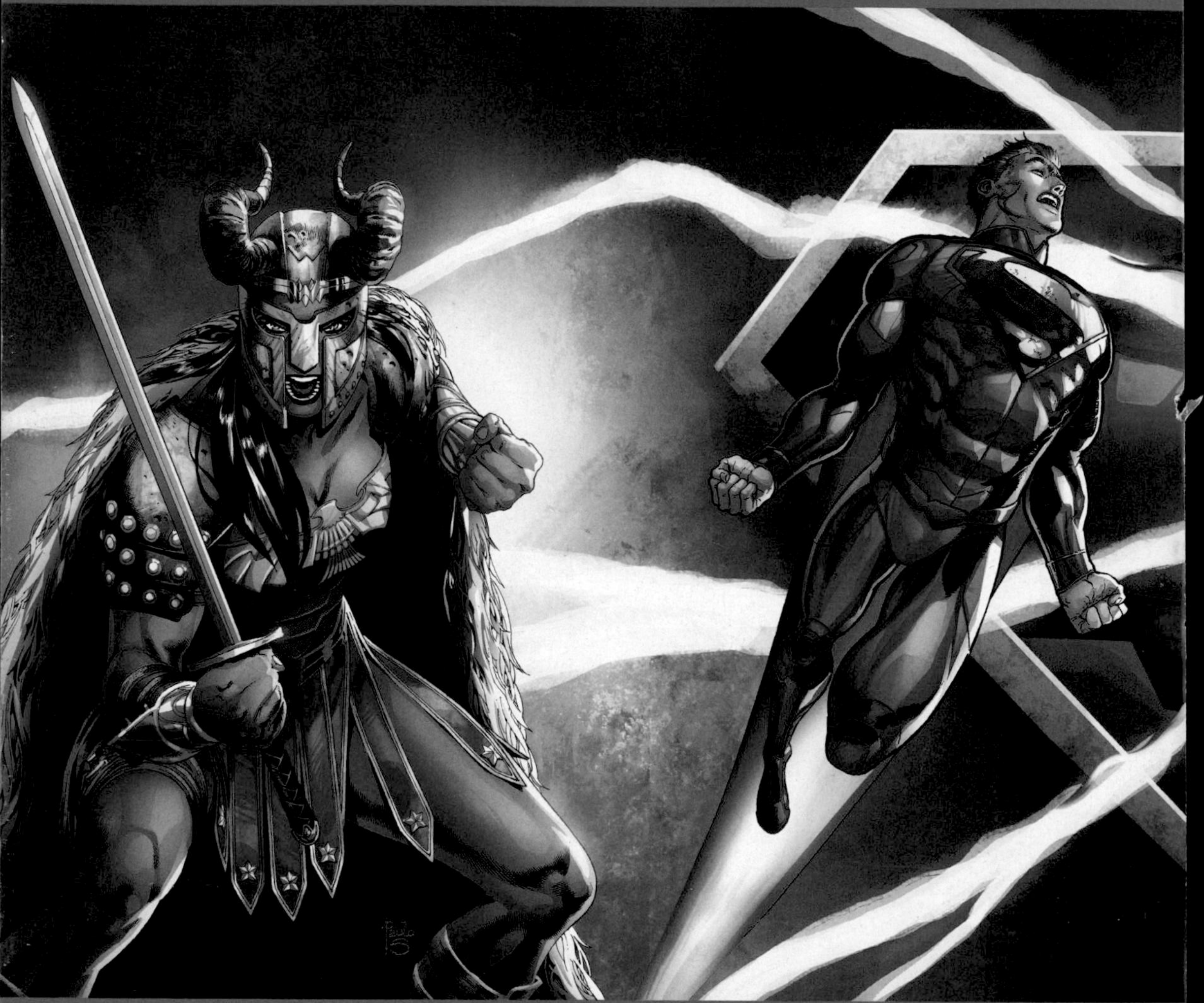

Convention cover for issue #43 by **JOHN ROMITA JR., KLAUS JANSON** and **PAULO SIQUEIRA.**

Second cover for issue #40 by **JOHN ROMITA JR.**, **KLAUS JANSON** and **DEAN WHITE.**

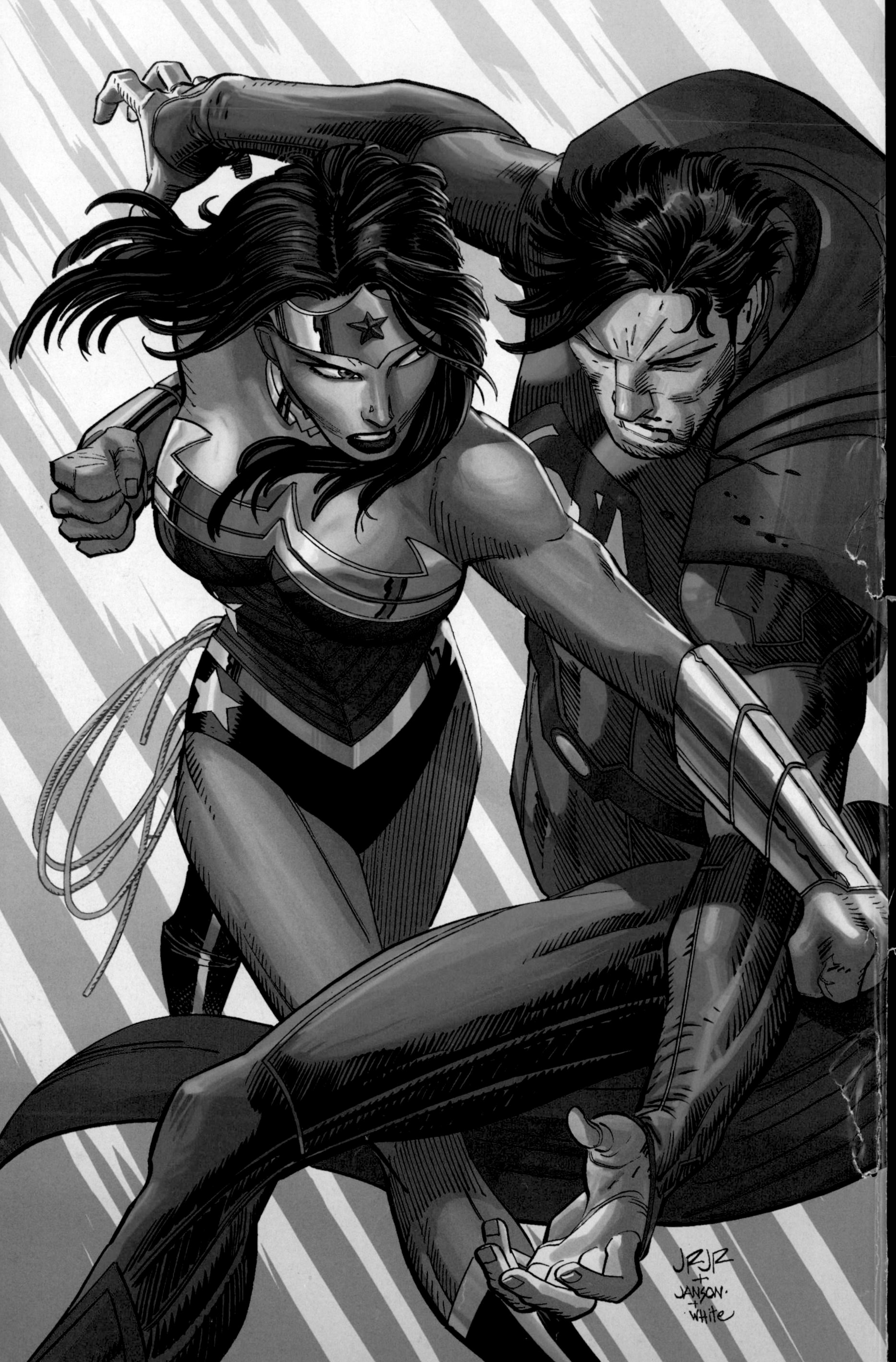
JRJR
+
JANSON.
+
White

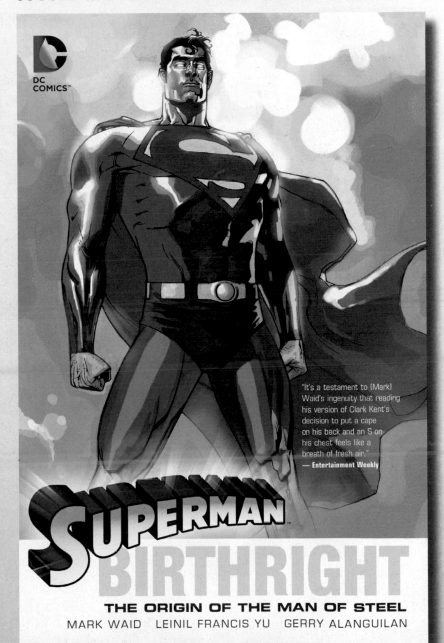

"An invigorating, entertaining an
modern take on the Man of Steel.
—VARIET

"Grade: A-.
—ENTERTAINMENT WEEKL

FROM THE WRITER OF *JUSTICE LEAGUE* & *GREEN LANTERN*

GEOFF JOHNS
with GARY FRANK

SUPERMAN: THE LAST SON OF KRYPTON

with RICHARD DONNER & ADAM KUBERT

SUPERMAN & THE LEGION OF SUPER-HEROES

with GARY FRANK

SUPERMAN: BRAINIAC

with GARY FRANK

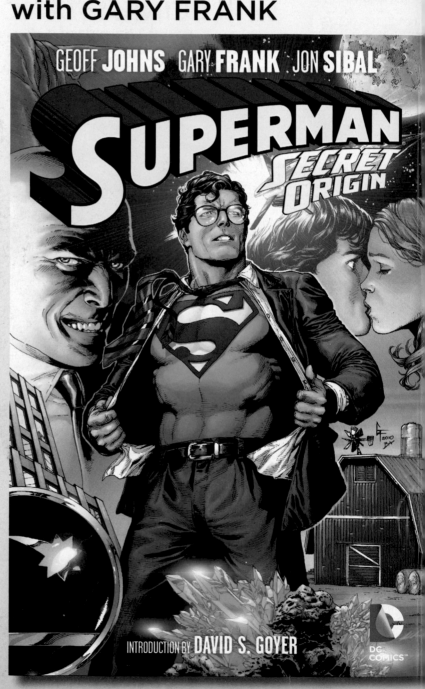

GEOFF **JOHNS** GARY **FRANK** JON **SIBAL**

SUPERMAN
SECRET ORIGIN

INTRODUCTION BY **DAVID S. GOYER**

"It's fresh air. I like this all-too-human Superman, and I think a lot of you will, too."
—SCRIPPS HOWARD NEWS SERVICE

START AT THE BEGINNING!

SUPERMAN: ACTION COMICS VOLUME 1: SUPERMAN AND THE MEN OF STEEL

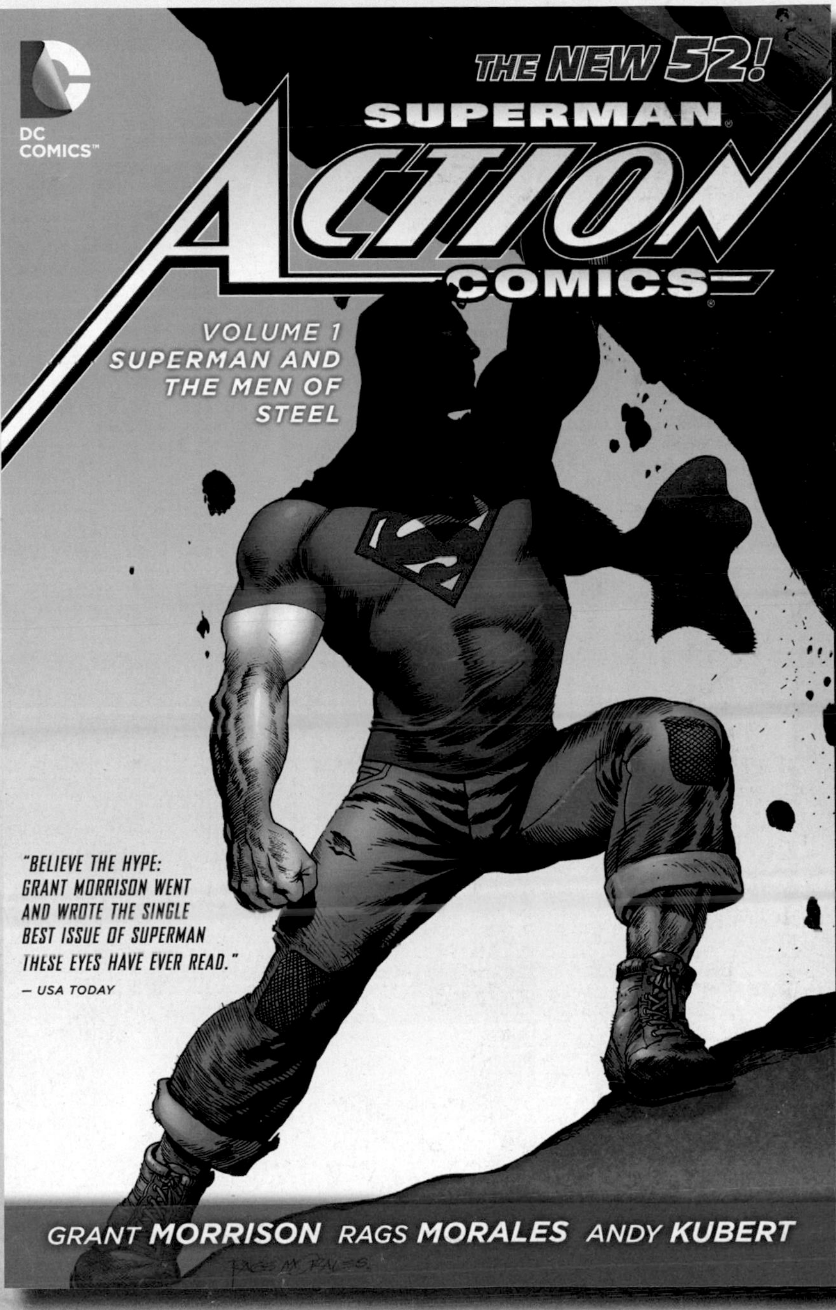
DC COMICS™
THE NEW 52!
SUPERMAN
ACTION COMICS
VOLUME 1
SUPERMAN AND THE MEN OF STEEL
"BELIEVE THE HYPE: GRANT MORRISON WENT AND WROTE THE SINGLE BEST ISSUE OF SUPERMAN THESE EYES HAVE EVER READ."
— USA TODAY
GRANT MORRISON RAGS MORALES ANDY KUBERT

SUPERMAN VOLUME 1: WHAT PRICE TOMORROW?

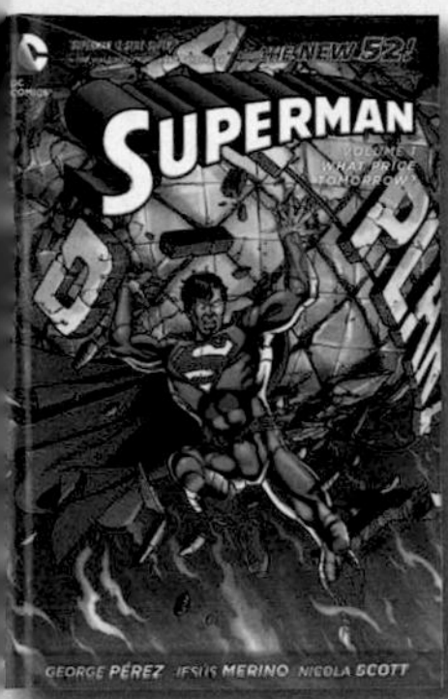
THE NEW 52!
SUPERMAN
GEORGE PÉREZ JESÚS MERINO NICOLA SCOTT

SUPERGIRL VOLUME 1: THE LAST DAUGHTER OF KRYPTON

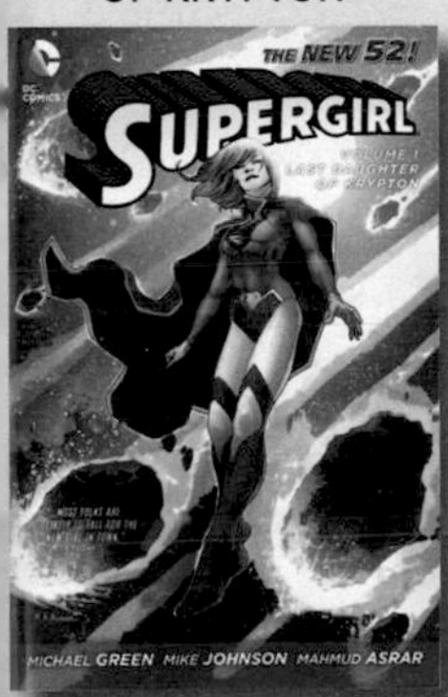
THE NEW 52!
SUPERGIRL
MICHAEL GREEN MIKE JOHNSON MAHMUD ASRAR

SUPERBOY VOLUME 1: INCUBATION

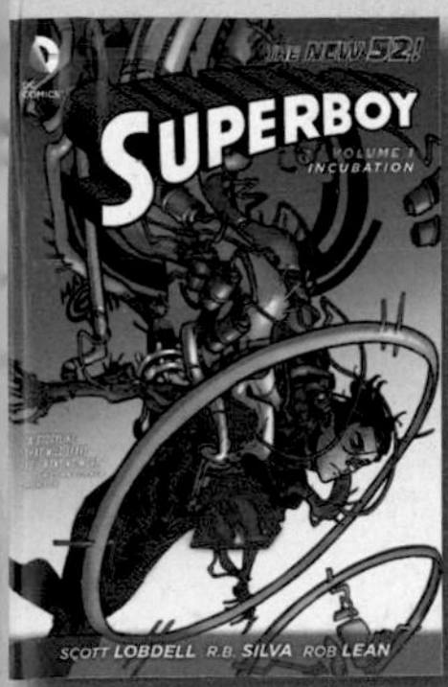
THE NEW 52!
SUPERBOY
VOLUME 1 INCUBATION
SCOTT LOBDELL R.B. SILVA ROB LEAN

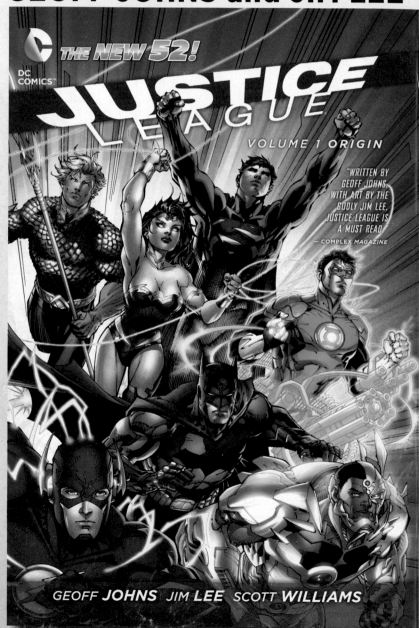